THE POLITICS OF RIGHTS
Lawyers, Public Policy, and Political Change

THE POLITICS
OF RIGHTS

*Lawyers, Public Policy, and
Political Change*

Second Edition

STUART A. SCHEINGOLD

With a Foreword by Malcolm M. Feeley

THE UNIVERSITY OF MICHIGAN PRESS

Ann Arbor

Copyright © by the University of Michigan 2004
First published in 1974 by Yale University Press
All rights reserved
Published in the United States of America by
The University of Michigan Press
Manufactured in the United States of America
∞ Printed on acid-free paper

2011   2010   2009   2008   6   5   4   3

A CIP catalog record for this book is available from the British Library.

Library of Congress Cataloging-in-Publication Data

Scheingold, Stuart A.
The politics of rights : lawyers, public policy, and political change /
Stuart A. Scheingold ; with a foreword by Malcolm M. Feeley — 2nd ed.
p.   cm.
Includes bibliographical references and index.
ISBN 0-472-03005-1 (paper : alk. paper)
1. Civil rights—Political aspects—United States.   2. Civil rights—
Social aspects—United States.   3. Lawyers—United States.
4. Social change.   5. Law and politics.   I. Title.

KF4749.S32   2004
342.7308'5—dc22   2004044000

ISBN13 978-0-472-03005-7 (paper)
ISBN13 978-0-472-02553-4 (electronic)

For Thres and Pat,
My Mom and Dad

CONTENTS

PART TWO: THE POLITICS OF RIGHTS

PART THREE: THE STRATEGISTS OF RIGHTS

EPILOGUE

FOREWORD

Like much good social theory, the arguments in this volume were born in the crucible of pressing events of a particular time and place. The book was conceived at the University of Wisconsin in the late 1960s, when Scheingold was inside Bascom Hall lecturing on constitutional rights and liberties, while outside, on the mall, National Guard troops were dispensing tear gas to disperse chanting students demanding their rights. These students had not heard and would not have listened to Scheingold's lectures about rights that had been realized by the Constitution and the Supreme Court. Increasingly his lectures fell on deaf ears, as his students chose to join those outside. Eventually, these distractions— National Guard troops, tear gas, student chants, and mounting skepticism—led Scheingold to rethink conventional understandings of legal rights and to explore the myths of rights and the politics of rights. He turned away from the words of the Constitution and the courts to explore what was in the minds of the chanting students. Thus was *The Politics of Rights* conceived. And by this move, Scheingold relocated the study of law in American political science.

The book opens boldly:

> The law is real, but it is also a figment of our imaginations. Like all fundamental social institutions it casts a shadow of popular belief that may ultimately be more significant, albeit more difficult to comprehend, than the authorities, rules, and penalties that we ordinarily associate with law.

What then follows is an extended essay elaborating on this insight, exploring that figment of our imaginations and the long shadow it casts. Divided into two parts, the book explores the *myth* of law, the symbolic, ideological, and rhetorical features of legal rights, and the *politics* of law, the law as resource and the appeal to rights as catalysts for political mobilization.

This combination was — and remains — stunning. No one until then had formulated a robust cultural analysis of American law in such an eloquent and sustained manner. A number of earlier commentators had explored aspects of Scheingold's complex argument before. Thurman Arnold's brilliant and quirky book *The Symbols of Government,* initially published in 1935, touched on some of the themes developed more systematically by Scheingold. Murray Edelman, Scheingold's colleague at Wisconsin, published *The Symbolic Uses of Politics* in 1964. It provides a penetrating analysis of how political language offers soothing condensation symbols that foster public quiescence. No doubt Scheingold was heavily influenced by this path-breaking book, though it differs substantially from Edelman's analysis in that its focus is on the distinct and powerful appeal of "rights," both as myth and as a political resource. Shortly after publication of *The Politics of Rights,* E. P. Thompson, in his great 1975 study, *Whigs and Hunters,* showed how the landed elite constructed the criminal in order to dominate the working class, but nevertheless concluded in something of a coda that this experience instilled a belief in the efficacy of the "rights of Englishmen" even as it was used to repress them. But before the *Politics of Rights,* no one, at least in American sociolegal scholarship, had offered such a thorough and deep analysis of law as ideology, law as myth, and law as politics. The closest work in this vein came later. The Critical Legal Studies Movement was founded several years after publication of *The Politics of Rights.* This movement could greatly have profited from careful consideration of Scheingold's analysis, since he anchors his work in core concerns of political psychology and a deeply rooted sense of American history. In contrast, Critical Legal Studies began and remained largely a reaction to conventional doctrinal legal scholarship, and soon withered away as a distinct form of analysis once this conventional approach made some concessions to the Crits.

A distinct and original book, the *Politics of Rights* draws on and synthesizes several quite different traditions. Indeed it was Scheingold's luck and brilliance, and the reader's good fortune, that he read so widely and so diversely. A small but marked tradition in political psychology appears to have influenced him, though perhaps by osmosis rather than any direct lineage. As already noted, his colleague Murray Edelman had begun his explorations of the symbolic uses of politics in the 1960s, and his 1964 book appears to have influenced Scheingold. But Edelman's work is anchored in a tradition of political psychology that does not focus on law and especially rights. Similarly, Harold Lasswell's and others' pioneering work in political psychology did much to recognize the symbolic functions of politics and to underscore that one important basis of successful public policies is not that they provide concrete and material benefits to the intended beneficiaries, but that they produce powerful condensation symbols that provide public comfort for personal insecurities.

More generally, of course, post–World War II social science was preoccupied with the analysis of the politics of mass society. One of its major missions was to ask how such tiny elites in Nazi Germany and the Soviet Union could at one and the same time foster the politics of mass arousal as well as the politics of passivity. This diffuse field had its origins in a number of different disciplines, psychoanalysis, German phenomenology, neo-Marxist historical and cultural studies inspired by the prewar Frankfurt school and its postwar presence in the United States, and the emerging study of public opinion and survey research. Scheingold's study reverberates with the echoes of each of these traditions.

In addition, Scheingold draws on a long and important tradition in anthropology, beginning perhaps with Émile Durkheim and continuing through to Clifford Geertz, a tradition that seeks to interpret symbols and myths of primitive societies, to take them as "facts" that shape the mental landscape of a society's inhabitants and serve important social functions. Scheingold's analysis is deeply and self-consciously indebted to this tradition. As he notes in his original preface, Dan Lev, a colleague at Washington working on the politics of Southeast Asia, helped him lace together and incorporate this diffuse body of work into his own project. In this process, Scheingold was introduced to Geertz's writings on ideology and its functions. At the time, the idea of ideology was somewhat out of fashion in much of American social science, at least as applied to contemporary democratic societies. Important scholars of that time argued that the late twentieth century had ushered in the "end of ideology," and functionalism, still the reigning social theory of the day, associated ideology with distortion and the manipulative selectivity characteristic of totalitarian or otherwise pathological societies, not modern democratic societies. In contrast Geertz and others saw ideology as ubiquitous, a necessary component of social life because it provides a means by which to evaluate complex social reality and give expression to deep cultural predispositions. Scheingold recognized the value of the concept of ideology as Geertz and others used it to account for the enduring appeal of the myth of rights in contemporary American society. He writes, "[L]ike other ideologies, [the myth of rights] elicits support, mobilizes energies, and coordinates the activities of its adherents. . . . [It] furnishes explanations for the past, standards for evaluating the present, and programs for social action in the future" (14–15). The analysis of rights as ideology thus provides the key for understanding the enduring appeal of the Constitution, the Supreme Court, and the law more generally. It reveals a deep insight into contemporary American political life.

But Scheingold did more than meld these diverse traditions of political psychology, anthropology, and cultural studies into a framework for examining law. His work is firmly anchored in an intimate knowledge of American history and the American political and legal tradition. He knows and draws on the best in this tradition, Alexis de Tocqueville, Louis Hartz, Daniel Boorstin, the Legal Realists, Judith Shklar. All these shrewd observers and many others working in their wake recognized the distinct salience of law in American culture, the powerful appeal of rights, and the connection of law to politics in the American experience. Some embraced it as expansive and liberating, others like the realists were cynical, and still others—Judith Shklar—warned that legalism was always just a short step away from fetishism, and thus could crimp if not cripple robust political discourse and analysis.

Scheingold's singular contribution is to harness these various traditions, to draw from each of them and present a stunning and original analysis of rights in America as a real symbol and as a force in politics. Others had caught glimpses of this and occasionally described this process. Scheingold offers an elaborated framework in which to consider it, and a sustained analysis employing the framework. Although much of his analysis draws on pressing issues of the day—the Warren Court's rights revolution and reactions to it; Watergate and reactions to it—the book transcends these events. Scheingold's genius is his ability to stand back, remain detached, and use pressing particulars to illuminate if not generic features of all societies, at least enduring features of American political and legal life. Scheingold wisely leaves it to his reader to figure out just how general his theory might be.

Because of all this, *The Politics of Rights* merits a place on the small list of indispensable sociolegal studies of American law and politics. Indeed, it leads the list. Scheingold's analysis of the function of "rights" in American political life remains unequaled. It was a liberating experience to read it when it first appeared thirty years ago. It is the single best book on law and politics in the United States. And it will remain an indispensable book—a must read—well into the future.

Once there was only *The Politics of Rights*. Today there is a library of materials on legal consciousness, the symbolic uses of law, the myths of rights, legal ideology, critical legal studies, law and political mobilization, cause lawyers, and the politics of law. Much of this literature is directly traceable to this path-breaking study. Scheingold not only wrote a classic, but with this book helped establish an expansive field that is by far the most exciting and rich area in the diverse sphere of American sociolegal scholarship. I do not mean to denigrate this vibrant new tradition in any way when I assert that *The Politics of Rights* is in a class by itself. Scheingold's breadth, perspective, and range, the book's tight structure, voice, and perfect level of generalization, and its carefully crafted prose, all place it in a category by itself. The library of work created in its wake is good, but even the best of it remains commentary on Scheingold's text. *The Politics of Rights* is the source. As important as this commentary is, the serious student must always and repeatedly return to the original text.

This book has already exerted an enormous influence on two generations of scholars. It has had an immense impact on political scientists, sociologists, and anthropologists, as well as historians and legal scholars. With this new edition, its influence is likely to continue for still more generations. *The Politics of Rights* has, I believe, become an American classic.

MALCOLM M. FEELEY
Claire Sanders Clements Dean's Professor
Boalt Hall School of Law
University of California at Berkeley

PREFACE TO THE SECOND EDITION: THE NEW POLITICS OF RIGHTS

Michael McCann was the first to call my attention to the way in which *The Politics of Rights* had become something of a Rorschach test among rights scholars. He pointed out that there were those who saw the book largely in terms of its first part, which explored the *myth* of rights, according to which legal entitlements were represented as a kind of a political confidence game—all promise and no delivery. Others focused on the *politics* of rights—that is, Part 2—where rights were analyzed as a contingent political resource, which, when opportunistically deployed, could contribute usefully to social change. Meanwhile, relatively little attention was given to Part 3, where I explored the likelihood that activist lawyers—cause lawyers, I would call them today—could act as effective agents of rights by utilizing them in a politically savvy fashion on behalf of meaningful social change.

While one of the objectives of this preface will be to provide my own take on the *old* politics of rights, my more fundamental objective will be to present a *new* politics of rights. This new politics of rights is derived from the rights scholarship that has developed in the years since the first edition was published in 1974. Fortunately, the two objectives converge because insofar as I am able to clarify the old politics of rights, it is due to the theoretical breakthroughs, the conceptual insights, and the empirical findings that constitute the new politics of rights. In the analysis that follows, I will begin by briefly summarizing my original intentions and by explaining what it was that may have obscured those intentions and, thus, conveyed an insufficiently complex vision of both the cultural resonance and political impact of rights.

THE POLITICS OF RIGHTS IN A NUTSHELL

As explained in the original preface (1974, xiii), I stumbled rather fortuitously on the myth of rights. At the time, I was largely unaware of the profoundly rich body of social theory from which I could have drawn. Accordingly, I constructed the myth of rights largely from the literature of American exceptionalism—and, in particular, from Louis Hartz's *The Liberal Tradition in America* (1955). I had always been struck by his claim that in the United States, "law has flourished on the corpse of philosophy" (ibid., 10), and the consonance between this claim and the nineteenth-century observations of Alexis de Tocqueville (1959) about the elemental role of law in American politics.

What I only dimly perceived when I began work on *The Politics of Rights* was that it was *not* useful to think about the American love affair with the law as a description of the way in which law and politics actually work. As the writing progressed, however, I came to understand the value of separating myself from the essentially descriptive aspirations of de Tocqueville, Hartz, and a bevy of functionalist scholars of the 1950s and 1960s. Insofar as I, thus, became aware of the ideological presence of law, it was from Judith Shklar's wonderfully evocative *Legalism* (1964) and Murray Edelman's seminal exploration, *The Symbolic Uses of Politics* (1964). Then, with Dan Lev's help I was led to the work of Clifford Geertz (1964) and came to appreciate the mythic character of both law and ideology and, thus, became sensitive to what the lore of law both reveals and conceals. It was in this sense that I began the prologue to *The Politics of Rights* by asserting that "the law is real, but it is also a figment of our imaginations."

More specifically, I went on to argue that the myth of rights— according to which legal rights are *directly* empowering—is misleading. More often than not, rights entitlements articulated by courts go unrealized when they are embedded in contested matters of public policy. The preeminent example at the time was the right of African Americans to desegregated schools, to equal access to justice, and to unfettered voting rights

˜ However, I further argued that what was not available directly through rights was available indirectly. Again, taking civil rights as a case in point, I argued that the belief of Americans in rights—that is, the myth of rights—was itself available as a kind of resource. In particular, I argued that this belief constituted a resource that could be deployed politically so as to procure indirectly through the political process what was unavailable through legal channels. More concretely, I argued that indignation generated by television reports of "massive resistance" to the civil rights decisions of the U.S. Supreme Court fueled a civil rights movement. In other words, the televised spectacles of rabid crowds at schoolhouse doors, the use of cattle prods and the unleashing of dogs during desegregation demonstrations, as well as the murders of civil rights workers were indirectly instrumental in the civil rights progress from 1964 onward.

In the final portion of the book my focus was on cause lawyers. I noted the tendency of the NAACP Legal Defense Fund lawyers to privilege litigation and to oppose the politicization of legal rights. Other examples of resistance to politicization and the resultant cooptation of rights campaigns include early Indian treaty rights activities (Medcalf 1978; Bruun 1982) and New Deal labor reform (Forbath 1991 and Klare 1978). This tendency was traced to the legalistic socialization of lawyers in law school and within the organized profession. Accordingly, I hypothesized that cause lawyers were more likely to be captives of the myth of rights than its opportunistic, strategically motivated political maximizers.

It is widely agreed that constitutional entitlements affirmed by the Supreme Court were in themselves largely ineffectual and that desegregation proceeded only after the civil rights movement gathered momentum (Rosenberg 1991). The distinctive message of *The Politics of Rights* is, however, that constitutional litigation did, by way of a politics of rights, contribute *indirectly* to the emergence and success of the civil rights movement (see also Scheingold 1988). On the one hand, the judicial validation of civil rights claims generated hopes that fed the organizing efforts of African Americans and their supporters. On the other hand, the "massive" legal resistance to judicial decrees — not to mention the television-documented spectacle of *extralegal* resistance — sparked the support of northern liberals. Taken together, these *unintended* consequences of constitutional litigation helped to destabilize the political stalemate that had protected segregation since the end of the Reconstruction.

TRANSCENDING *THE POLITICS OF RIGHTS*

Some of the recent rights scholarship, most notably Gerald Rosenberg's *Hollow Hope* (1991) and portions of Critical Legal Studies work, has denied that rights could, whether directly or indirectly, promote political and social change. My concern is not, however, with this research, which in effect rejects the premises and perspectives of *The Politics of Rights*. Instead, I want to focus on the scholarship that I see as enriching and transcending my own understanding of rights.

In the remaining pages of this preface I will, therefore, provide a kind of thumbnail sketch of a *new politics of rights* — as it emerges from the conceptual and empirical work of the last quarter of a century. *My* guiding vision was of a *society* that believed in the myth of rights, was sensitive to its violation, and could be readily mobilized on its behalf if only cause lawyers themselves were sufficiently shrewd not to fall under its spell. Subsequent work has provided a conceptual schema and empirical findings that clarify and qualify the inchoate premises and speculative assertions of *The Politics of Rights*. The net effect of this more recent research is to lend credence to, and provide an enhanced understanding of, the *constitutive* capabilities of the myth of rights while also problematizing my largely unqualified claims about the political utility of rights. Rights emerge as less predictable but not as less politically significant.

Necessarily my review of this literature will be selective rather than exhaustive. I can only hope that even a selective sampling will reveal at least the basic contours of a new politics of rights that is both more complex and more convincing than the original. An exhaustive account would have taken me beyond a preface and to the brink of an entirely new book. John Brigham's *The Constitution of Interests: Beyond the Politics of Rights* (1996) is just such a book. At the conclusion of this preface I offer my own suggestions for a new volume that would diverge significantly from Brigham's. We are, however, in complete agreement that the shift to a constitutive conception of the politics of rights is a major step forward.

A Constitutive Theory of Rights and Legality

The initial scholarship of the law and society movement, in reaction to legal formalism, sought to demonstrate how and why the law on the books should be, and ultimately and inevitably is, decisively shaped and altered by shifts in underlying structural forces—be they economic, political, or social. Thus, the mission of sociolegal studies was to uncover and to specify the role of structural forces in explaining, and in closing, the gap between the law on the books and the law in action. This legal realist message as translated into the terms of social science meant that law was understood as the dependent variable—thus making formal legality largely irrelevant.

In contrast, both the old and the new versions of the politics of rights are associated with a constitutive theory of law. To think in terms of the mythic and ideological properties of rights is to see them as *constitutive* of, rather than simply as a reflection of, social practice. It is, however, only in more recent work that the constitutive conception of law and politics has been expressly formulated.

The decentering of law by sociolegal studies was a necessary but insufficient step toward constitutive legality, which required

the *radical* decentering of law. To decenter law is to refocus—as
sociolegal studies has done since its inception—from the hierarchy of authoritative institutions and formal doctrine to the more
fluid terrain of their multidimensional interaction with intermediate institutions—lower courts, bureaucratic agencies, and so
forth. In this way, a top-down understanding of law is, in effect,
redirected toward a bottom-up perspective. In calling attention to
the thwarting of authoritative rulings of the U.S. Supreme Court
by the intermediate institutions of the law and politics, *The
Politics of Rights* was, then, deploying the findings and conceptual premises of a decentered conception of the law—as pioneered by legal realist and sociolegal scholarship.

To *radically* decenter legality is to move beyond the sociolegal studies paradigm in two ways. On the one hand, both the top-
down and the bottom-up perspectives are deemed inadequate and
replaced by a vision of the interpenetration of multiple levels of
legality. On the other hand, law is understood as "a continuous
part of social practice," meaning that, "first, law is *internal* to the
constitution of those practices, linked by meaning to the affairs it
controls; [and] second, and correlatively, law largely influences
modes of thought rather than conduct in any specific case. Law
enters social practices and is, indeed, imbricated in them, by
shaping consciousness, by making law's concepts and commands seem, if not invisible, then perfectly natural and benign"
(Sarat and Kearns 1993, 31, emphasis in the original; see also
McCann and Silverstein 1993, 133).

From this perspective *The Politics of Rights* emerges as a step
toward the constitutive perspective. In directing attention beyond
both formal legality and institutional hierarchy and, indeed,
beyond the informal legality of, for example, "street-level
bureaucracy"—police, social workers, and the like (Lipsky
1980)—the myth of rights incorporates legal consciousness into
the legal field. Still, *The Politics of Rights* falls short of the essential elements of the constitutive perspective identified by Sarat
and Kearns. It does not fully apprehend how and why legal consciousness constitutes legal meaning, and it is in essence bottom-

up in its emphasis on the extent to which a politics of rights from below can contribute to redistributive goals.

The more robust constitutive conception that I see as the hallmark of a new politics of rights has, however, emerged from three bodies of subsequent scholarship.

1. Rights in Everyday Life: Research on the ways in which individuals mobilize (or fail to mobilize) rights (and law) to resolve disputes focuses on, and uncovers multiple versions of, *rights consciousness*. Rights emerge from this work as discursive resources of varying utility and multiple meanings. That is to say, rights consciousness is shown to vary dramatically from person to person and place to place. This research lends credence to the constitutive power that I attribute to the myth of rights. However, in uncovering multiple iterations of rights consciousness, the disputing literature suggests that the sweeping generalization of the myth of rights must be qualified.

2. Rights and Collective Political Mobilization: In contrast to research on rights in everyday life with its largely nonpolitical account of rights, research on collective political mobilization is situated squarely within the political process. Here the focus is on campaigns to deploy rights to pursue a progressive political agenda—desegregation, gender equity, protection of people with disabilities, improvement of working conditions, defense of the environment, and the like. This research analyzes rights as both discursive and institutional resources and also identifies the conditions and circumstances that are conducive to a successful politics of rights. The result is a vastly more complex and fluid understanding of rights than I envisaged, and it leads to a more conditional and problematic understanding of the nature and the possibilities of the politics of rights.

3. Countermobilization: Whereas the dominant message of collective mobilization research is a positive, albeit qualified, endorsement of rights as a progressive political

resource, there are arguments and evidence that reveal conservative versions of, and reactions against, the politics of
rights. There is, on the one hand, evidence of a backlash
against progressive rights strategies. On the other hand, both
their indeterminacy and the quid pro quos attached to rights
reveal them as double agents — amenable to serving *anti-
egalitarian* as well as egalitarian purposes.

The following sections will consider and clarify each of these
elements of the emergent new politics of rights. For the moment,
I will simply reiterate that the constitutive scholarship does not
so much challenge as enrich the politics of rights paradigm —
providing an enhanced understanding of the properties, processes, and contingencies that are intrinsic to it.

Individual Legal Mobilization: Rights in Everyday Life
Whereas the premise of *The Politics of Rights* was that
Americans believed in, and were favorably disposed toward,
rights, a substantial body of research has revealed a multiplicity
of varied and often contradictory responses to rights. As Michael
McCann points out, these findings have emerged primarily from
research on the "mobilization of the law by individuals seeking
resolution of mostly 'private' disputes" (1994, 5). This disputing
literature reveals varied, complex, and context-specific patterns
of legal consciousness in the United States — a "polyvocal" legal
consciousness, as Patricia Ewick and Susan Silbey put it.

> The polyvocality of legality, that is, the varieties of legal con-
> sciousness and multiple schemas of and by which it is consti-
> tuted, permit individuals wide latitude in interpreting social
> phenomena, while at the same time still deploying signs of
> legality. (1998, 52)

Similarly, by focusing on "individual autobiographies over a
broad sweep of time," Engel and Munger's research on the
Americans with Disabilities Act discloses "the variety of ways in

which rights can become active or remain inactive" (2003, 10). Thus, legal consciousness and *rights* consciousness vary from individual to individual, group to group, time to time, relationship to relationship, and so forth (Merry 1990). The net effect is that a mélange of different and contradictory strains of rights consciousness regularly coexist in society.

This research demonstrates the necessity of qualifying the myth of rights—but how to do so is hardly self-evident. As a starting point, one could reasonably think of the rights consciousness of individuals as constituent elements of the myth of rights. However, insofar as these constituent elements are as fluid and varied as the disputing literature demonstrates, my assertions about the breadth, depth, and consensual resonance of the myth of rights are put in substantial doubt. In short, it is difficult to see how the suasive power of the myth of rights can be anywhere near as compelling and decisive as I claim in *The Politics of Rights*. The disputing literature does not, however, simply destabilize my formulation of the myth of rights. In addition, these findings reveal patterns that suggest alternative formulations while at the same time reaffirming the constitutive understandings that are the driving force behind the overall politics of rights project.

Ewick and Silbey (1998) find three such patterns of legal consciousness among their respondents. Each pattern lends credence to the constitutive power of rights while at the same time qualifying and, indeed, destabilizing the myth of rights as such. Of the three variants identified by Ewick and Silbey, only one, the *before-the-law* narrative, is consistent with the myth of rights. Whereas these before-the-law narratives emphasize the preeminence of the law and the inappropriateness of questioning it, *against-the-law* narratives envisage law as an instrument of domination, an enemy of justice, and, accordingly, deserving of resistance. Finally, Ewick and Silbey uncover a third narrative that is more consistent with the politics of rights than with the myth of rights—with the efficacy of legality requiring that it be "played like a game, to draw from and contribute to everyday life, and yet exist as a realm removed and distant from the commonplace affairs of particular lives" (1998, 234). In short, *with-the-law* narratives recognize legality as inextricable from strategic action.

John Gilliom's research on welfare mothers in Appalachia reveals an interesting variation on against-the-law narratives. While not asserting a right of privacy against the intrusive surveillance of, and denial of benefits by, welfare officials, they did develop their own survival strategies that were *against the law* in distinct but related ways. On the one hand, some of these mothers subverted the rules by, for example, working off the books for income necessary to provide for their children and themselves. On the other hand, Gilliom reports that in court, they invoked not rights but "stories of need, caring, and personal offense" (2001, 117). While Gilliom deplores the inaccessibility of rights to these women, he calls attention to their alternative route to resistance:

> [W]e found patterns of critique and action drawn from the experiences and conditions of everyday life and directed toward meeting the impact of the surveillance bureaucracy in the terms that mattered most. . . . [W]e explored how this everyday critique and resistance was an important and productive form of politics advancing the daily needs of the poor, building and reflecting a collective identity, and both working from and strengthening a principled and ethical ideology. (135)

Clearly, Gilliom's own narrative is not only against the law but against the politics of rights as well. His is definitely a constitutive theory, but the collective identity that he uncovers is rooted in material need and, thus, looks more like the politics of class than the politics of constitutional entitlement (see also Kristin Bumiller's [1988] account of rights as an agent of victimization).

The work of Carol Greenhouse, Barbara Yngvesson, and David Engel (1994) further destabilizes the myth of rights—

revealing not only multiple and contested versions of rights consciousness but also providing a glimpse of a myth that competes with the myth of rights. Thus, Engel's research in Sander County reveals that newcomers who turn to the law and litigation to deal with personal injury claims are labeled troublemakers by long-time residents who argue that rights-claiming by the newcomers is a threat to the community. Yet, as Engel points out,

> In Sander County, the philosophy of individualism worked itself out quite differently in the areas of tort and contract. If personal injuries evoked values emphasizing self-sufficiency, contractual breaches evoked values emphasizing rights and remedies. Duties generated by contractual agreements were seen as sacrosanct and vital to the maintenance of the social order. Duties generated by socially imposed obligations to guard against injuring other people were seen as intrusions . . . as inappropriate attempts to redistribute wealth, and as limitations on individual freedom. (1994, 50)

In short, acting on settled rights claims was a routine and, indeed, praiseworthy practice for insiders. Conversely, rights-claiming by newcomers was deemed illegitimate; they were expected to subordinate rights to community solidarity and coherence.

All of this adds up, in Greenhouse's words, to the transformation of "what would otherwise be defenses of hierarchy in opposition to democratic values into defenses of community (and country) in opposition to selfishness and anarchy" (1994, 130). Thus, this research demonstrates differential cultural resonance for rights-claiming as between the haves and the have-nots. For the former it resonates positively while for the latter it can be inflected with disapproval and can extract discursive costs. This selective approval of rights-claiming, in effect, contests the presumably settled meaning of rights as a social institution. In addition, the work of Greenhouse, Yngvesson, and Engel (1994) can be read as introducing a competing myth, the *myth of commu-*

nity, that trumps the myth of rights and serves to reinforce the prevailing hegemony. I will, as suggested earlier, return to this issue of contested meanings and competing myths later.

Collective Legal Mobilization: Rights as Egalitarian Political Resources

Sociolegal research on rights-based campaigns on behalf of pay equity (McCann 1994), gays (Goldberg-Hiller 2002; Brigham 1996; Herman 1996), people with disabilities (Olson 1984), animals (Silverstein 1996), and the mentally ill (Milner 1986) has revealed how, why, and to what extent an egalitarian politics of rights can be successful. At the core of collective mobilization is what Helena Silverstein characterizes as "the indeterminate and malleable nature of legal language, and the various manifestations of legal symbols and actions . . . frequently characterized by imagination and re-creation" (1996, 7). It is, then, in this contested discursive space that legal meanings take on shapes.

> Legal meaning is constituted by and in state institutions during the process of drafting, interpreting and enforcing specific laws. Various players influence these official processes . . . [and thus] [l]egal meaning becomes constitutive of society as it permeates, informs and structures the social realm . . . [but] people do not simply absorb legal meaning into their consciousness. Incorporating legal meaning . . . involves reconstruction. . . . Hence, just as legal meaning constitutes individual and social identity, so too does individual and social identity constitute legal meaning. (9)

In each of the rights-based campaigns mentioned earlier, activists capitalized on the indeterminacy of legal meaning to construct expansively egalitarian readings of rights. Feminists have constructed conceptions of affirmative resistance to sexual violence that transcend conventional understandings of self-defense by recognizing compelling differentials of physical strength between men and women (Schneider 1986). In this same way, civil rights claims have moved beyond the perpetrator perspective to affirmative action and toward a victim perspective that takes account of the underlying conditions of institutional racism (Freeman 1998). Similarly, McCann (1994) has demonstrated that rights were a useful vehicle for developing pay equity (or comparable worth) claims that recognized gender bias in the job market and thus transcended more traditional claims of equal pay for equal work.

McCann goes on to specify both the preconditions for, and the limitations of, rights-based campaigns for collective political mobilization. Interestingly, McCann does not see success in court as a precondition. Thus, one message of his research is that judicial *defeats* can be leveraged by political activists for movement-building purposes (McCann 1994). What was, however, essential was a cadre of union activists.

> The key actors were not judges but movement organizers, who skillfully utilized litigation in a wide variety of movement building activities. . . . Lacking such organizational supports . . . the new constituency would not have been "ripe" for activation around the new rights claims. (279–80)

A second message is that, although the pay equity movement's politics of rights campaign generated wage concessions, it was never possible to establish pay equity, per se, as the guiding principle of wage compensation. This was due in part to the increasingly conservative political and judicial ethos during the 1980s.

McCann concludes, therefore, that the principal "legacy of pay equity reform" was political rather than legal. McCann's empirical evidence reveals that a rights-based campaign can contribute significantly to movement building.

> My primary finding was that the political advances in many contexts matched or exceeded wage gains. One important advance was at the level of rights consciousness. . . . Legal

rights thus became increasingly meaningful both as a general
moral discourse and as a strategic resource for ongoing challenges to the status quo power relations. (1994, 281)

Thus, McCann's research provides empirical confirmation of the
claims made in *The Politics of Rights* about the indirect, rather
than the direct, payoff of legal tactics.

At the same time, this research qualifies those claims in illu-
minating ways. To begin with, McCann specifies as preconditions what I took for granted—namely, a preexisting organized
leadership cadre of political activists and a supportive political
and legal ethos. The pay equity movement's claim of "equal pay
for work of comparable worth derived in large part from previous battles" was effectively deployed "to raise the expectations
and channel the energies of working women already well aware
of their unfair treatment" (1994, 279–80).

And from this foundation, the movement cultivated additional
resources—including financial and organizational support
from allies in government, community groups, and the public
at large—which sustained defiant action for new rights even as
the initial judicial support faded. (280)

Charles R. Epp, in the context of comparative research, makes an
analogous point—arguing that "a vibrant support structure is a
necessary condition" for politically effective rights advocacy
(1998, 21). Thus, he hypothesizes that "rights revolutions have
occurred only where and when and on those issues for which
material support for rights litigation—rights advocacy organizations, supportive lawyers, and sources of financing—has developed" (23).

McCann also distinguishes movement-building outcomes
from policy outcomes and from the creation of new rights and
argues that the payoff of the former is more significant in the
long term than the latter:

Ideological reconstruction became institutionalized in the very process of struggle. It is important to recognize in this regard that the campaign for rights not only altered official workplace policies and practices but also greatly fortified organizational ties among women workers and with their allies. This newly developed solidaristic strength in many contexts quickly facilitated a variety of other successful struggles for new workplace rights and reforms. Even though the overall equity movement was contained, my case studies thus revealed a variable but broadly significant pattern of political empowerment. (282)

Finally, McCann's evidence reveals that a rights-based campaign contributes to movement building by generating both internal solidarity and by enlisting external support.

Silverstein (1996) comes to similar conclusions in her study of the animal rights movement. She acknowledges the burdens imposed by attempting to deploy a politics of rights on behalf of nonhumans. She argues, however, that "the emphasis [of animal rights activists] on a broadened notion of community and on the responsibility we have in our relations with members of the community may be important in advancing causes beyond animals" (238). Specifically, she perceives "a general challenge and resistance to dominant constructions of meaning from which other movements may learn and draw support" (238).

The overall message of the research on collective mobilization is that rights are a distinctly qualified political resource. Under appropriate conditions, however, rights can be deployed to promote collective political mobilization on behalf of an egalitarian agenda. By lending their discursive and institutional support, courts can make an important contribution to this process—as they did with respect to civil rights. When the courts validate an expansive interpretation of the kind that McCann discovered in the pay equity cases, they provide both institutional leverage and discursive legitimation. However, without a favorable political ethos and a cadre of movement activists to take advantage of the leverage and legitimation, collective mobilization will not occur. Conversely, given the necessary conditions, mobilization can succeed even in the face of judicial opposition.

Countermobilization: Competing Myths and Contested Meanings

The collective mobilization research makes a convincing case for the conditional character of a progressive politics of rights — providing empirical evidence of the circumstances conducive to the success or failure of rights campaigns. What gets less attention in this research are the potential downsides of the politics of rights — that successful politics of rights campaigns can, on the one hand, generate a backlash and that, on the other hand, the politics of rights can serve right-wing purposes as readily as those of the liberal-left. Pointing to the latter, Jon Goldberg-Hiller puts it this way:

> The vast majority of [legal mobilization] studies have approached law from an implicit civil rights model in which law's utility for social action is evaluated from the standpoint of progressive groups seeking fundamental political and social reform. [There are] interesting questions rarely asked in these studies, however. Primary among these is how some social movements mobilize *against* the law and seek to transform discourses about rights — particularly civil rights — into exclusionary limits. (Goldberg-Hiller 2002, 34; emphasis in the original; see also Bakan 1997)

While hitherto neglected, the research cupboard on countermobilization is by no means bare. There is both analytic and anecdotal evidence about when and how the politics of rights can go wrong. At the heart of this emerging revisionist literature are two key elements — the indeterminacy of rights and their negation through competing myths.

Although there is ample evidence that the myth of rights does resonate positively, there is also evidence that it is not universally well received and is subject to external challenges from competing myths—and, in particular, a myth of community. The myth of community comes in a variety of forms. Consider, for example, the ascendance of a discourse of law and order beginning in the 1960s—when a myth of crime and punishment regularly trumped the rights of defendants legally and politically (Scheingold 1984; 1991). At its core, the underlying message of this communitarian counter to rights is a discourse of individual responsibility and social solidarity (Glendon 1991; 1994).

Just as the indeterminacy of rights accommodates their egalitarian expansion, so too can rights be inflected in anti-egalitarian ways. Note, to begin with, that it was only in the latter part of the twentieth century that rights took on an egalitarian tone. One need not accept the characterization of this development as a "rights revolution" to acknowledge that rights have historically had more to do with the protection of property and privilege than with their redistribution. Accordingly, it should come as no surprise that rights can readily be inflected with nonegalitarian meaning—in both the legal and the political arenas.

In sum, the right has taken its cues from the left—constructing its own cultures of victimization and resistance and deploying them both legally and politically. (On cultures of resistance, see Merry 1995.) It is to these matters that I now turn.

Conservatives have, in effect, successfully mobilized an anti-egalitarian politics of rights—although they have done so in part (and paradoxically) by repudiating rights. How and why is this possible, and under what conditions can a conservative backlash in effect trump the myth of rights and capture the political initiative? The answer can be readily traced both to the discursive indeterminacy of rights (contested meaning) and to the ambivalent resonance of rights in American culture (competing myths).

Conservatives challenge egalitarian inflections of rights and propose culturally resonant alternatives. In claiming that the fetus has rights, abortion foes are, of course, attempting to expand the meaning of rights beyond its traditional boundaries—

altogether analogous to the efforts of their egalitarian counterparts on the left. Affirmative action opponents argue for a color-
blind interpretation of rights—a return in effect to a formal,
decontextualized conception of equal rights and equal opportunity.
Gay rights and American Indian treaty rights are reinterpreted as
special rights and thus at odds with equal rights. Political mobilization proceeds from these contested meanings with the
objective of enlisting support not only from a core of true believers but also from the political mainstream. In sum, conservative
countermobilization, while politically at odds with egalitarian
evocations of the politics of rights, is analytically indistinguishable from them.

Jeffrey Dudas's research on the backlash in the state of
Washington against Indian treaty rights provides a particularly
thorough analysis of countermobilization. Litigation of treaty
rights, he points out, has been successful in enhancing the material well-being of tribal nations—initially by way of commercial
fishing and subsequently, and much more dramatically, through
casino gambling.

> However, the successes that many tribal governments have
> recently experienced in pursuit of their treaty rights have also
> exacted significant costs. Some of the most substantial of
> these costs, as I have detailed throughout, revolve around the
> mobilization of well-financed, resentful, and zealous opposi-
> tion groups. Encouraged by local politicians and persuaded by
> the core American cultural values of equal treatment and indi-
> vidual merit that treaty rights claims are illegitimate forms of
> political activity, these opposition groups have consistently
> acted in ways that work to delay the realization of tribal inter-
> ests and expunge scarce tribal resources; their efforts counter
> the efficacy of treaty-rights claims. (Dudas 2003, 12–13)

Dudas focuses then on the competing myth of individual responsibility to explain the cultural resonance of the backlash against
treaty rights.

Note that countermobilization is as much about what is wrong with rights—their tendency to sow social discord—as about the virtues of individual responsibility. As Dudas puts it,

> Opponents frequently allege that treaty rights are un-American. Treaty rights are thus understood to be "violations of the basic tenets of our civic culture," with opponents emphasizing how treaty rights affront the moral and political sensibilities that underwrite American community. (2003, 5)

In other words, countermobilization against treaty rights rejects rights-claiming as such, because it is said to privilege social conflict and encourage dependence on the state. Of course, whether countermobilization around competing myths is successful depends (like mobilization itself) on the cultural resonance of the myths, on opportunistic advocacy, and on the political context.

There is, however, a deeper meaning to the increasingly widespread reaction against rights—namely that the rights revolution and the rights reaction are dialectically entangled with one another. Just as the denial of rights tends to legitimate rights-claiming, so too does the granting of rights undermine rights-claiming. As Greenhouse points out, the success of civil rights has made rights appear to be not only superfluous but also actually subversive of citizenship.

> Since the Brown generation has now reached middle age, the benefits of equality having been made available (so this reasoning seems to go), inequality is no longer the public's responsibility, but the lifestyle choice of intrinsically inferior citizens. (1997, 186)

To claim and to gain rights is to make oneself and one's social group "beneficiaries of opportunities made available by federal power" (182). This dependency on federal power is meant to be self-correcting—necessary and sufficient to transform the dependent citizen, the citizen manqué, into a fully responsible citizen.

Put another way, once rights are granted, continued rights-claiming becomes ever more culturally suspect. The marginalized are, thus, trapped in a discursive field that gives them a Hobson's choice between acknowledging a deficient identity and accepting the burdens of marginality. The former choice, *victimhood* (Bumiller 1988), is just as unwelcome as the latter in that victimhood imposes "psychological impediments to pursuing legal remedies . . . [and thus] an unwillingness to accept 'the image of the victim as powerless and defeated'" (Sarat and Kearns 1993, 58).

Leonard Feldman demonstrates how this Hobson's choice has been formalized within the jurisprudence of homelessness—specifically in the Chicago practice of indiscriminate confiscation of the property of the homeless living on the streets. The courts affirmed the city's right to confiscate all property except for what is required to sustain "bare life"—that is, everything beyond "items essential for physical survival . . . 'such as a sleeping bag and several blankets, required to live on the sidewalk'" (2000, 68). The justification for this "dispossessive individualism" was that because the homeless had made a "lifestyle choice" to live on the streets, rather than entering the shelters provided by the city, they also had to accept the responsibility to minimize the resultant inconvenience to their fellow citizens. In this way, Feldman argues, "agency is converted into a form of blame" (2000, 88). Similarly, Greenhouse argues that Clarence Thomas's life story, as constructed during his confirmation hearings, served as evidence that it is appropriate to blame since "the need for civil rights is now gone" (1997, 171).

And once blaming begins, exclusion readily follows. Greenhouse connects the racialized discourse of street crime in the United States to the end of the civil rights era. Insofar as civil rights are granted but the favored group fails to fit in, their "otherness" must be managed by the state (1997, 184–85). Social control takes precedence over rights-claiming by those who have abused their freedom (Rose 1999) and *chosen* to threaten the social and moral orders through predatory street crime, welfare dependency, and the like. Similarly, while abortion opponents do inflect their campaign as rights in conflict, opposition to abortion is rooted at its core in the moral imperatives of the religious right—less about rights than about individual responsibility to maintain community standards of morality. In much the same way, the tort reform movement has sought to discredit trial lawyers and personal injury litigation as a threat to, for example, the health care system (Haltom and McCann, forthcoming). It is, thus, in the nature of rights to be both agents of equality and perpetuators of inequality. Put another way, rights consciousness and anti–rights consciousness are part of the same discursive field.

If rights thus emerge as something of a two-edged sword, the same is true albeit in a different way of cause lawyers, who constitute the final element of this new politics of rights. Cause-lawyering research reveals that right-wing cause lawyers have modeled their tactics and strategy on the successes of liberal-left cause lawyers going back to the civil rights era. In so doing, cause lawyering emerges as both an agent of equality and redistribution and the inspiration and model for resisting egalitarian and redistributive changes.

Cause Lawyers: From Litigation to Politicization

My analysis of cause lawyers, whom I referred to as activist lawyers, in *The Politics of Rights* resulted in two significant miscalculations that have been corrected by subsequent research. To begin with, I argued that cause lawyers were socialized in ways that privileged litigation and marginalized the politicization that was essential to a politics of rights. This conclusion was rooted *historically* in the example of the NAACP Legal Defense Fund lawyers, who actively resisted extrajudicial tactics, and *analytically* in my understanding of legal education and legal practice. I also took it for granted that cause lawyering was by definition a left-liberal phenomenon. My thinking was based on the assumption that only society's have-nots had to resort to a cumbersome and contingent politics of rights while society's haves had ready and direct access to political power. Neither argument has held up very well to empirical scrutiny.

Michael McCann and Helena Silverstein (1998) argue convincingly that the "lure of litigation" is not irresistible, and they have specified the circumstances conducive to the politicization of rights campaigns. They do not deny that cause lawyers tend to privilege litigation, but point out that, like other lawyers, cause lawyers view litigation as one arrow in a quiver that includes, for example, leveraging the threat of litigation, lobbying, and under the right circumstances, political mobilization. They note, in particular, that lawyers working with and within organized social movements (such as labor movements) are willing and able to deploy rights politically.

Research findings from the cause-lawyering project lead in the same direction. A case in point is Neta Ziv's project on the legislative and bureaucratic advocacy of disability cause lawyers. She concludes that the Americans with Disabilities Act legislative campaign "illustrates how cause lawyers, as representatives of disadvantaged social groups and movements, can develop mechanisms that ameliorate imbalances between disadvantaged and privileged segments of society through mainstream political institutions" (2001, 215). Still closer to the politics of rights, per se, is Susan Coutin's finding that "cause lawyers' advocacy work was not limited to helping immigrants discover ways to manipulate U.S. immigration law and thus to win in court" (2001, 132).

> This work required cause lawyers to participate in broad-based movements that sought justice for Central American immigrants. These movements were transnational in character, drew on both official and clandestine networks, and promoted multiple models of statehood, membership, and legitimacy. Attorneys sometimes participated in these movements directly. In addition, as members of organizations that were involved in political advocacy, attorneys were implicitly supporting this work. (133)

Coutin's account of "political advocacy" by immigration cause lawyers also reveals how and why cause lawyers regularly cross and recross the line dividing legal from political cause lawyering.

Comparable findings have emerged from research in Latin America (Meili 1998), Israel (Morag-Levine 2001), and Japan. The Japanese example (Kidder and Miyazawa 1993) is particularly instructive. Japanese cause lawyers, persuaded that adversarial legalism was ineffective given Japan's neocorporatist state, strongly believed that even the most modest results are possible only when it can be demonstrated outside the courtroom that their claims find resonance in the polity. Thus, Japanese cause lawyers regularly, if reluctantly, take on the onerous chore of organizing plaintiffs and helping them to orchestrate campaigns to raise public consciousness—and in this way to get the attention of the government. In sum, cause lawyers do not necessarily see political and legal strategies as mutually exclusive, as I originally suggested—and, thus, often willingly engage in the strategic calculations that are essential to a successful politics of rights.

On the other hand, my own research with Anne Bloom (Scheingold and Bloom 1998) reveals that cause lawyers are well aware of the impact of their choice of strategies on their social capital. As Jack Katz (1982) noted some years back, appellate litigation is seen by lawyers as much more prestigious than grassroots community organizing. Moreover, political mobilization is seen as suspect in some of the sites where cause lawyers practice—in particular in the pro bono programs of corporate firms and in social advocacy organizations, which rely on politically moderate funding sources. Finally, many cause lawyers do, as I originally argued, honor the law-politics distinction—leading them to privilege litigation over the mobilization of social movements, electoral politics, and lobbying. For both practical and principled reasons, then, litigation is the path of least resistance for cause lawyers. Consequently, it seems fair to conclude that it is mostly in the kind of supportive practice settings identified by McCann and Silverstein (1998) that cause lawyers are likely to engage directly with the politics of rights.

We know less about right-wing cause lawyering—that is, lawyers working on behalf of property rights, the religious right, a variety of libertarian causes, and the like. The research findings that have emerged, however, strongly suggest that these right-wing cause lawyers, despite their similarities to their left-liberal counterparts (Southworth 2003), are even less likely to undertake a politics of rights. Generally speaking, it might be said that right-wing cause lawyers, with the exception of Christian evangelicals, do not need and/or do not believe in the politics of rights.

To begin at the beginning, the phenomenon of right-wing cause lawyering can reasonably be seen as backlash—counter-mobilization against left-liberal rights activism. In some cases, however, this backlash amounts to fighting fire with fire, while in other cases backlash is about going against the grain of liberal-left cause lawyering. Consider Laura Hatcher's contrasting characterizations of the Pacific Legal Foundation (PLF) and the Institute for Justice (IFJ):

> The PLF's position makes the legislature the arena for all political debate, deferring to elected legislators to know what is in the best interest of the people. . . . IFJ, on the other hand, views the judge as an active participant in the law-making process, reviewing and striking down any legislation that is unconstitutional (2003, 25–26).

In neither case, however, is there any evidence of a politics of rights, as such.

Simply put, the PLF is sufficiently well connected politically to eschew the cumbersome, conditional, and indirect modus operandi of the politics of rights. Instead, they campaign against courts and exercise their ready and direct access to the political process to limit government regulation and vindicate property rights. The IFJ, in contrast, believes that conservative courts can curb both legislative excess and liberal judicial activism by simply returning to strict constitutional construction. Accordingly, it is both necessary and sufficient to participate vigorously in judicial recruitment and selection while at the same time deploying litigation to reconstruct the meaning of rights so as to reflect conservative values.

On the right, the available research suggests that only evangelical Christian cause lawyers have pursued a politics of rights. Unlike the civil rights lawyers of the 1960s and 1970s, however, the political organization of Moral Majority preceded legal mobilization (den Dulk, n.d.) and, more fundamentally, the result has been an ideologically coherent political and legal social movement (Scheingold and Sarat, forthcoming, chap. 5). Still, the overall process is in keeping with McCann and Silverstein's (1998) findings, that political mobilization is most likely to occur among those lawyers who are both politically engaged and associated with an organized social movement like Operation Rescue (Van Dyk 1994).

Except for Malcolm Feeley's foreword and my preface, this second edition of *The Politics of Rights* is indistinguishable from the original 1974 version. In the intervening years I have more than once considered a substantially revised second edition. Why then has the text remained unchanged? To begin with, there is a way in which it is too late to systematically revise the original. The subsequent rights scholarship that is the focus of this preface amounts in effect to a multiplicity of second editions. This work has so expanded the purview of what we know about the politics of rights that there would be no way to do a revision without completely dismantling and reconstructing the original to such an extent that it would be less a second edition than an entirely different book.

What might such a book, a *New Politics of Rights,* look like? Ideally, it would be comparative and empirical—reaching beyond the U.S. experience to analyze rights in other national settings, and in transnational settings as well. Its goals would be to identify common ground and to explain variation in the cultural resonance and political utility of rights. This would require crafting a conceptual schema less tethered to the United States—and, indeed, to Western—experience and tradition. I see Charles Epp's *Rights Revolution* (1998), with its emphasis on uncovering macroanalytic patterns, as an important step in the comparative, empirical, and explanatory directions. The cause-lawyering volumes contribute in analogous ways—albeit with a more qualitative and microanalytic approach that seeks out and celebrates variation. The individual disputing literature seems the most conceptually ambitious and has recently taken a comparative turn. In sampling these literatures and juxtaposing their findings, this preface makes the case for a *New Politics of Rights*.

To close on a more personal note, the multiple "second editions" of *The Politics of Rights* are especially gratifying because of the prominence of research done by Michael McCann, my longtime friend and colleague, and by our graduate students at the University of Washington. It has also been a particular pleasure to work with the talented and congenial multidisciplinary, multinational, and multigenerational cohort of scholars in the Cause-Lawyering Project, which Austin Sarat and I have been codirecting for almost a decade. Taken together, the many flourishing bodies of rights scholarship—irrespective of whether they have invoked, ignored, corrected, superseded, or denounced my work—have given the politics of rights a deeper and longer life than I would have ever imagined possible.

I will be forever grateful to Malcolm Feeley, who not only provided a foreword but also conceived of the idea for a second edition. He thus added to the many, many personal and intellectual debts I have incurred to him through the years. At the University of Michigan Press, Jeremy Shine steered this venture safely through its initial stages and Jim Reische and Sarah Mann graciously saw me through subsequent stages of the publication process.

REFERENCES

Bakan, Joel. 1997. *Just Words: Constitutional Rights and Social Wrongs.* Toronto: University of Toronto Press.

Brigham, John. 1996. *The Constitution of Interests: Beyond the Politics of Rights.* New York: New York University Press.

Bruun, Rita. 1982. "The Boldt Decision: Legal Victory, Political Defeat." *Law and Policy* 4:271–98.

Bumiller, Kristin. 1988. *The Civil Rights Society: The Social Construction of Victims.* Baltimore: Johns Hopkins University Press.

Coutin, Susan Bibler. 2001. "Cause Lawyering in the Shadow of the State: A U.S. Immigration Example." In *Cause Lawyering and the State in a Global Era,* ed. Austin Sarat and Stuart Scheingold, 117–40. New York: Oxford University Press.

Den Dulk, Kevin R. N.d. "In Legal Culture, But Not of It: The Cause Lawyering of Evangelical Conservatives." Unpublished ms.

Dudas, Jeffrey. 2003. "Rights, Resentment, and Social Change." Chapter 1 (draft) of "Rights, Resentment, and Social Change: The Politics of Treaty Rights." Ph.D. dissertation, University of Washington.

Edelman, Murray. 1964. *The Symbolic Uses of Politics.* Urbana: University of Illinois Press.

Engel, David M. 1994. "The Oven Bird's Song: Insiders, Outsiders, and Personal Injuries in an American Community." In *Law and Community in Three American Towns,* ed. Carol J. Greenhouse, Barbara Yngvesson, and David M. Engel, 27–53. Ithaca: Cornell University Press.

Engel, David M., and Frank W. Munger. 2003. *Rights of Inclusion: Law and Identity in the Life Stories of Americans with Disabilities.* Chicago: University of Chicago Press.

Epp, Charles R. 1998. *The Rights Revolution: Lawyers, Activists and Supreme Courts in Comparative Perspective.* Chicago: University of Chicago Press.

Ewick, Patricia, and Susan S. Silbey. 1998. *The Common Place of Law: Stories from Everyday Life.* Chicago: University of Chicago Press.

Feldman, Leonard. 2000. "Homelessness and the Public Sphere: The Politics of Displacement and the Domestication of Citizenship." Ph.D. dissertation, University of Washington. Forthcoming as *Homeless Politics: Democratic Pluralism and the Predicament of Bare Life.* Ithaca: Cornell University Press.

Forbath, William E. 1991. *Law and the Shaping of the American Labor Movement.* Cambridge: Harvard University Press.

Freeman, Alan. 1998. "Antidiscrimination Law from 1954 to 1989: Uncertainty, Contradiction, Rationalization, Denial." In *The Politics of Law: A Progressive Critique,* ed. David Kairys, 285–311. 3d ed. New York: Basic Books.

Geertz, Clifford, 1964. "Ideology as a Cultural System." In *Ideology and Discontent,* ed. David E. Apter, 47–76. New York: Free Press.

Gilliom, John. 2001. *Overseers of the Poor: Surveillance, Resistance, and the Limits of Privacy.* Chicago: University of Chicago Press.

Glendon, Mary Ann. 1991. *Rights Talk: The Impoverishment of Political Discourse.* New York: Free Press.

Glendon, Mary Ann. 1994. *A Nation under Lawyers: How the Crisis of the Legal Profession Is Transforming American Society.* New York: Farrar, Straus, and Giroux.

Goldberg-Hiller, Jonathan. 2002. *The Limits of Union: Same-Sex Marriage and the Politics of Civil Rights.* Ann Arbor: University of Michigan Press.

Greenhouse, Carol J. 1994. "Courting Difference: Issues of Interpretation and Comparison in the Study of Legal Ideologies." In *Law and Community in Three American Towns,* ed. Carol J. Greenhouse, Barbara Yngvesson, and David M. Engel, 91–110. Ithaca: Cornell University Press.

Greenhouse, Carol J. 1997. "A Federal Life: Brown and the Nationalization of the Life Story." In *Race, Law and Culture: Reflections on Brown v. the Board of Education,* ed. Austin Sarat, 170–89. New York: Oxford University Press.

Greenhouse, Carol J., Barbara Yngvesson, and David M. Engel. 1994. *Law and Community in Three American Towns.* Ithaca: Cornell University Press.

Haltom, William, and Michael McCann. Forthcoming 2004. *Distorting the Law: Politics, Media, and the Litigation Crisis.* Chicago: University of Chicago Press.

Hartz, Louis. 1955. *The Liberal Tradition in America: An Interpretation of American Political Thought Since the Revolution.* New York: Harcourt, Brace, and World.

Hatcher, Laura. Forthcoming. "Economic Libertarians, Property and Institutions: Linking Activism, Ideas and Identities among Property Rights Advocates." Unpublished paper for inclusion in *The Worlds Cause Lawyers Make: Structure and Agency in Legal Practice,* ed.

Austin Sarat and Stuart A. Scheingold. Stanford, CA: Stanford University Press.

Herman, Didi. 1996. *Rights of Passage: Struggles for Lesbian and Gay Legal Equality.* Toronto: University of Toronto Press.

Katz, Jack. 1982. *Poor People's Lawyers in Transition.* New Brunswick, N.J.: Rutgers University Press.

Kidder, Robert, and Setsuo Miyazawa. 1993. "Long-Term Strategies in Japanese Environmental Litigation." *Law and Social Inquiry* 18:605–27.

Klare, Karl E. 1978. "Judicial Deradicalization of the Wagner Act and the Origins of Modern Legal Consciousness, 1937–1941." *Minnesota Law Review* 62:265–339.

Lipsky, Michael. 1980. *Street-Level Bureaucracy: Dilemmas of the Individual in Public Service.* New York: Russell Sage Foundation.

McCann, Michael. 1994. *Rights at Work: Pay Equity Reform and the Politics of Legal Mobilization.* Chicago: University of Chicago Press.

McCann, Michael, and Helena Silverstein. 1993. "Social Movements and the American State: Legal Mobilization as a Strategy for Democratization." In *A Different Kind of State? Popular Power and Democratic Administration,* ed. Gregory Albo, David Langille, and Leo Panitch, 131–43. Toronto: Oxford University Press.

McCann, Michael, and Helena Silverstein. 1998. "Rethinking Law's Allurements: A Relational Analysis of Social Movement Lawyers in the United States." In *Cause Lawyering and the State in a Global Era,* ed. Austin Sarat and Stuart Scheingold, 261–92. New York: Oxford University Press.

Medcalf, Linda. 1978. *Law and Identity: Lawyers, Native Americans, and Legal Practice.* Beverly Hills: Sage Publications.

Meili, Stephen. 1998. "Cause Lawyers and Social Movements: A Comparative Perspective on Democratic Change in Argentina and Brazil." In *Cause Lawyering and the State in a Global Era,* ed. Austin Sarat and Stuart Scheingold, 487–522. New York: Oxford University Press.

Merry, Sally Engle. 1990. *Getting Justice, Getting Even: Legal Consciousness among Working-Class Americans.* Chicago: University of Chicago Press.

Merry, Sally Engle. 1995. "Resistance and the Cultural Power of Law." *Law and Society Review* 29:11–26.

Milner, Neal. 1986. "The Dilemmas of Legal Mobilization: Ideologies and Strategies of Mental Patient Liberation." *Law and Policy* 8:105–29.

Morag-Levine, Noga. 2001. "The Politics of Imported Rights: Transplantation and Transformation in an Israeli Environmental Cause-Lawyering Organization." In *Cause Lawyering and the State in a Global Era,* ed. Austin Sarat and Stuart Scheingold, 334–53. New York: Oxford University Press.

Olson, Susan M. 1984. *Clients and Lawyers: Securing Rights of Disabled Persons.* Westport, Conn.: Greenwood Press.

Rose, Nikolas. 1999. *Powers of Freedom: Reframing Political Thought.* Cambridge: Cambridge University Press.

Rosenberg, Gerald N. 1991. *The Hollow Hope: Can Courts Bring about Social Change?* Chicago: University of Chicago Press.

Sarat, Austin, and Thomas R. Kearns. 1993. "Beyond the Great Divide: Forms of Legal Scholarship and Everyday Life." In *Law in Everyday Life,* ed. Austin Sarat and Thomas R. Kearns, 21–62. Ann Arbor: University of Michigan Press.

Scheingold, Stuart A. 1984. *The Politics of Law and Order: Street Crime and Public Policy.* New York: Longman.

Scheingold, Stuart A. 1988. "Constitutional Rights and Social Change: Civil Rights in Perspective." In *Critical Perspectives on the Constitution,* ed. Michael W. McCann and Gerald L. Houseman, 73–91. Boston: Little, Brown.

Scheingold, Stuart A. 1991. *The Politics of Street Crime: Criminal Process and Cultural Obsession.* Philadelphia: Temple University Press.

Scheingold, Stuart A., and Anne Bloom. 1998. "Transgressive Cause Lawyering." *International Journal of the Legal Profession* 5:209–53.

Scheingold, Stuart A., and Austin Sarat. Forthcoming. *Something to Believe in: Professionalism, Politics, and Cause Lawyers.* Stanford, CA: Stanford University Press.

Schneider, Elizabeth. 1986. "The Dialectics of Legal Repression: Perspectives from the Women's Movement." *New York University Law Review* 61:589–652.

Shklar, Judith N. 1964. *Legalism.* Cambridge: Harvard University Press.

Silverstein, Helena. 1996. *Unleashing Rights: Law, Meaning, and the Animal Rights Movement.* Ann Arbor: University of Michigan Press.

Southworth, Ann. Forthcoming. "Professional Identity and Political Commitment among Lawyers for Conservative Causes." Unpublished paper for inclusion in *The Worlds Cause Lawyers Make: Structure and Agency in Legal Practice,* ed. Austin Sarat and Stuart A. Scheingold. Stanford, CA: Stanford University Press.

Tocqueville, Alexis de. 1959. *Democracy in America.* New York: Vintage.
Van Dyk, Robert A. 1994. "Challenging Choice: Abortion Clinic Blockades and the Dynamics of Collective Action." Ph.D. dissertation, University of Washington.
Ziv, Neta. 2001. "Lawyers, Clients, and the State: Congress as a Forum for Cause Lawyering during the Enactment of the Americans with Disabilities Act." In *Cause Lawyering and the State in a Global Era,* ed. Austin Sarat and Stuart Scheingold, 211–43. New York: Oxford University Press.

PREFACE TO THE FIRST EDITION

This book investigates the political role of legal rights. The inquiry is conducted on two levels—corresponding to what I choose to think about as the two lives of the law in the United States. The concrete institutional existence of the law is the more familiar; it is readily researched and therefore better understood. Law, however, also has a symbolic life; it resides in the minds of Americans. The symbolic life of the law is often acknowledged but seldom analyzed, and the impact of legal symbols on political life accordingly remains obscure.

What I shall argue is that the influence of legal symbols is indirect but powerful. Legal values condition perceptions, establish role expectations, provide standards of legitimacy, and account for the institutional patterns of American politics. To understand the political importance of American law, it is not enough to consider the concrete manifestations of legal institutions or to take into account the immediate reactions to or compliance with legal rulings. These are important matters, to be sure, but they must be understood in connection with the patterns of belief evoked by legal symbols. In its symbolic form, the law shapes the context in which American politics is conducted.

An adequate examination of the place of the law in American politics must, in other words, take seriously the interplay between values and behavior. I have sought to focus this amorphous task by concentrating on the efforts of lawyers to put litigation and legal rights at the service of redistributive political goals. Neither litigation nor political change is, however, examined for its own sake but rather for the light shed on the broader problem of understanding the influence of legal values on political outcomes. Similarly, this is not a detailed historical inquiry but a self-conscious attempt to develop a new and useful perspective on the relationship between law and politics.

I draw upon familiar facts and generally accepted concepts. What matters is the way these pieces are fitted together. I have deliberately chosen to sacrifice detail in order to present the big picture in a coherent and persuasive fashion. If, as one reader suggested, there could be more meat on the bones, I can only hope that the result is not slim pickin's.

In short, this book should be taken as a point of departure —one that raises questions rather than provides answers. That is not to say that I have avoided taking a position. Indeed, I have adopted a direct and assertive style in order to make my case. The assertions are not meant to close issues, however, but to frame them.

While I have explored some new terrain in this study, it is primarily a work of synthesis. A deliberate effort has been made to draw widely upon the relevant literature in the field of public law, although my synthesis has been selective rather than exhaustive. Even the more novel aspects of this study build on insights and inquiries of other scholars. While these direct debts are acknowledged in footnotes, the work of two scholars, Judith Shklar and Murray Edelman, deserve special mention.

The personal origins of this study, my first published work on law and politics in the United States, extend back into the distant past. When I was a graduate student in Berkeley, it was Charles Aikin who introduced me to the puzzles of law and politics; Yosal Rogat who provided the jurisprudential perspectives that helped me piece together and understand the importance of those puzzles; and John Schaar who encouraged me to explore the cultural roots of legal values in America.

All of this graduate student searching did not really begin to pay off, however, until I found myself in the stimulating and congenial intellectual environment offered by the law and society program at the University of Wisconsin. To name individual friends and colleagues from those days would be, however, to betray the whole collective spirit of that experience.

As for work on the manuscript itself, I must acknowledge particular debts. Ken Dolbeare was the first person to suggest that I lay aside my work in international relations and undertake this study. Dick Flathman read the manuscript in draft and was kind enough to go over the whole of it in painstaking detail. Victor Bernstein and Victor Rosenblum each provided me with extensive critiques of the manuscript. I fear that I was more receptive to their encouragement than to their many sensible suggestions. Finally, Dan Lev's contribution to this book has been enormous and invaluable. He patiently explained just what I was trying to do and thus helped me lace together a body of diffuse material into what I trust is a coherent whole. To underscore the weight of his contribution, I shall break with precedent and demand that he accept responsibility for the shortcomings of this book as well as for its merits.

The only continuous link between graduate school and this study has been provided by my students in Davis, Madison, and Seattle. In particular, it was the students who led me to reexamine the cultural myths about American law which I was all too inclined to accept as descriptions. What seemed of fundamental importance to me often struck them as academic irrelevance. Because they, especially the minority students, would not (and often quite literally could not) relate to my truths, I was forced to rethink and refine some of my most cherished political premises. Because my debt to these students is so heavy, I must also acknowledge a debt to several foundations which, as a result of their unwillingness to fund this project, kept me in the classroom while work was proceeding on the manuscript.

The publication process has added still further to my

indebtedness. Marian Ash has been remarkably flexible and responsive in the face of a number of unusual problems. Moreover, she has provided me with a superb copy editor. To Ruth Kaufman, who wields a precise but understanding blue pencil, I owe enthusiastic thanks for all the help she has provided in the publication of this book—as well as belated thanks for her work on an earlier tome.

Only Lee knows in how many ways this is our book.

Seattle   S.A.S.
April 1974

Prologue

1. LEGAL RIGHTS
AND POLITICAL ACTION

This is a book about the law. The law is real, but it is also a figment of our imaginations. Like all fundamental social institutions it casts a shadow of popular belief that may ultimately be more significant, albeit more difficult to comprehend, than the authorities, rules, and penalties that we ordinarily associate with law. What we believe reflects our values; it also colors our perceptions. What we believe about the law is related directly to the legitimacy of our political institutions.

Traditional views about the law in America see it as beneficent and tend to reinforce legitimacy and stabilize the polity. Surely these views have, at least until quite recently, dominated the literature on law and politics in the United States.[1] But now a radical interpretation which equates law with repression has begun to gain support.[2] Thus, myth and countermyth compete for our attention and acceptance.

The purpose of this study is not necessarily to choose

1. See, for example, Alexander M. Bickel, *The Least Dangerous Branch: The Supreme Court at the Bar of Politics* (Indianapolis: Bobbs-Merrill, 1962); Theodore J. Lowi, *The End of Liberalism: Ideology, Policy, and the Crisis of Public Authority* (New York: Norton, 1969); and the works of J. Willard Hurst, such as *Law and the Condition of Freedom in the Nineteenth-Century United States* (Madison: University of Wisconsin Press, 1956).
2. The Cornerstone of a radical analysis of American law is (or should be) Charles A. Beard, *An Economic Interpretation of the Constitution of the United States* (New York: Free Press, 1965). Two recent collections are Robert Lefcourt, ed., *Law Against the People* (New York: Vintage, 1971) and Jonathan Black, ed., *Radical Lawyers* (New York: Avon, 1971). See also Ralph Miliband, *The State in Capitalist Society* (New York: Basic Books, 1969).

between these competing visions, each of which seems to be flawed in significant ways. If, however, we can understand how the law lends itself to such dramatically contrasting interpretations, a more satisfactory appraisal of the relationship between law and change in America will surely be possible.

The specific aim of this book is to assess the part that lawyers and litigation can play in altering the course of public policy. While this problem has been considered in a number of previous studies, each of them has provided only a partial glimpse of the process. Their tendency has been to concentrate on a particular institution—most frequently the Supreme Court—or a single policy problem like civil rights. There has also been a pronounced inclination to separate theory (or jurisprudence) from empirical analysis.[3] The result has been a proliferation of data and theories but no efforts at general synthesis. At a time when serious questions are being raised about the role of law in the United States, a systematic look at the total picture is surely in order.

The most important distinguishing feature of this study is that it abandons the conventional legal perspective and replaces it with a political approach to the problem of law and change. In the United States we have long been accustomed to associating lawyers (albeit a small minority of the bar) with programs to alter the status quo. The lawyers'

3. There is a large body of literature and I cite only a few titles which illustrate the partial nature of these studies. Frederick M. Wirt, *The Politics of Southern Equality: Law and Social Change in a Mississippi County* (Chicago: Aldine, 1970); Joseph L. Sax, *Defending the Environment: A Strategy for Citizen Action* (New York: Knopf, 1970); Kenneth M. Dolbeare and Philip E. Hammond, *The School Prayer Decisions* (Chicago: University of Chicago Press, 1971); Alexander M. Bickel, *The Supreme Court and the Idea of Progress* (New York: Harper and Row, 1970). The relevant works of jurisprudence would include such titles as Judith N. Shklar, *Legalism: An Essay on Law, Morals and Politics* (Cambridge: Harvard University Press, 1964); H. L. A. Hart, *The Concept of Law* (London: Oxford University Press, 1961); and perhaps a recent collection, Robert Paul Wolff, ed., *The Rule of Law* (New York: Simon and Schuster, 1971).

basic tool has been litigation, and it has been used doggedly and inventively on behalf of goals like school desegregation, free speech, and the rights of defendants. The successes and failures of these efforts to influence public policy have provided the raw material for studies of law and change in the United States, and analysts have, for the most part, accepted the actors' legal frame of reference.

THE MYTH OF RIGHTS

Legal frames of reference tunnel the vision of both activists and analysts leading to an oversimplified approach to a complex social process—an approach that grossly exaggerates the role that lawyers and litigation can play in a strategy for change. The assumption is that litigation can evoke a declaration of rights from courts; that it can, further, be used to assure the realization of these rights; and, finally, that realization is tantamount to meaningful change. The *myth of rights* is, in other words, premised on a direct linking of litigation, rights, and remedies with social change.

There are a number of difficulties with this myth of rights approach to change. Judges cannot necessarily be counted upon to formulate a right to fit all worthwhile social goals. Even when a right exists, it can hardly be taken for granted that a remedy is close behind. Activist attorneys and those who chronicle their work are ordinarily unwilling to face up to these problems. They prefer to believe that persistence and legal ingenuity will ultimately be rewarded. The result is an ad hoc search for targets of opportunity rather than a careful sorting out of priorities as they relate to long-range goals.

But even rather sophisticated strategies of litigation have been flawed in a fundamental way by the confining legal perspective. Rights-and-remedies is primarily a test of wills and resources between the parties to suits, and it is not directly assimilable to a program of social action. Legal approaches and the rules under which courts operate tend to reduce political conflicts to disputes between parties at a given time. While these encounters are often symptomatic of underlying social struggles and ordinarily reflect more general forces, success depends on establishing a personal entitlement and often turns on distinguishing one's cause from others with similiar claims. In thus driving a wedge between potential allies, litigative tactics can impose a heavy burden on the process of political organization. There are still other problems that flow from mistakenly identifying isolated courtroom victories with real progress. Confusion of the symbolic with the real diverts attention from the inertial forces which sustain the status quo. Lawyers are, moreover, reinforced in their natural inclinations to think of litigation apart from other political tactics rather than as part of a coordinated strategy.

The Politics of Rights

The simplicities and exaggerations of the myth of rights have led in the past to overrating the progressive capacities of the law. These days, it is fashionable to employ evidence and premises that are every bit as questionable to identify legal processes with reactionary forces in the society. Neither approach will do. So basic and pervasive a social institution as the law obviously merits careful and systematic scrutiny.

To this end, I propose a political approach to analyzing the utility of litigation. No framework is adequate if it fails to attach primary importance to the redistribution of power. If litigation can play a redistributive role, it can be useful as an agent of change. If not, its political utility must be heavily discounted. The political approach thus prompts us to approach rights as skeptics. Instead of thinking of judicially asserted rights as accomplished social facts or as moral imperatives, they must be thought of, on the one hand, as authoritatively articulated goals of public policy and, on the other, as political resources of unknown value in the hands of those who want to alter the course of public policy. The direct linking of rights, remedies, and change that characterizes the *myth of rights* must, in sum, be exchanged for a more complex framework, the *politics of rights,* which takes into account the contingent character of rights in the American system.

To think about rights as officially articulated goals of public policy leads directly to a more politically sensitive perspective. It is immediately clear that the courts are only one of a number of authoritative agencies that articulate goals for the polity. Formal recognition by the courts may therefore improve the bargaining position of those upon whom the judges look with favor. Judicial acceptance does not, however, mean that the goal will be embraced more generally nor that the social changes implied will be effected. If there is opposition elsewhere in the system, the judicial decision is more likely to engender than to resolve political conflict. In that conflict, a right is best treated as a resource of uncertain worth, but essentially like other political resources: money, numbers, status, and so forth. The value of a right will therefore depend in all likelihood on the circumstances and on the manner in which it is employed, and for the social scientist this boils down to a matter for careful empirical analysis.[4]

If it is assumed that on important matters of public policy a political struggle will follow a judicial decision, then the task of the analyst is to determine how that struggle is affected by the articulation of rights, and in this way to develop a comprehensive understanding of the utility of litigation. The

4. This political approach to rights departs from conventional legal and philosophic usage. My intention is to convey the idea that all official rules imply legal rights (as well as obligations) and to call attention to the contingent character of these official "promises." From this perspective, the distinctions made by lawyers and philosophers among categories of rights are less important than the opportunities and expectations that attach to all official enactments. For a compact presentation of conventional approaches to the analysis of rights, see Stanley I. Benn, "Rights," *The Encyclopedia of Philosophy* (1967), 7:195–99.

legal perspective encourages concentration on the implementation of judicial decrees alone. The courts are, however, only
modestly endowed with coercive capabilities—adequate, perhaps, for dealing with recalcitrant individuals but probably
insufficient for bringing large groups or powerful institutions
into line. Moreover, the tendency of litigation to break
political action down into a multiplicity of individual transactions stretches out the process of implementation to the point
that it can become not only tedious but counterproductive—
one step forward, two steps back. The politics of rights
implies a much more comprehensive assessment which includes but transcends the simple straight-line projection from
judicial decision to compliance.

The broader question is whether litigation can be useful for
redistributing power and influence in the political arena. Such
possibilities exist, and they deserve careful attention and
investigation. Litigation can be useful for political mobilization and can in this way affect the balance of forces. Court
decrees often articulate as a right that which has been
traditionally withheld—like integrated schooling—or granted
only as a favor—like an adequate income for welfare
recipients. These judgments can therefore alter expectations
and/or self conceptions and may be useful as well in creating
a new sense of collective identity. Mobilization can surely not
be taken for granted as the normal and necessary consequence of litigation. Nor should it be seen in isolation from
other political tactics. Even the relationship between mobilization and more traditional compliance goals poses some
interesting problems. The key point is, in any case, that there
are implications of litigation suggesting that it may be useful
in reshaping the political arena.

The politics of rights focuses on distinctive forms of
political action which are closely associated with lawyers and
litigation. Attention is directed to the articulation of public
policy goals by courts and to the post-judgment political
process. In investigating that process it is necessary to

examine both the symbolic and the coercive capabilities which attach to rights and to consider tactics that can maximize these capabilities. The utility of litigation may be expected to vary from one policy arena to another. What is useful at one stage in a process of change may be worthless or even counterproductive at another stage. In the final analysis, success may well turn on how skillfully litigation is employed and especially on how well it is coordinated with other tactics. In practice, this may all depend on the political sensitivity of lawyers and on how well they are able to work with other activists.

The organizational plan of the book flows directly from this introductory analysis. Part One, comprised of four chapters, provides a detailed analysis of the *myth of rights,* which is treated as a political ideology. The purpose of this section is to indicate how deeply and with what effect the roots of the myth of rights extend into the mainstream of American political thinking.

Part Two, also comprised of four chapters, sets the myth of rights into the political perspective that is required for an understanding of the *politics of rights.* Starting from the premise of the opening section—that the myth of rights is most sensibly treated as a political ideology—a frame of reference is developed for investigating the interplay between the ideology of rights and political action. The main message of this section is that litigation is more useful in fomenting change when used as an agent of political mobilization than when it is employed in the more conventional manner—that is, for asserting and realizing rights.

The activist lawyers who are ordinarily associated with programs of litigation are the subject of the next two chapters, which make up Part Three. The inquiry begins with an investigation of the impact of the myth of rights on legal education and professional standards. All American lawyers, including activists, are subjected to these influences—albeit in varying degrees. The focus narrows in the following chapter to the programs and prospects of the activist lawyers and, more specifically, to the ways in which their approach to litigation is shaped by ideology and socialization. These *strategists of rights,* it turns out, tend to distrust politics in general and mobilization in particular.

The concluding Epilogue assesses the contribution that rights can reasonably be expected to make to a strategy for change. Once the analysis is broadened so that litigation, rights, and mobilization are put in the context of American politics more generally, it becomes immediately clear that it is not realistic to think in terms of a *strategy of rights* as such. Legal tactics which capitalize on rights can, however, make an important ancillary contribution. Beyond simple utilitarian calculations, the ethical costs and benefits of relying on legal tactics and on political mobilization must also be considered. What I am undertaking then is a comprehensive and value-sensitive balance sheet.

Part One

THE MYTH OF RIGHTS

2. LAW AS IDEOLOGY: AN INTRODUCTION TO THE MYTH OF RIGHTS

The essential premises of this study are (1) that the law furnishes American politics with its most important symbols of legitimacy, and (2) that these symbols reflect values which are the building blocks of a political ideology. I refer to this ideology as the myth of rights.

At the core of the myth of rights is the legal paradigm—a social perspective which perceives and explains human interaction largely in terms of rules and of the rights and obligations inherent in rules.[1] Lawyers are, naturally, most self-consciously caught up in the legal way of doing things. Most Americans, however, are responsive to legal symbols— owing, I think, to distinctive cultural predispositions that Alexis de Tocqueville noticed more than a century ago. These symbols fuse the law with our formal constitutional order. The result is to lend political coherence to a singularly legal approach to politics and social intercourse. There is a strong current of belief in rights—both constitutional rights and the generality of legal rights. We believe that politics *is and should be* conducted in accordance with patterns of rights and obligations established under law.

Its coherence and legitimacy impart to the myth of rights a

1. The entire first section of this study draws heavily on the insights of Judith N. Shklar, who first systematically exposed the ideological implications of the legal frame of reference in *Legalism* (Cambridge: Harvard University Press, 1964). See also Thurman Arnold, *The Symbols of Government* (New York: Harcourt, Brace, 1962).

popular resonance that justifies the characterization as a
political ideology. As Clifford Geertz puts it, ideology provides "a symbolic framework in terms of which to formulate,
think about, and react to political problems." [2] "The function
of ideology is to make an autonomous politics possible by
providing the authoritative concepts that render it meaningful, the suasive images by means of which it can be sensibly
grasped." [3] What the myth of rights offers is an integrated set
of assertions about the nature and workings of American
politics, intimately linked to legal processes and firmly rooted
in cherished values.

The principal institutional mechanism of the myth of rights
is litigation, which we are encouraged to view as an effective
means for obtaining declarations of rights from the courts, for
assuring realization of those rights, and for building a more
just social order. The focus of the myth of rights is preemi-
nently on courts and on the maintenance of a stable system of
rules. The "political" branches of the government are, in
contrast, viewed with mistrust. Their intrinsic flaws—tendencies to steer an erratic course and to aggregate power—are
seen as threats to a viable constitutional order.

This preoccupation with courts, rules, and litigation—with,
in other words, the legal paradigm—stems from an elusive
distinction between law and politics which is so much a part
of myth of rights thinking. To the extent that this line of
thought does tap cultural predispositions, the myth of rights,
like other ideologies, elicits support, mobilizes energies, and
coordinates the activities of its adherents. It has the power to
confer legitimacy, to "bind . . . both cognitively and affec-

2. Clifford Geertz, "Ideology as a Cultural System," in David E. Apter, ed.,
Ideology and Discontent (New York: Free Press, 1964), p. 65. As used in this
manuscript, the term ideology combines normative, descriptive, and horta-
tory elements. This usage is derived largely from Geertz. See also Harry M.
Johnson, "Ideology and the Social System," in *International Encyclopedia of
Social Sciences* (1968), 7:76–85.

3. Geertz, "Ideology as a Cultural System," p. 63.

tively, providing a *basis* for discussion and action." [4] The myth of rights furnishes explanations for the past, standards for evaluating the present, and programs for social action in the future.

LEGAL SYMBOLS AND POLITICAL LEGITIMACY

Legal symbols are all around us: the Constitution, the Bill of Rights, the courts, and justice itself. The connotations of legitimacy which attach to these symbols are readily apparent. It comes as no surprise when the president of the United States has recourse to them in an effort to extricate himself from a crisis that threatens his administration and perhaps even the office he holds. Thus, President Nixon on Watergate:

> Some people, quite properly appalled at the abuses that occurred, will say that Watergate demonstrates the bankruptcy of the American political system. I believe the opposite is true.
>
> . . . It was the system that has brought the facts to light and that will bring those *guilty* to *justice.*
>
> It is essential now that we place our faith in that system, and *especially in the judicial system.*
>
> It is essential that we let the *judicial process* go forward, respecting those *safeguards that are established to protect the innocent as well as to convict the guilty.* [5]

As the president's appeal suggests, these symbols take on coherence and consistency by their association with the ongoing processes of the law. Legal symbols, in other words,

4. Douglas H. Rosenberg, "Arms and the American Way: The Ideological Dimensions of Military Growth," in Bruce Russett and Alfred Stepan, *Military Force and American Society* (New York: Harper Torchbook, 1973), p. 153. Rosenberg, also working from Geertz's formulation, offers an ideological analysis of American cold war foreign policy.

5. *The New York Times,* 2 May 1973, p. 32. Italics added.

attach to operative institutions and to the values that these institutions typify.

The integral linking of political and legal processes in our constitutional order lays the basis for what amounts to a legal theory of governance. At the core of this theory is the United States Constitution, which spells out the relationships that are supposed to obtain among institutions and individuals in the polity. Since the Constitution is also the measure of legality in our system, the interpenetration of legal and political processes is assured. It quite reasonably follows that a government of laws under the Constitution is a necessary and perhaps even a sufficient condition of political legitimacy. Legitimate authority totally outside the confines of law would naturally be altogether inconsistent with this theory, as would be a political order resting primarily on such alternative sources of authority as religion, charisma, or the general will.[6]

The theory of constitutional government also implies a legal approach to political change. If the Constitution does actually express our most fundamental political ideals, it becomes a timeless document. Properly interpreted by the judiciary, constitutional standards encourage us to constantly reexamine and upgrade the ethical tone of our society. As such, they enable us to adjust peacefully to changing conditions, but in a manner consistent with values we have agreed to live by as a people. Rather than tying us irrevocably to the past, constitutional standards are presented as indispensable guides to the future.

The ideological overtones of all this should by now be clear, as should my reasons for characterizing this ideology as

6. As J. P. Nettl has written with regard to the legal tone of political legitimacy in constitutional regimes: "Authority is perceived as vested in manifestly political institutions. Politics is viewed in terms of the relationship between institutions, and in turn between institutions and individuals and groups. This process of interrelation between individuals and institutions will be as clearly defined and as openly symbolized as possible." *Political Mobilization: A Sociological Analysis of Methods and Concepts* (New York: Basic Books, 1967), pp. 83–84.

the myth of rights. *The myth of rights rests on a faith in the political efficacy and ethical sufficiency of law as a principle of government.* According to this way of thinking, the political order in America actually functions in a manner consistent with the patterns of rights and obligations specified in the Constitution. The ethical connotations of this rule of law system are based on a willingness to identify constitutional values with social justice. It encourages us to break down social problems into the responsibilities and entitlements established under law in the same way that lawyers and judges deal with disputes among individuals. Once the problem is analyzed, the myth, moreover, suggests that it is well on the way to resolution, since these obligations and rights are not only legally enforceable but ethically persuasive, because they are rooted in constitutional values. Like all ideologies, then, the myth of rights "define[s] a particular program of social action as legitimate and worthy of support." [7]

The myth of rights, again like other ideologies, seeks to be all things to all people—or at least as many things to as many people as possible. Its success depends on its capacity to tap the predispositions of Americans. Ideologies and other cultural patterns, as Clifford Geertz has persuasively argued, provide a "template or blueprint for the organization of social and psychological processes." [8] People are responsive to that blueprint and, therefore, influenced by the ideology if there is some congruence between social reality as they perceive it and the images engendered by the ideology.[9] These images or "ideological figures" are successful if they strike compelling chords, and thus the political significance of the myth of rights is rooted in its capacity to evoke familiar patterns and cherished values.

One reason that Americans support programs of social

7. Johnson, "Ideology and the Social System," p. 81.
8. Geertz, "Ideology as a Cultural System," p. 62.
9. Ibid., p. 60.

action associated with the myth of rights is to be found in our
tradition of constitutional government. The American constitutional order is based on institutional relationships, role
conceptions, and standards of legitimacy that are all defined
in legal terms and are thus consistent with the myth of rights.
As we observe politics ostensibly marching to a constitutional
drummer, we see in the law the normal frame of political
reference. Consider, for example, our penchant to export
constitutionalism as a tool of civilization and good government to such culturally diverse nations as Japan, Germany,
and Vietnam. Probing deeper, it seems reasonable to trace the
attraction of the myth of rights to the deeply rooted
involvement of Americans with things legal. De Tocqueville
noted these cultural concerns early in the nineteenth century:

> The language of the law thus becomes, in some measure, a
> vulgar tongue; the spirit of the law, which is produced in
> the schools and courts of justice, gradually penetrates their
> walls into the bosom of society, where it descends to the
> lowest classes, so that at last the whole people contract the
> habit and tastes of the judicial magistrate.[10]

While there is no way of locating the ultimate source of these
preoccupations, the impetus that such faith in the law would
lend to the myth of rights is clear. The most convincing
explanation for the attractions of the myth of rights has not
yet been touched upon, however. It is to be found in the basic
compatibility of legal values and other mainstream American
values.

LEGAL VALUES AND POLITICAL VALUES

The traditional American beliefs in individualism, private
property, the market economy, and limited government mesh

10. Alexis de Tocqueville, *Democracy in America* (New York: Vintage,
1959), 1:290.

in a political creed that can reasonably be identified with the mainstream of American politics.[11] Private property is identified as the secret of individual achievement and satisfaction; it provides the individual with a stake in the existing system and is the cornerstone of stable government. Private property also provides the incentive for exercising entrepreneurial initiative, which leads to a thriving market and hence to economic progress. Belief in limited government—meaning minimal official intrusion into the personal, economic, and social life of the country—is the clearest symptom of our distrust of the coercive character of the power of the state as well as the final tribute to the individual and the market. The priorities of the mainstream are private, and the purpose of politics is to serve needs defined from a personal perspective.

The myth of rights tends to partake of these same mainstream values and assures us that the path of the law is consistent with our fundamental political ideals as they are enshrined in various provisions of the Constitution and the Bill of Rights. The integrity of the individual is embodied in the idea of equality before the law and protected against governmental intrusion in a variety of ways spelled out in provisions of the Bill of Rights. The constitutional concern for private property is most explicitly expressed in the Fifth Amendment, which forbids deprivation of "life, liberty, or property without due process of law" as well as the taking of "private property for public use, without just compensation." The construction and protection of a national market were, of course, major considerations for the men who drafted the Constitution, as evidenced in a number of provisions. Finally, the preoccupation of the founding fathers with limited

11. This is the kind of argument which is developed at length in such studies as Louis Hartz, *The Liberal Tradition in America: An Interpretation of American Political Thought Since the Revolution* (New York: Harcourt, Brace & World, 1955), and Richard Hofstadter, *The American Political Tradition and the Men Who Made It* (New York: Vintage, 1955). See also Kenneth M. and Patricia Dolbeare, *American Ideologies: The Competing Beliefs of the 1970s* (Chicago: Markham, 1971), pp. 22–106 in particular.

government is displayed in the way the Constitution frag-
ments government authority by counterposing one institution
against another, as well as in the efforts to circumscribe
carefully the areas of governmental concern.

The legitimacy of the myth' of rights is not, however,
unassailable. Its vulnerability is rooted in the tension between
government by consent and constitutional truths proclaimed
by courts. Courts are, after all, our most overtly countermajor-
itarian institutions. Whereas other agencies of government
retain unambiguous, if indirect and attenuated, links with the
electorate, courts invariably are the most insulated agencies
of government.[12] Federal judges are appointed for life and
thus purposefully removed from electoral checks. State
judges, while often subject to some such checks, usually face
the electorate less frequently and in less compellingly partisan
circumstances than other officials. Judicial insulation is
rooted in the assumption that legal rights may be jeopardized
by the insistent demands of an intemperate majority. Since
only a constitutional majority composed of two-thirds of the
Congress and three-fourths of the state legislatures is entitled
to alter rights, it is presumed that judges must be protected
against lesser majorities. This distrust of the free play of
political forces and ideas which is built into the myth of rights
is what led Judith Shklar to stigmatize the legal frame of
reference as inimical to "social diversity" and "effective social
choice." [13]

There are, in sum, both affinities and tensions between the
myth of rights and the mainstream values of the American
polity. The underlying conflict between government by
consent and constitutional truths is, however, softened by a
well-entrenched tradition of indirect democracy—one of our
most basic constitutional truths. We have learned to live with

12. For a brief discussion, see Alexander Bickel, *The Least Dangerous
Branch: The Supreme Court at the Bar of Politics* (Indianapolis: Bobbs-Merrill, 1962), pp. 16–23.
13. Shklar, *Legalism*, pp. 5–6.

these kinds of contradictions and even to extol them as a tribute to our pragmatism and inventiveness. At times of crisis such contradictions tend to surface, but in the normal course of events there is no reason that the American people cannot be responsive to both legal and democratic symbols— particularly since each of them is validated by our constituent act as a nation.

In Search of the Myth of Rights

The difficult task of establishing the place of the myth of rights in American culture is fourfold:

1. To detail the premises about the relationship between law and politics upon which the myth of rights rests.
2. To consider the values associated with this particular view of politics.
3. To offer a plausible explanation of this distinctively American faith in the law.
4. To provide evidence of the extent to which Americans are responsive to the myth of rights.

All of these themes—description, evaluation, explanation, and substantiation—will be woven into the three remaining chapters of Part One. Each chapter will, however, provide a different perspective on the themes and on the myth of rights generally. These perspectives should be mutually reinforcing and cumulate to a more convincing picture of the myth of rights.

Many legal scholars and writers who are continually analyzing and evaluating the interaction between law and politics in the United States can reasonably be thought of as ideologists of the myth of rights, and they will be so treated in Chapter 3. They view politics from a legal perspective and ordinarily can be counted upon to celebrate—although not altogether uncritically—the political role of law. While systematic and perhaps intellectually persuasive, the picture provided by the ideologists is not necessarily accurate; its detailed and abstract quality makes it in many ways a rather poor reflection of the social reality of the myth of rights.

Insofar as the myth is rooted in our culture we can confirm its existence by simply looking within ourselves; Chapter 4 is an invitation to just this sort of introspection. It employs an allegory to encourage readers to relate personally to the myth of rights: to reflect on the political values embodied in this approach to politics and to assess the persuasiveness of legal symbols to themselves and other Americans.

Chapter 5 is based on survey data that are at once empirical and subjective. From these data it is possible to learn in a comprehensive and orderly way how a cross-section of Americans responds to legal symbols. Although subjective perceptions of this sort come quite close to constituting the social reality of any ideology, this chapter cannot stand alone. There are, in the first place, some deficiencies in the data, not the least being the fact that the complex and nuanced responses of human beings to major social issues cannot be adequately captured by survey research. More fundamentally, subjective perceptions tell us a good deal about the public reality of the ideological blueprint but not about the blueprint itself. Consequently, they are not very useful in coming to terms with the social ideal that infuses the myth of rights.

To seek verification of a social ethic is, at once, to belabor the obvious and to aspire to the impossible. Impressionistic and purposefully subjective approaches must be combined with empirical techniques and rigorous analysis, resulting in a convergence of perspectives. That is the task of these opening chapters.

3. AN IDEOLOGIST'S EYE VIEW
OF THE MYTH OF RIGHTS

Those who speak for American law provide us with a coherent explanation and a reasoned defense of the theory of government under law. They argue in particular that the capacity of American politics to adjust peacefully to changing conditions is attributable in large measure to a penchant for channeling serious conflict into legal procedures. They see legal processes as the primary source of reason in our governmental system and peaceful progress as dependent on a reasoned response to the insistent pressures of technological advance and to shifting cultural expectations.

The position of the law writers rests on three key ideas. The first is that the American Constitution lays the foundation for a just political order. The second is that legal reasoning as employed by our judges provides a subtle tool for updating constitutional principles. The third is that American politics is responsive to constitutional principles—or, in other words, that when the judges talk the politicians listen.

Taken together, these three ideas comprise an ideologist's eye view of the myth of rights. My purpose here is to present these ideas and the arguments that have been offered in their defense. Since there is no single voice of American law, it has been a task of selection and synthesis, attempting to present the myth of rights from the perspective of law writers—in a sense, to make this chapter their chapter.

To present the work of respected legal scholars as political ideology is to impose a frame of reference which they may understandably find offensive and unfair. By characterizing it as ideology, however, I simply wish to call explicit attention

to a point of view which permeates this particular body of
scholarly writing. All scholarship develops within premises
that focus energies and provide distinctive points of view; law
writers are neither more nor less vulnerable on these grounds
than political scientists or other scholars.

THE CONSTITUTION

The law writers trace the justness of our constitutional
document to the very careful balances it strikes between
stability and change and between freedom and social responsibility. Any constitution is supposed to have a stabilizing
effect on the polity, because it specifies in advance the rights
and obligations of citizens and of authorities as well. Our
Constitution is additionally defended on more substantive
grounds. The particular mix of rights and obligations is said
to promote a decent relationship between the people and
their government—one anchored firmly in mutual respect
and responsibility; one in which the citizen has a stake in the
system and is, in turn, respected by its officials.

The case for constitutionalism rests on the alternative it
offers to force and violence as a means of resolving conflict
within the polity. The claim of constitutionalists is that in
bringing the protean world of politics under the influence of
legal norms, a constitution lends a welcome measure of stability to the political order. The guiding premise is of course
rooted in Hobbes: systems that respond only to current
distributions of power are, in the long run, unsatisfactory to
everyone. Accordingly, the strong as well as the weak can see
the advantages of foregoing momentary gains in return for
the security provided by reciprocal acceptance of the rules of
the game. So long as the rules of the game are enforced in a
systematic and even-handed fashion—so long as the authorities take the rights seriously—all those with a stake in the
existing system will have good reason not to take the law into

their own hands. Forbearance and restraint are, in other words, the price of a secure social setting.

The constitutionalization of political relationships promises more than just the elimination of violence, however. The Constitution provides principled legal standards for judging political action and thus can serve as a counterpoise to the incessant pulling and hauling among entrenched interests. Theodore Lowi, one of the severest critics of this bargaining, which he terms "interest group liberalism," looks hopefully to legal and constitutional processes to "eliminate the political process at certain points. . . . Clear statutes that reduce pluralistic bargaining also reduce drastically the possibility of scientific treatment of government as simply part of the bundle of bargaining processes and multiple power structures." [1] Not all of those who partake of the myth of rights desire to eliminate politics, but there is an inclination to look to the law as a corrective—a way of tempering the erratic impulses of our pluralist democracy. The mission of the law is to foster a creative tension between constitutional principles and the expediential tendencies of politics. The Constitution, in other words, puts at the disposal of our judges principled arguments with which to persuade and restrain shortsighted political operatives.

Constitutionalization does not offer peace at any price, but peace and reason in behalf of the public interest. The Constitution is, in the first place, seen as the repository of our national heritage, thus providing an enduring vision of our public interest that can be used to test, shape, and understand political action. More specifically, the Constitution reflects the classic liberal distrust of government and politics combined with the celebration of society and economy. According to this essentially Lockean view, social and economic relationships are perceived as products of individual choice

1. Theodore J. Lowi, *The End of Liberalism: Ideology, Policy, and the Crisis of Public Authority* (New York: Norton, 1969), p. 127.

within a pattern of mutually rewarding interaction among groups and their members. Government, on the other hand, is seen typically as acting through imperative commands backed by force. The polity is associated with coercion while society and economy are looked upon as bastions of freedom.[2] When set against this philosophic background, the broad outlines of the Constitution take on a certain coherence—in particular, the distrust of concentrations of official power evidenced in the separation of powers and the checks and balances designed to maintain that separation. The Bill of Rights, in particular, stands out both as a demonstration of distrust of those in power and as a tribute to the importance of protecting and nurturing private spheres of endeavor. The general boundaries of the polity are difficult to determine by a search of the Constitution, since the mission of the federal government was limited not just by liberal doctrine but by the powers retained by the states in the federal union. One thing is clear from both constitutional provisions and federal practice, however. While regulation of the economy and the society may be suspect, governmental support of entrepreneurial initiative warrants praise—presumably because it promotes the welfare of sectors in which freedom tends to be maximized. Indeed, the impetus for building a federal union could be seen as stemming primarily from the need for a truly national economy.[3]

2. For a superb analysis of the debilitating impact of classic liberal thought on political vision, see Sheldon S. Wolin, *Politics and Vision: Continuity and Innovation in Western Political Thought* (London: George Allen & Unwin, 1961), chap. 9.

3. If this analysis tends to blur distinctions between Hamiltonians and Jeffersonians, it is not because I perceive that conflict as unimportant. Surely the mercantilist features of our system raise questions about its liberal credentials, and the tensions between classic and mercantilist liberalism continued to surface long after the constitutional period. On the other hand, a serviceable consensus seemed to emerge in the mainstream of American politics even in the face of these underlying contradictions. For the definitive presentation of this position, see Louis Hartz, *The Liberal Tradition in America* (New York: Harcourt, Brace and World, 1955).

Finally, we are urged to think of constitutional values as timeless. The nineteenth century is represented as the testing period for the Lockean assumptions that are at the heart of our constituent act. In the twentieth century our constitutional wisdom has proven its adaptability.

During most of the nineteenth century, it is argued, legal and constitutional solutions encouraged private entrepreneurial initiative and promoted economic growth in a number of ways. The constitutional system set the framework for a national economy in which the factors of production could flow freely across state boundaries, while legal and constitutional doctrines secured private property and guaranteed contractual relations.[4] Law, so the argument runs, released and organized the energies required for dynamic growth. At the heart of this argument is a curious anomaly that has been effectively analyzed in James Willard Hurst's discussion of the Supreme Court's protection of "vested rights."

"Vested Rights" sounds like pure standpattism, as if it connoted merely protection of what is because it is, because nothing is valued more than stability. But on the whole, the nineteenth-century United States valued change more than stability and valued stability most often when it helped create a framework for change. . . . Thus, the more one looks at the lines along which the vested rights doctrine grew, the less satisfied is he to appraise it as a simple expression in favor of the status quo. Dynamic rather than static property, property in motion or at risk rather than property secure and at rest, engaged our principal interest.[5]

In short, the law promoted change by securing for the entrepreneur the fruits of his labor subject only to the general

4. Arnold M. Paul, *Conservative Crisis and the Rule of Law: Attitudes of Bar and Bench 1887–1895* (New York: Harper Torchbook, 1969).
5. James Willard Hurst, *Law and the Conditions of Freedom in the Nineteenth-Century United States* (Madison: University of Wisconsin Press, 1956), p. 24.

warning that his property had an economic mission and that property "at rest" was subject to regulation insofar as it stood in the way of growth and progress.

By the close of the nineteenth century, however, it became increasingly clear that a system of largely uninhibited entrepreneurial initiative had destructive tendencies. National resources were ravaged; many in the society were shamelessly exploited; and increasing concentration of economic power seemed likely to choke off entrepreneurial initiative itself by limiting access to the marketplace. It was at this critical juncture, according to the myth of rights, that law displayed its remarkable capacity to adapt. We are offered as the prototypical event the Supreme Court's reluctant accommodation to the introduction by the New Deal of social security, minimum wage laws, a modicum of government ownership, and a modest amount of planning. Enlightened reinterpretation of common law and constitutional doctrine thus legitimated positive acts by the state and federal governments designed to protect our system from its own self-destructive tendencies. The result of these adjustments, the law writers assure us, is a Constitution which is the key to beneficent social order in the twentieth century just as it was in the nineteenth.

JUDGES, COURTS, AND LEGAL REASONING

Practically speaking, it is the judges who are responsible for drawing the enduring values from an eighteenth-century constitutional document and adapting them to contemporary circumstances. A task of this sort calls for habits of mind geared to both the retrospective and prospective implications of political action. It also requires institutional structures and a cultural setting capable of maintaining the integrity and independence of constitutional values. What reasons have we to believe that our judges are ready, willing, and able to assume these heavy burdens? Alexander M. Bickel assures us that our system is arranged in a way which provides judges with "the leisure, the training, and the insulation," that is necessary.[6]

Judges are, of course, trained in law school to reason in a legal fashion. Generally speaking, legal training teaches lawyers a concern for precedent (looking backward) while at the same time sensitizing them to the precedential implications of current judgments (looking forward). More specifically, legal reasoning focuses attention on three components: rules, facts, and analogy.[7] The judges' job is to look at a given set of *facts,* and decide on the basis of *analogy* whether these facts call for the application of one *rule* or another. The result is supposed to be a system of rules which both updates and preserves fundamental American values.

A couple of examples which illustrate the interaction among the three components of legal reasoning will make this clearer.

1. Although there are laws against homicide in most jurisdictions, taking a life in self-defense is not ordinarily subject to punishment. In attempting to dispose of a case before him in which the accused has pleaded self-defense, the judge must decide whether the behavior of the accused falls within the rule against homicide or is excepted as self-defense. In making this decision, the judge is supposed to compare the facts of the current case to previous cases, and since the facts are unlikely to be substantially identical, he must reason by analogy.

6. Alexander M. Bickel, *The Least Dangerous Branch: The Supreme Court at the Bar of Politics* (Indianapolis: Bobbs-Merrill, 1962), p. 25.

7. Edward H. Levi, *An Introduction to Legal Reasoning* (Chicago: University of Chicago Press, 1963), pp. 1, 2. There are probably as many accounts of the nature of legal reasoning as there are legal scholars, and the conflicts among them are intense. For our purposes, however, it is the similarities more than the differences that are of interest. If, therefore, the analysis given is drawn primarily from Levi, that is not because it is deemed "correct" but because it is more or less typical, on the one hand, and because he uses legal reasoning to lead into a discussion of the interaction between judicial and political decisions.

2. The First Amendment to the United States Constitution prohibits the Congress from making any law "abridging the freedom of speech." Very early in its history the Supreme Court decided that this ostensibly absolute prohibition was not without exceptions. These exceptions have themselves been formulated into what might be loosely termed rules—like that one which permits restrictions on speech when there is a "clear and present danger" or that one which excludes "fighting words" from the protection of the First Amendment. In any case, when dealing with a First Amendment challenge, judges must struggle by way of analogy to assess the compatibility of facts in the current case with earlier decisions in order to decide which rule to apply.

This cursory glance should dispel two common misconceptions about legal reasoning: (1) that the judge simply uncovers and applies preexisting rules, and (2) that judicial decision-making is a precise calculation. While the resultant ambiguity might seem to be a serious fault, this "open texture" can also be viewed as the key to the law's capacity to adapt.

No matter how carefully drafted, legal rules are never without a certain range of ambiguity or open texture. In documents like contracts ambiguity is readily acknowledged as a shortcoming, but the law writers explain that ambiguity is a virtue in a constitution or even in a statute. The classic American statement of this position came early in our history when Chief Justice John Marshall declared in *McCulloch* v. *Maryland:*

> A constitution, to contain an accurate detail of all the subdivisions of which its great powers will admit, and of all the means by which they may be carried into execution, would partake of the prolixity of a legal code, and could scarcely be embraced by the human mind. . . . Its nature, therefore, requires that only its great outlines should be

marked, its important objects designated, and the minor ingredients which compose those objects, be deduced from the nature of the objects themselves. . . . In considering this question, then, we must never forget that it is a *constitution* we are expounding.[8]

Our Constitution is, in other words, necessarily and happily a supple document. Patterns of collective action are too varied and the course of events too unpredictable to be caught and held within the confines of precise rules. The open texture permits judges to make the constant small corrections necessary to shape rules to the infinite variety and ever-changing conditions of political existence.[9]

The application of rules is difficult to distinguish in practice from the making of rules. Each exception can be viewed either as an application or a deviation depending on one's perspective. No matter, say the law writers. To the extent that consistent patterns of exception begin to emerge, a new rule is taking shape. Legal and constitutional provisions are to be thought of in terms of a hard core of meaning and a penumbra of uncertainty. The judges' job is to see to it that the words of the law not allowed to undermine its spirit. What we must rely on to keep the system "honest," as the fabric of the law is woven and rewoven by judicial decision, is the analytic power of legal reasoning. The judges are expected to perform as competent and committed professionals. They are to work within the established constitutional system of rules—neither as prisoners nor as free spirits but as responsible harmonizers and synthesizers relying on the tools of their trade.

Analogy is, in this perspective, the key to understanding the contribution that legal reasoning can make to a flexible

8. McCulloch v. Maryland, 4 Wheaton 316, 407 (1819). Italics in the original.

9. My presentation of these matters is based on the lucid analysis of H. L. A. Hart, *The Concept of Law* (London: Oxford University Press, 1961), pp. 120–50.

and stable constitutional order. As the social context changes,
so too does the comparability of factual situations. Technical
innovations like wiretapping, to consider the most obvious
kind of example, could not possibly have been foreseen by
the founders (except perhaps Benjamin Franklin) when they
guaranteed us all security "against unreasonable searches and
seizures." More broadly, the status and conditions of minorities have undergone substantial transformation in the last two
hundred years. While the tool of analogy is not a precision
instrument, arguments made to the judges which do not take
account of contextual changes will, we are told, tend to be
unpersuasive. It is in this spirit that E. H. Levi concludes his
analysis by asserting that "Legal reasoning has a logic of its
own. Its structure fits it to give meaning to ambiguity and to
test constantly whether the society has come to see new
differences or similarities. . . . The words change to receive
the content which the community gives to them." [10] Thus
attorneys are encouraged to rethink yesterday's precedents in
terms of the circumstances and values of today. The judges in
their turn have an opportunity, perhaps an obligation, to
draw "progressive" decisions from the competing analogies
presented by counsel. Reasoning by analogy may not be
exact but neither should we think of it as a process devoid of
guidelines. Those schooled in the ways of the law share
common if somewhat inchoate standards of argumentation.

Complementing the judges' training in law is the judicial
setting which encourages them to apply legal standards to the
political conflicts they are asked to resolve. Legal logic is
infused into judicial decision-making in a number of ways.
Lawyers offer and defend "competing analogies." Evidence is
screened to focus on the relevant facts—that is, those related
to the analogies that are proposed. Judges are subjected to
continuing scrutiny on professional grounds in the nation's
law reviews. At the same time, procedures are established to

10. Levi, p. 104.

insulate judges from at least the grosser forms of political pressure. (If Chief Justice Warren could so disappoint President Eisenhower, then is a "Nixon Court" inevitable, even given four appointments in his first term of office?) Finally, according to Bickel, there is a certain "leisure" inherent in the judicial situation—not time on their hands, but time on their side, time that may drain problems of at least a portion of their political urgency. If judges act after issues have peaked, they are, Bickel tells us, better able to take the long view—that is, to test the expedient and random outcomes of pluralist bargaining against the basic principles of the American polity as these principles are found in the Constitution. Judges are, moreover, not normally confronted with a problem until it has taken on a certain concreteness. Judges do not deal with rules as abstractions, but as they come to life in relationships among real people in actual conflicts. The case method is thus defended as a way of reinforcing the pragmatic tendencies of legal reasoning and of providing a setting congenial to the analogy.[11]

CONSTITUTIONAL POLITICS

Whatever the virtues of law and constitutionalism, they must finally compete in the political arena with traditional forms of power and influence if they are to have any impact on public policy. The myth of rights leads us to believe that judicial decisions come off quite well in such competition— that both those in power and the general citizenry tend to defer to judicial decisions. We are all, in other words, supposed to be sensitive in some significant measure to the value of resolving our political conflicts through legal processes in accordance with constitutional norms.

The political appeal and ostensible vitality of legal processes is in part explained by their public and rational

11. Bickel, chap. 4 in particular.

character. The courtrooms of the nation are open; the rules that focus litigation are a matter of public record; the judgments that emerge are generally available: they are preceded by the careful argumentation of the adversary process and are accompanied by a reasoned defense of the decision. If cameras are excluded from the halls of justice and the seating capacity restricted, it is, we are told, in the service of decorum—that is, to create an atmosphere in which reason will prevail—not for purposes of secrecy.

While the esoteric language of the law and the vagaries of legal reasoning might seem to make the process less accessible than its public character leads us to believe, the myth of rights offers reassurance. Influential elites are often trained in the law and always have legal staff at their disposal. Consequently, there is nothing preventing the reasoned judgments of courts from feeding directly into political controversy at the highest level. The path to the people is more devious but not necessarily less certain. Judgments are also picked up by working journalists who are trained to apply the standards of legal reasoning. Their reactions are relied upon to set the tone of public response in a manner generally in keeping with the spirit of reasoned argument that is associated with the courtroom.

Taken altogether, the myth of rights contrasts the openness of judicial proceedings to the secret bargaining of interest group pluralism so as to underscore the integrity and incorruptibility of the judicial process. The aim, of course, is to enhance the attractiveness of legal and constitutional solutions to political problems. The courts' claim to legitimacy is traced deeper still. The justices of the Supreme Court are likened to "teachers in a vital national seminar," and the power of the Court is discussed in "mystic" terms. What is implied is that courts in general and the Supreme Court in particular draw upon a fund of good will and respect which amounts to a kind of public reflex action. Consider, for example, the response of *The New York Times* to the Supreme Court's 1965 birth control decision:

> The Supreme Court's 7-to-2 decision invalidating Connecticut's birth-control law is a milestone in the judiciary's march toward enlarged guardianship of the nation's freedoms. It establishes a new "right to privacy."
>
> The Court was divided on its authority to declare the Connecticut statute unconstitutional but unanimous in finding the law a bad one.[12]

Never mind a murky legal situation; let us rely on the moral wisdom of our judges. To the extent that the judges are associated in this way with wisdom and justice, they need not rely on coercion to enforce their decisions, nor must they settle for simple acquiescence. Deference to judicial decisions can instead be seen as the natural consequence of genuine respect.

Respect, of course, has its price, and the myth of rights would have us believe that only so long as our judges follow the path of the law—evidencing a serious concern with precedent, a firm commitment to the Constitution, and a subtle appreciation of our enduring values—can they expect to have political influence. History can be and regularly is read in a way that lends support to these arguments. Franklin Roosevelt's attack on the Hughes Court in the 1930s, as well as the more recent assaults on the Warren Court, are often explained in such terms.[13] When the judges venture beyond the limits of constitutional decorum, so the argument goes, they forfeit their relative immunity and make themselves

12. Editorial comment, *The New York Times*. 9 June 1965, p. 46.
13. Alexander Bickel is the most thorough and subtle exponent of this theory. On the problems of the Warren Court, see *The Supreme Court and the Idea of Progress* (New York: Harper and Row, 1970). There are innumerable accounts of the legal transgressions and political recompense of the Hughes Court. See, for example, Walter Murphy, *Congress and the Court* (Chicago: University of Chicago Press, 1962), pp. 53–62.

vulnerable to political repudiation in the form of congressional legislation reversing individual decisions or limiting the basic powers of the Court.[14] Excesses by the judges are also seen as the route to disaffection among the general public. Opinion sampling is used, in this connection, to provide evidence that the "Warren Court was viewed unfavorably by most of its critics in the public as too liberal and too activist. The criminal procedures area was particularly a source of increasing negative support of the Supreme Court and American court systems (federal and state) in general." [15] While our preoccupation with constitutional regularity puts some obvious limitations on the power of courts, it also creates opportunities.

In a system which takes its constitutional norms so seriously, it follows that a special form of political action is possible, indeed appropriate. Constitutional politics need not depend on conventional political resources, since judges are not supposed to respond to differences in wealth, to distinguish winners from losers according to majoritarian criteria, or to yield to the more blatant forms of coercion. Before the bench it is intellectual rather than financial or martial resources that count. Groups wishing to stake a claim to something or other need only demonstrate that their needs correspond with constitutional norms or lesser rules derived from or consistent with the Constitution. Once the judges are enlisted, the battle is not necessarily over but the opportunities for success are good. The judges' function is to call the other branches to constitutional account—to engage them in a continuing colloquy having to do with the fundamental

14. Walter F. Murphy has chronicled the Supreme Court's problems with Congress in *Congress and the Court*. For a more recent study focusing on the period after World War II, see John R. Schmidhauser and Larry L. Berg, *The Supreme Court and Congress: Conflict and Interaction, 1945–1968* (New York: Free Press, 1972).

15. Sheldon Goldman and Thomas P. Jahnige, *The Federal Courts as a Political System* (New York: Harper and Row, 1971), p. 137.

goals and methods of American politics.[16] Striking illustration is provided by the Watergate intervention of Federal District Judge John J. Sirica. Constitutional politics is, thus, the politics of reason rather than of power, and if the realization of rights cannot be taken for granted, the myth of rights assures us that the inertial forces of American politics are basically supportive of established rights.

The myth of rights, in sum, encourages the view that the United States Constitution is a beneficent document which is in a large measure responsible for both our affluence and our domestic tranquility. Our constitutional order is said to be responsive to reason rather than power, to promote the public interest, and to nurture change within a reassuring framework of continuity.

What this chapter indicates most clearly is that the ideologists of the myth of rights are, above all, optimists, who provide us with reassuring interpretations of our political past and with hope for the future. Even our darkest moments are given a soothing gloss. Eugene Rostow of the Yale Law School struck a typically sanguine note in speaking of efforts to make amends for the outrageous treatment of Japanese-Americans during World War II, offering his

> congratulat[ions to] the Attorneys General who have carried programs of financial restitution through to success and, even more important, have speeded up and completed the program for restoring citizenship to those who renounced it *in the heat of a troubled moment.* . . . They have made this battle their own, with a fervor which bespeaks

16. This process is developed most exhaustively in Bickel, *The Least Dangerous Branch.* Others seem to take it as a given. In this connection, see Joseph L. Sax, *Defending the Environment: A Strategy for Citizen Action* (New York: Knopf, 1971). Surely the strategy of the NAACP campaign to bring civil rights to black Americans was premised on some such belief in the political influence of judicial decisions.

their dedication to the highest value of our culture—the conviction that the most exalted office of the state is to do justice to the individual, *however small his cause.*[17]

What Professor Rostow tells us is that the law is a living institution capable of learning from its own mistakes. Its deficiencies can be acknowledged and, at the same time, discounted by the law's own regenerative powers.

To some, the temptation is overwhelming to scoff at the sweeping claims of the myth of rights. As one radical critic sarcastically puts it, "Law therefore modestly suggests that it is all-changing, yet always constant; it is both all-knowing and all seeing, old and new combined." [18] The utopian note struck by the myth of rights can in this fashion be played back to us as a kind of reality test.

The success of an ideology does not depend, however, on the objective accuracy of the theory it presents but on the response it evokes. It is to these essentially subjective reactions that we turn in the next two chapters. They suggest that it would be most unrealistic to shrug off the persuasive appeal of the myth of rights, for Americans seem to be significantly responsive to its vision of government under law.

17. Eugene V. Rostow, *The Sovereign Prerogative: The Supreme Court and the Quest for Law* (New Haven: Yale University Press, 1962), pp. 265–66. Italics added.

18. Kenneth Cloke, "The Economic Basis of Law and State," in Robert Lefcourt, ed., *Law Against the People* (New York: Vintage, 1971), p. 76.

4. THE CALL OF THE LAW: THE MYTH OF RIGHTS AS POLITICAL RHETORIC

The myth of rights has been presented as the belief system that dominates the thinking of Americans about the interplay of legal and political forces in our society. Belief systems are tricky things to deal with. It is one thing to agree that cultures tend to perpetuate themselves by inculcating patterns of values and favorable perceptions of social institutions, but quite another to specify with any degree of confidence the contours of that belief system. I have chosen to use the writings of legal scholars as the initial source of information about the myth of rights. The scholars provide an orderly picture, but how accurately does it reflect the inchoate images locked away in the minds of Americans? The elaborate scholarly presentations are far removed from people's daily lives; the myth of rights as it penetrates those lives takes on quite a different tone. It is less coherent, more impressionistic, but surely better suited to engaging the attention and capturing the imaginations of significant numbers of people.

The myth of rights filters into our daily life as legal slogans like "clear and present danger," "with all deliberate speed," "government of laws," "fair trial," "one man, one vote," and so forth. At first glance, it might seem that the popular artifacts of the legal world do no more than debase and caricature the careful theories of the law writers, but that is not the case. The rhetoric of rights, as an integral part of political discourse in the United States, introduces constitutional values into politics in an imperfect but salient and engaging fashion.

In order to portray the impressionistic public face of the myth of rights, this chapter begins with an allegory drawn from the problems of university life in the United States in the late 1960s. Anyone familiar with those times will recognize that while the events discussed did not *happen,* the scenario presented does accurately reflect the temper of the period as well as themes that might recur both within universities and more broadly within the polity. I have deliberately gone outside the normal context of politics to provide a manageable setting and also to underscore just how widespread legal symbols are. Universities are, of course, rather special kinds of social institutions, but I would contend that they are typical in their ambivalent concern with rights and rules.[1] University politics like the politics of other social organizations in the United States can be viewed at least for our limited purposes as American politics in microcosm. Thus the allegory invites us to ponder pervasive and enduring political tendencies.

The allegory reveals in a preliminary fashion the claims that are made on behalf of the legal approach to political problem-solving as well as the manner in which legal slogans symbolize such claims. There are three essential advantages claimed for legal ordering and, taken together, they comprise the call of the law in American politics.

1. The legal approach is realistic. It is based on a willingness to accept things as they are rather than as one might ideally wish them to be.
2. The legal approach is neither complicated nor demanding. The principles to guide action are easily understood; their implementation may be confidently left to professionals.

1. See Lon L. Fuller, "Human Interaction and the Law," in Robert Paul Wolff, ed., *The Rule of Law* (New York: Simon and Schuster, Clarion Book, 1971), p. 171.

3. The legal approach rests firmly on an ethical base. Typical American values like personal responsibility and equality of opportunity inhere in the legal frame of reference.

While other approaches to political problems may lay claim to one or another of the above virtues, the three in combination define the law's special claim to legitimacy.

The special claim of the law is not, however, unchallenged. The allegory is meant to convey a sense of the political arena in which legal symbols must compete with other standards of legitimacy. The persuasive power of legal rhetoric can be assessed best in the context of claim and counterclaim which normally characterizes political conflict. In addition, to begin to understand and appraise the values associated with the myth of rights may require giving some consideration to alternative social visions. The allegory affords an opportunity to ponder the virtues of the law together with the claims of its competitors, thus laying the basis for the more systematic discussion that follows.

THE RHETORIC OF RIGHTS: AN ALLEGORY

BANG (Basic Action Noncompliance Group) has decided to begin the academic year with a ROW (Radical Organizing Week) in order to build a radical constituency for the nine months of struggle lying ahead. The result is a series of noisy, nonviolent, on-site sit-ins aimed at designating and dramatizing BANG's objectives. The university president refuses requests from embattled faculty and administrators to call in the police. He offers to negotiate throughout the ROW, but BANG refuses to meet with the president unless he agrees publicly to comply with all of the demands. Finally, at the end of the ROW the president moves unilaterally on several of BANG's grievances:

1. No students are to be henceforth admitted to ROTC, thus guaranteeing the end of the program in three years.

2. The university will sign no more contracts for classified research and will allow all current contracts to lapse.
3. Investigatory committees are to be appointed to look into other grievances, including the alleged exploitation of black athletes.
4. No disciplinary action is to be taken against BANG or against any of the other student participants in ROW.

Following the president's announcement, a sizable student meeting called by BANG votes overwhelmingly against a second ROW. During the second week of school there is an apparent return to normality. BANG rallies draw fewer participants; the library reports that its facilities are being taxed by an unprecedented influx of students; and for the first time in several years the stadium is sold out for a season-opening football game. But beneath this tranquil surface a faculty revolt is brewing. Powerful senior professors are calling for the ouster of the president. PRRR (Professors for Rights, Rationality, and Reflection) calls for an emergency faculty meeting and proposes that disciplinary action be taken against BANG as well as other "disruptive" participants in the ROW. According to this proposal, the law school faculty is to be charged with responsibility for establishing hearing procedures that insure due process and the dean of the Law School is to serve as the chief magistrate of the hearing process. The law faculty is to be further charged with preparing a code which would specify and prohibit disruptive activities in the future.

The emergency faculty meeting is long, disjointed, and bitter—even a little tedious, some think. No summary can do justice to the endless subtlety of academic debate. Like ships in the night, argument and counterargument float harmlessly past one another, but the general configurations of the discussion look something like this. The president reminds the faculty that an overwhelming majority of students and faculty participating in a referendum the previous spring expressed opposition to ROTC and classified research. More-over, he argues that his tactics of the first week were directed at disarming BANG and preventing a series of ROWs that would polarize the campus and effectively end the academic year before it really began. Since this was in his judgment the real goal of BANG but not of many of the participants in ROW, he saw his tactics as the most effective way of separating BANG from its potential constituency and thus of opposing militance on campus.

PRRR responds that the president has compromised the academic environment. They argue that the referendum of the previous spring was conducted under the auspices of the outgoing student government and was therefore not relevant to this year, much less authoritative. Moreover, since faculty and student votes had been counted equally, the long-term faculty interests in the university would have been badly understated—even if a majority of faculty and students had participated. In fact, less than 40 percent of the students had voted and barely 20 percent of the faculty. Accordingly, the actions of the president can be accurately seen in only one light. He has yielded to pressure and thus undermined the orderly processes of university governance. At the same time, the president has utterly failed to protect the rights of faculty members whose classes have been disrupted and of students who have been denied access to university facilities. While most of the faculty line up behind either the president or PRRR, isolated voices from the left and right are raised in defense of or in opposition to ROTC, classified research, the athletic department, the Vietnam War, and the racial policies of the university, the state, and the current administration in Washington.

Happily, there is no reason to pursue this conflict in detail to its temporizing anticlimax. Suffice it to say that the president retains his position, a Code Against Disruption (CAD) is promulgated, and the law faculty decides that both evidentiary and ex post facto considerations make discipli-

nary action against BANG inadvisable. What is relevant to our
purposes are the symbols evoked by the opposing sides to
defend their interests and legitimate their positions. It is even
more important to understand the values that inhere in these
symbols. We could, of course, simply dismiss PRRR as
hopelessly conservative and the president as an opportunist.
Indeed, in the heat of battle this is most likely what many of
us would do. But if we did so we would be missing an
opportunity to reflect on some of the more enduring problems
of political organization as they emerge in this hypothetical
academic struggle.

Think a bit about the position taken by PRRR. Does it not
have a distinctly legal ring to it? Legalistic, an opponent
might be tempted to say. But it is not legal in the usual sense
of the term since no appeal to state or federal courts is
contemplated, nor is legislation being sought. If we think of
law solely in terms of the authoritative agencies of the state,
then the professors seem content to function in the strictly
extralegal world of the university. If, however, we broaden
our perspective and consider the symbols employed by PRRR,
do we not recognize the language of the law? The problem
facing the university is seen largely in terms of the rights that
have been violated and the obligations that have not been
fulfilled, punishment of the guilty and vindication of the
innocent. The future, moreover, will be assured by a CAD.

PRRR is no doubt defending its own interests; it is arguing
for the maintenance of the academic status quo; there is even
a measure of vengeance in its insistence on punishment. But
these facets of the PRRR position do not surface in the debate.
PRRR perceives that the language of the law is more useful in
public discourse. In part, PRRR is no doubt banking on
rhetoric and employing its legal symbols loosely. The rights
that PRRR is defending are not authoritatively established; a
lawyer could not, in all likelihood, build a winning case.
Indeed, the need for a new code is symptomatic of the

looseness of the legal usage adopted by PRRR—as is the determination of the law faculty that disciplinary action would have an ex post facto note to it. But the PRRR stand is not simply empty rhetoric. The effort is to evoke among their wavering colleagues an image of an academic society to support and defend.

To understand this image, reflect briefly on both sides of the debate. The president has, in essence, argued that the success of his tactics is its own justification. BANG has been broken; there have been no more ROWS. Order has been restored to the campus and students and faculty have returned to education—or whatever else they normally do. The president invites us to think about what he has achieved rather than the way in which he has done it. PRRR, on the other hand, insists that we think beyond expediency to principle and inveighs against using a desirable end to justify disreputable means. The president is not insensitive to the strong ethical appeal of this assault on what is merely expedient. Consequently, he tries to invoke an alternative symbol of legitimacy at the same time that he exposes a weakness in the legal approach adopted by PRRR. He reminds the faculty of his mandate to act as expressed in the referendum of the previous spring. His means may have been somewhat irregular in that they did not conform to existing rules. On the other hand, the procedures that he used were consistent with the wishes of the majority and he did not allow himself to be trapped into the self-defeating and formalistic legal logic employed by PRRR. The point is that in public discourse the law conveys both an attractive commitment to principle and the foolish consistency associated with small minds.

The ambivalence conveyed by the symbols of the law in public discourse reflects quite accurately, in my judgment, important aspects of the nature of legal ordering. The law as an enterprise is characterized by a distinctive way of doing things and, in particular, by a preoccupation with procedures. To some this is the glory of the law and its single most important contribution to public life:

> Procedure is the bone structure of a democratic society; and the quality of procedural standards which meet general acceptance—the quality of what is tolerable and permissible and acceptable conduct—determines the durability of the society and the survival possibilities of freedom within the society.[2]

But not everyone shares former Supreme Court Justice Abe Fortas's enthusiasm for procedure. Even so ardent a defender of the legal faith as Lon L. Fuller, resident jurisprudent at the Harvard Law School, asserts that "If it is empty of ends, the law can hardly be attractive in the means it employs." [3] Professor Fuller does not admit that the law is devoid of purposes but he understands why it often seems that the law is "all means and no ends." [4] Surely no student of the law can deny its procedural priorities. We are thus left with a number of questions. Just what is the relationship between means and ends in legal ordering? Is the legal approach conservative, progressive, or simply neutral as to ends? Is excessive formalism inherent in the legal approach to problem solving or is it pathological? Although an image of the legal enterprise has begun to emerge, it remains blurred and incomplete. One way of bringing the image into better focus is to consider in turn the three virtues which comprise the call of the law.

THE VIRTUE OF REALISM

For those who pride themselves on being realistic, the legal approach is appealing because it seems to be both descrip-

2. Abe Fortas, *Concerning Dissent and Civil Disobedience* (New York: Signet Special Broadside, 1968), pp. 60–61.
3. Lon L. Fuller, *Anatomy of the Law* (New York: New American Library, 1969), p. 11.
4. Ibid.

tively accurate and tough-minded. The legal approach, as Raymond Aron has said in another context, has "genuine appeal to the mind" but a "feeble echo in the heart." [5] Of course, the empirical integrity of any world view is likely to be more apparent than real, since they all tend to screen out dissonance as they focus and simplify. The mind to which the legal view appeals has perhaps been conditioned to pick up the signals that confirm the paradigm and to dismiss those which suggest that rules do not in fact make the world go 'round. We are not, however, concerned with the objective accuracy of the legal paradigm but with its persuasiveness in the American milieu. On what grounds, then, does the ostensible authenticity of the legal approach rest?

In the first place, the legal perspective, unlike most other world views, is linked directly if somewhat imperfectly to the authoritative institutions of the society. The law game thus becomes more "tangible" than the class struggle or economic determinism, for example. The reality of the law game is constantly before our eyes; its rules are officially recognized as "oughts" by the system and are often if not inevitably implemented by those institutions. If it could be publicly and popularly demonstrated that people are more loyal to their class than to the rules of the system, the hold of the legal paradigm would no doubt be shaken. But the perceived need for rules in a complex impersonal society probably runs deep. How else can we develop the minimal patterns of reciprocal expectation that permit us to order and plan our lives? We can hardly anticipate the behavior of those whom we do not know.

And what of human nature? The law appeals to the tough-minded with a no-nonsense view of the roots of human behavior. People being as they are (and let us be realistic) will take unfair advantage of their position and resources. They

5. Raymond Aron, *The Century of Total War* (Garden City: Doubleday, 1954), p. 316.

will fulfill their obligations to the extent that they are forced to, or at least only insofar as they can be reasonably sure that others will reciprocate. In a large-scale society where the bonds of human community are weak, rules become the key to reasonably harmonious relationships. Rules define the nature of the social contract and are, at the same time, our assurance that if we live up to our part of the bargain so too will others.

What I am suggesting is that Americans have a kind of common-sense inclination to impute rules—written or un-written—to most ongoing social relationships. Think back to the university dispute. The Professors for Rights, Rationality, and Reflection (PRRR) took it for granted that the disruptive features of ROW were contrary to the established practices of the university—with or without a formal rule. Similarly, when Pentagon documemts were released without authorization to *The New York Times*, was it necessary to cite a specific law in order to evoke a feeling that a rule had been broken—that something illegal had taken place? Even in the ostensible anarchy of war, it can usually be argued with some hope of rallying a constituency that "crimes against humanity" are contrary to existing rules. There is, in short, a tendency in the United States to see rules as a kind of universal precondition to organized human endeavor. This universality seems, moreover, to be confirmed by what we see all around us, even by "smaller systems—at least 'law-like' in structure and function—to be found in labor unions, professional associa-tions, clubs, churches, and universities." [6]

There is, of course, a distinctly conservative bias to this approach, rooted as it is in established patterns of rights and obligations. But if we look no further than the association of legal processes with the status quo, we shall fail to fully understand the call of the law to Americans who are neither lawyers nor conservatives. Thus, the association with author-

6. Fuller, "Human Interaction and the Law," p. 171.

ity provides constant confirmation that the legal world view is accurate and real—tangible referents which attest to the enduring need for rules. Moreover, while change is inevitable and often desirable, it must take place within a framework of rules. It is one thing to support innovation and progress but quite another to open the door to chaos. For anyone willing to tell it like it is, the choice is between law and anarchy. The law is not pie-in-the-sky; it simply takes people as they are: in need of guidelines and limits.

THE VIRTUE OF CONVENIENCE

Convenience, I have argued, is the second virtue projected by the legal approach. Let us, however, not be misled by this characterization. There is no reason to believe that the solutions provided by legal analysis will themselves be convenient. Quite the contrary, the law game often calls upon us to avoid those solutions which are "merely" convenient or expedient. Such was the case in the university ROW considered at the outset of this chapter. Although the legal approach may not promise a convenient solution, it does specify the issues simply and directly, thus promising maximum understanding for minimum expenditure of intellectual energy. Similarly, the legal approach promises maximum control with minimum expenditure of participatory energy. After all, the detailed work of the law must, can, and should be left to others with professional qualifications working under well-established guidelines embodied in the law. Citizens are therefore encouraged to believe that they are fully competent to understand and even loosely monitor, but not to participate in acts of governance. We must now consider just how the legal approach offers the citizen this feeling of competence and understanding while at the same time assuring him that public affairs can be safely left to others.

The key to understanding is, of course, simplification. The legal approach simplifies complex situations by stripping away all those elements which do not pertain to existing or potential rules. Moreover, this quest for rules builds on a ready inclination to accept the pivotal importance of rules in organized societal activity. It is, no doubt, true that the law game simplifies in its own inimitably complex fashion, that law students take upwards of the three years in law school to learn the game, and that only those well schooled in the case method can play the game successfully. But, then, *we* are not really expected to *play* the game; we are only to be spectators or, at the most, critics.

The language of the law in political discourse is largely metaphorical. No one can realistically expect public debate to sort effectively through the claims and counterclaims over what is, in fact, the applicable rule. Instead, legal symbols are used to persuade those involved in the conflict that it makes sense to think of the problem at hand in terms of rights and obligations—thus tapping that latent sensitivity to the need for rules and, at the same time, framing the issue in readily comprehensible fashion. Lurking behind this appeal to everyone's common sense, however, is the machinery of government (or of university governance) which *can* produce an authoritative determination of the controlling rule. The underlying purpose of the debate is to channel dispute into established institutions.

Clearly, once the formal processes are invoked the game becomes much more complicated. Lawyers and judges (or their surrogates in bureaucracies) are required to determine just what kinds of behavior are consistent with existing rights and obligations. The parties may be forced to fall back from the relevant rule to some higher law or even to principles which inhere in that higher law. They may be forced to ask whether the rule is constitutional or to decide between two constitutional provisions. All this is very esoteric business and must be turned over to the authoritative institutions: "It would seem that the judge is peculiarly qualified to render decisions because he knows what many of the rules are, where the others may be readily located, and how to use the canons of logic to discern valid arguments." [7] The layman is asked to wait for and comply with the decision ultimately churned out by the legal process. A common response to civil disobedience, for example, is that the citizen has a duty to accept the judgment of the Supreme Court as final:

> Just as we expect the government to be bound by all laws, so each individual is bound by all of the laws under the Constitution. He cannot pick and choose. He cannot substitute his own judgment or passion, however noble, for the rules of law. Thoreau was an inspiring figure and a great writer; but this essay should not be read as a handbook on political science.[8]

In other words, if we leave the job to professionals, problems will be resolved and resolved well—according to rules and procedures that we all, at least tacitly, recognize as legitimate. We will be spared endless hours of participation in faculty meetings, citizen groups, and the like, dealing with problems that we understand only in the most general sense and invoking rules that we grasp imperfectly at best.

This curious mixture of respect and contempt for even the well-informed citizen is typified by a stern rebuke issued by Professor Philip Kurland of the University of Chicago Law School to a well-known journalist and a high public official who characteristically jumped too quickly toward the defining rules in a conflict concerning release of the Pentagon Papers.

> Anyone with the self righteousness of a Melvin Laird or a Tom Wicker has little difficulty determining the proper outcome of the present controversy between the Govern-

7. Richard A. Wasserstrom, *The Judicial Decision: Towards a Theory of Legal Justification* (Stanford: Stanford University Press, 1961), p. 15. It should be noted that in this passage Wasserstrom is tapping the common-sense rationale rather than arguing the point himself.
8. Fortas, *Concerning Dissent*, p. 33.

ment and the *New York Times*. But certitude is only an
anagram and not a synonym for rectitude. The respective
battle cries of "free speech" and "national security" frame
the question; they do not answer it.

Professor Kurland, let it be noted, does not answer it either,
but he does get us all on the right track by stripping the
problem down to its essentials: the conflict between "two
primary values of a democratic society." In the public forum,
Professor Kurland uses legal logic only to "frame the
questions." In the classroom or the courtroom, he would no
doubt pursue this logic to its inexorable conclusion: a rule
appropriate to the dispute at hand and one that we can live
with in at least the proximate future. Indeed, in this short
article he clearly implies that the final determination must be
made in the courts by judges working with the Constitution
and with those rules developed through the years to make
that document more precise and workable.[9]

In sum, legal symbols in political discourse divert attention
from fundamental conflicts by focusing on established procedures. Should the president be impeached? We need only let
the professionals hammer out a satisfactory interpretation of
that curious constitutional formulation, "high crimes and
misdemeanors." How much neater than getting mired in
dispute over the performance of the Nixon regime. Indeed, is
it not rather curious that the relatively petty crimes of
Watergate and not the unspeakable horrors of Vietnam could
bring a president to the brink of impeachment? The law, in
other words, calls upon a prior procedural consensus to
resolve or perhaps to sublimate a current conflict of sub-
stance. Citizens are asked to cut short what will necessarily be
an endless debate over controversial issues, like the propriety
of the Vietnam War, about which men of good will inevitably
differ; they are asked instead to settle for a determination of

9. *The New York Times*, 23 June 1971, p. 43.

who is entitled to what according to existing rules that are beyond dispute.

THE VIRTUE OF MORALITY

So far it has been argued that the call of the law is realistic and convenient, but there is an ethical theme to be examined as well. We have, one might say, considered the legal paradigm's "genuine appeal to the mind" and will now ponder its "feeble echo in the heart." The ethical theme is clear enough. Judith Shklar has devoted an entire book to "legalism," which she defines as "the *ethical* attitude that holds *moral* conduct to be a matter of rule following, and *moral* relationships to consist of duties and rights determined by rules." [10] Whether the echo in the heart is feeble or not remains, however, a matter of controversy. Clearly, the echo in Professor Shklar's heart is feeble, since she sees the ethic as petty and confining. On the other hand, apparently she wrote her "polemic" against legalism precisely because she felt that for too many Americans the echo was strong though the ethic was weak. Lon Fuller has attempted to explain and defend what Professor Shklar wished primarily to condemn. In *The Morality of Law,* Professor Fuller has explored the ethical roots of legal ordering as well as the links between legal morality and traditional American values.[11] The analysis that follows will lean heavily on the insights of the Fuller approach although that dependence may not always be made explicit.

Let us begin by considering the symbol of justice in our

10. Judith Shklar, *Legalism* (Cambridge: Harvard University Press, 1964), p. 1. Italics added.

11. Lon L. Fuller, *The Morality of Law* (New Haven: Yale University Press, 1964). Professor Shklar's book also is explanatory and her attack on the counterproductive and confining character of legalism is extraordinarily insightful. On the other hand, her admittedly polemical purposes lead to the brink of caricature, to some extent obscuring what she is explaining. Fuller is equally partisan but his presentation is more balanced and systematic.

society. The scales and the sword are understandable enough;
they relate directly to the law's "genuine appeal to the mind."
The scales reassure us that judicial determinations are
precise, reliable, and even somewhat mechanical. The sword
suggests both deterrence and punishment: citizens must
choose between compliance and retribution. The sword is,
therefore, our promise of vigorous support by the state for the
rights and obligations embodied in our laws. But the blindfold? What purposes does it serve? Why not open the eyes of
our judges? Certainly we must hope that the blindfold is lifted
when the scales are read and before the sword is swung. Prior
to that time, however, it is fundamental to our system that
judges not be allowed to really see the persons who stand
before them. Judges are to concern themselves solely with
rules rather than with persons. Why?

At first glance the answer to that question seems obvious.
That which the judge can see with the blindfold removed is
simply irrelevant: age, skin color, perhaps some evidence of
social class. Instinctively, we know that it would be wrong for
the judge to respond to such invidious distinctions rather
than to the evidence. Part of what we object to is the note of
corruption which is implicit in giving favors to the rich or the
powerful, but beneath the surface there is the obvious
unfairness of applying rules on a hit-and-miss basis. Consider, for example, the following report of the position taken
by a New York City health official who had discovered
excessive concentrations of poisonous lead in several samples
of paint marketed in the New York area: "Dr. Guinee
declined to name the brands of paint with excess lead
because, he said, he had not tested all the paint on sale here
and it would be unfair to name some companies while others
that might also have excess lead were not included in the
sample." [12] It is only fair that we all be treated in the same

12. *The New York Times,* 24 July 1971, p. 1.

way by rules, since "all men are created equal and they are endowed by their creator with certain inalienable rights." Equality before the law—before judges, public officials, and before the rules themselves—is simply part and parcel of a basic American credo.

What at first glance appears incontestable seems on closer examination to be absurd and counterproductive. Take the eight offending paint companies. If their identity is released the incidence of lead poisoning will presumably be reduced. Is this not the purpose of the standards? Where is the ethical net profit in perfecting the fairness of the procedures at the expense of the obviously moral goal of minimizing the number of innocent deaths? But even the fairness of equality before the law does not stand up well under careful scrutiny. Clearly people are not, in fact, equal—intellectually, financially, or emotionally. In the criminal law, to treat the rich and the poor alike is to close one's eyes to distinctions which may be relevant in explaining *why* a crime was committed. The rich and the poor, as the saying goes, are equally prohibited from sleeping under the bridges. Why should the law react in the same way to the theft of a loaf of bread by the hungry and the well-nourished? More generally, the equality of opportunity implied by the evenhanded administration of rules has a largely illusory cast to it. When some of the contestants begin the race with a broken leg, can there be equality of opportunity? When, for instance, we admit "handicapped minorities" to our universities, in what sense is it "fair" to apply the same standards to them as to middle class, white students who are both better equipped to meet these standards and more comfortable with their use and abuse. Although it is simple enough to trace the ethic of equality before the law back to traditional American values— or at least to a basic American credo—it is more difficult to explain the attractions of this demonstrably fallacious principle.

More difficult, yes, but by no means impossible. In the first place, we should not be surprised that the ethical principle of equality before the law does not square with empirical reality. Ethics is, after all, concerned with aspirations—with what *should be* rather than with what *is*. Moreover, the fact that "fairness" in rule application is *in some instances* counterproductive from a moral standpoint, does not empty fairness of its ethical content. But beyond these rather tentative arguments in behalf of the legal ethic, there is a more direct defense to be made. The only problem is that the ethical points are difficult to extricate from an overlay of practical considerations.

In the first place, equality before the law is at one and the same time a doctrinal hedge against the temptation of judges to abuse their authority and an indication of the ethical relativism that lies at the root of the legal paradigm. How is the judge to decide which minorities are to be favored by law? That is to say, just which handicaps constitute a sufficient justification for benign discrimination? And if special treatment is justified, how much of it—and under what circumstances? If judges are left to answer these questions in whichever way they choose their discretionary powers are increased enormously and so too are the opportunities for abuse of judicial authority. But leaving aside this quest for certainty and control, what standards is the judge to use in determining who deserves special treatment? Should the law serve each according to need or should it favor those who have labored the most diligently? These are the kinds of basic moral questions that have been the source of controversy through the centuries.

Equality before the law thus can be seen as the last line of resistance against turning disputes into the kind of battles over first moral principles that have in the past torn societies apart. No one has made the point more effectively than Louis Hartz: "Law has flourished on the corpse of philosophy in

America, for the settlement of the ultimate moral question is the end of speculation upon it." [13] We are thus brought back to the practical convenience of the law game, but we see that it rests on an ethical premise—namely, that ultimate moral truths are out of reach. Consequently, we must be prepared to settle for the existing patchwork of values embodied in established rights, procedures, and institutions. We must accept the eclectic consensus which holds the society together rather than going to the moral mat at every occasion in search of real human community. The law game provides an answer for every question and at the same time cuts the debate off short of first principles. As such, it contributes to and reinforces tendencies in the system toward rather modest ethical aspirations.

But the law game is more than simply a pragmatic ethical echo of the general determination to settle for less than the best by avoiding the tough questions. Equality before law amounts to a systemic commitment to respect each human being as an individual. The decision to make special exceptions is patronizing as well as benign. From this perspective it is easy to understand why favors in behalf of minority students, for example, would be rejected as "unethical, racist, opportunistic, and utterly demeaning to both dispenser and recipient, because underlying it all is a fundamental denial of human dignity. It is rank paternalism." [14] The benign shading of grades is condescending, because it suggests that the students need special help and to the extent that certain minorities are, as groups, designated as being in need, it becomes difficult to escape racist overtones. At the same time, if compensatory arrangements become common knowledge

13. Louis Hartz, *The Liberal Tradition in America* (New York: Harcourt, Brace, 1955), p. 10.
14. From a letter written by Professor Pierre van den Berghe to *The Daily* (University of Washington) concerning the University's Special Education and Ethnic Studies programs, 29 July 1971, p. 7.

(as is the tendency), the practice denies individuals an opportunity to demonstrate that they can make it on their own. And what of the others involved in the grading process? Is it not true that "there is no way of being benign to one group without being malign to another, if they have to compete for the same scarce resources?" [15]

Clearly, there are societal dimensions to this ethic of individual responsibility and reward. What we all have in common is the fundamental uniformity of our rights and obligations. It is one thing to demand a job, to ask others to leave you alone, to ask for better housing, or to apply for a scholarship. It is quite another to claim that you have rights to these things—privacy, a college education and so forth. In the first instance, you personalize your claim and make it less than compelling, for we all recognize that society is overripe with unsated needs and desires. You come to those who are in a position to honor your claim as a supplicant—one who is in need. Why should *your* request be honored while others go unheeded? How much more compelling to assert a right. You are claiming only what is due to you and what others have an obligation to fulfill. There is dignity in asserting a right. Moreover, in asserting your right you imply a reciprocal relationship with others in the society. Your right is no longer personal but part of a more general set of societal rights and obligations, independent of and predating your particular need. To claim a right is thus to invoke symbols of legitimacy that transcend your personal problems. At the same time, you tacitly commit yourself to accept the obligations which inhere in the existing system—that is to say, the pattern of mutual and reciprocal commitments that defines the fabric of the society.

It can be argued that the system is built on a lie, in that citizens are not equally willing or able to accept responsibility or claim rewards. In part, the answer to this condemnation

15. Ibid.

has already been given. While by no means perfect, a system which refuses to make invidious distinctions among individuals at least avoids some obvious injustices about which there is little dispute. It may not be the best, but it keeps us safe from known evils. But more fundamental than this mini-max ethical stand is probably a deep-seated belief that such a system can actually be self-fulfilling: if the state does, in fact, treat its citizens as responsible human beings, they will in the long run rise to the challenge. And of course there would be no point in betting on this distant future if one were not initially committed to the beneficence and desirability of the responsible and striving individual as the cornerstone of the society.

The purpose of this chapter has been to convey a general sense of what is distinctive and what is attractive about the legal way of doing things. It has been argued that the legal view of the world perceives and explains human relationships in terms of rules and the rights and obligations which are inherent in these rules. This world view is, of course, readily associated with legal symbols and with institutions and processes in the American system. Whatever legitimacy inheres in these symbols, institutions, and processes presumably attaches automatically to the legal approach to political problem solving. Reinforcing this ingrained political reflex is the convenient, realistic, and principled approach to politics that is projected by the myth of rights.

The message that emerges is somewhat ambiguous. On the one hand, the appeal of the myth of rights is instrumental. A government of laws promises a stable political order and a reliable structure of authority. On the other, the myth of rights is rooted in a moral vision of a political society dedicated to maximizing individual freedom. The particular rights specified in the Bill of Rights serve as a protective shield against unwarranted governmental intrusion. More generally, our right to have rights imparts a certain equality of status to all individuals in the society. We are made equal before the law and invited to take advantage of whatever opportunities are thereby afforded us. While the instrumental and moral promises are distinct they are compatible and, in fact, complement one another. It is the stable social order and the reliable authority structure promised by a government of laws that releases individuals from a range of political concerns and burdens and thus increases energies available to pursue personal achievement.

The rhetoric of rights transmits this message in terms which are generally accessible. No doubt something is lost in the transmission. The piecemeal evocation of symbols and slogans hardly promotes and probably impedes systematic reflection on the total social vision implied by the myth of rights. On the other hand, the rhetoric of rights is singularly effective at penetrating the surface issues and conveying the value choices lurking beneath. Should we add a screening tribunal to the Supreme Court to reduce the workload of our overburdened justices? At first glance, this is a technical matter. Not so, warns former Justice Goldberg, invoking the rhetoric of rights to alert us to hidden dangers: "It is perhaps the greatest virtue of the Supreme Court as it now functions that it serves as a guarantee to all citizens of whatever estate, race, or color, that our highest court is open for consideration of their claim that equal and relevant justice under the Constitution is being denied them." [16] The problem posed by the rhetoric of rights is, as it is with other ideologies, the tendency to exaggerate the stakes of political conflict. Particular decisions may carry us closer to or farther from a society of rights and, in that sense, legal rhetoric accurately reflects what is at stake. Neither the total vision nor any fundamental component of it is, however, likely to be at risk in a given

16. Arthur J. Goldberg, "One Supreme Court: It Doesn't Need Its Cases 'Screened,'" *The New Republic*, 10 February 1973, p. 16.

political conflict. Nonetheless, the rhetoric of rights consistently will inflate the stakes by setting the present issue in the context of a perfect past.

In the final analysis it is not the accuracy of the image, but its attractiveness, that determines the success of the myth of rights. I have suggested that the rhetoric of rights does not compete unopposed, that other symbols are evoked with significant claims on our affections. The next chapter provides an empirical glimpse of the extent to which Americans are predisposed to respond affirmatively to the call of the law.

5. THE POLITICAL RESONANCE OF THE MYTH OF RIGHTS

The appeals made by the myth of rights for the support of Americans are rooted in traditional values and closely associated with venerable institutions. The symbolic voice of the myth of rights can, moreover, be easily understood and readily adapted to political discourse. But just how compelling is it? How pervasive, widespread, and uniform a grip do legal values have on the minds of Americans? These are obviously crucial and elusive questions.

The last chapter provided an opportunity to relate to them in a personal way. Now the questions will be confronted empirically through consideration of a wide variety of research findings. The focus will be on our legal culture, on "the network of values and attitudes relating to law, which determine when and why and where people turn to law or government, or turn away." [1]

The evidence tends to confirm the political significance of the myth of rights, but it also strongly indicates that broad generalizations about the responsiveness of Americans to the myth must be qualified in a variety of ways. Legal symbols do not resonate evenly, or with uniform intensity, throughout the body politic. Blacks and other minorities, for example, seem less caught up in these beliefs. The pattern of their disenchantment raises more questions than it answers, however.

1. Lawrence M. Friedman, "Legal Culture and Social Development," *Law and Society Review* 4 (August 1969): 34. The concept of legal culture is analogous to and most usefully perceived in connection with political culture. See Lucian W. Pye, "Political Culture," *The International Encyclopedia of the Social Sciences* (New York: Macmillan, 1968), 12:218–25.

Loss of faith in the operational integrity of legal institutions is often found in combination with a firm residual commitment to legal ideals. Even with all of the complications and qualifications that the data force upon us, if we take account of what we know and what we have reason to suspect, it is safe to say that the myth of rights significantly influences the perceptions and priorities of many and perhaps most Americans. At least that is the argument that will be made in the pages just ahead.

Before beginning the analysis an important cautionary note about the character of the data is clearly in order. The available findings are scattered; they bear directly but not systematically on the myth of rights. Because no survey has been conducted on the myth of rights as such, I have been forced into the somewhat dubious exercise of combining findings from a number of separate studies of the attitudes of children—linked to one another primarily by the tenuous bonds of socialization theory—with results of work on public perceptions of the Supreme Court. The resultant "synthesis" can hardly be taken as conclusive; it does, however, provide at least a glimpse of the underlying predispositions which ultimately determine responses to the myth of rights. So long as the endeavors of this chapter are taken as heuristic or hypothetical, perhaps obvious objections can be set aside, at least temporarily.

RIGHTS, RULES, AND LEGAL INSTITUTIONS

Research on the attitudes of children indicates that legal values take root early. Even young children tend to associate successful social ordering with rules.[2] There is a striking

2. June L. Tapp and Lawrence Kohlberg, "Developing Senses of Law and Legal Justice," in *Journal of Social Issues* (No. 2, 1971), pp. 73–77. The research in this special issue, "Socialization, the Law and Society," edited by June L. Tapp, will figure heavily in my analysis. Socialization research provides the most useful empirical findings on attitudes relating to the myth

purity to these early images of law. Rules are perceived as
immutable, imperative, and fair.[3] The policeman and the
president are the prototypical figures, and the rules are seen
in essentially negative terms—as a bulwark against societal
violence or the predatory impulses of aggressive individuals.[4]
In young children, visions of the law tend to be dominated by
connotations of obedience to authority.

Older children perceive rules in increasingly complex ways.
The sense of immutability is softened by perceptions of
movement and adaptation. Similarly, the obligation to obey
seems to be eroded with age as children become more
discriminating about rule following.[5] Age brings an enhanced
respect for individual freedom and a tendency to associate
the protection of individual freedom with legal and constitutional rights—suggesting, of course, that particular laws may
contravene individual rights, thus encouraging the emergence
of a conditional concept of obedience.[6] More broadly, older
children come to think of the law as a vital structuring agent
in social relations, and some take the further step of looking
at the law as a purposeful instrument for social action. Only
college students, however, seem prepared to abandon the
negative images and/or embrace instrumental notions of law
in significant proportions. Most characteristically, then, rules
emerge as facilitators of social interaction, and the college
students who "found it *impossible to imagine a world without
rules*" can be taken as typical, if somewhat extreme.[7] Finally

of rights. It is seriously marred, however, by the absence of blacks from most
of the samples.

3. Robert D. Hess and Judith V. Torney, *The Development of Political
Attitudes in Children* (Chicago: Aldine, 1967), pp. 52–54.

4. Tapp and Kohlberg, "Developing Senses of Law and Legal Justice," pp.
78–79.

5. Ibid., pp. 81–83.

6. Judith Gallatin and Joseph Adelson, "Legal Guarantees of Individual
Freedom: A Cross-National Study of the Development of Political
Thought," in *Journal of Social Issues* (No. 2, 1971), pp. 93–108.

7. Tapp and Kohlberg, "Developing Senses of Law and Legal Justice," p.
73. Italics in the original. This research tends to support a cognitive theory of

and altogether consistently, a tolerance for imperfection in legal processes seems to develop as children mature. That is, they begin to realize and accept the fact that legal institutions will not always operate as they should.

An increasingly complex vision of law does not seem to undermine the attraction of legal values or the perceived importance of legal institutions, although some revealing changes in orientation do develop among the older children. What emerges could be characterized as a distinction between law and laws. The recognition that all laws are not fair increases sharply and steadily with age.[8] So, too, does the feeling that those in power make mistakes—including policemen, senators, and even the president, who among the younger children is seemingly beyond reproach.[9]

> Though implicit trust in law decreases with age, it establishes the criteria a child may use later in assessing the performance of all authority figures. If, at a later age, he discovers that laws are not always just, he may nevertheless believe they should be; if he has experience with authority figures who enforce law arbitrarily, he may be disillusioned yet hold to the principle of fair administration of laws.[10]

Data on the Supreme Court suggest that age may not so much bring a loss as a transfer of faith. While the older children evidence a much more tough-minded approach to the police and the president, approval of the Supreme Court seems to increase with age and to be associated with qualities like "infallibility," "knowledgeability," and "power." [11] Inter-

---

legal development based on a three-stage progression from pre-conventional (the negative or "physical power" stage) through conventional (the facilitator or "interpersonal concordance" stage) to post-conventional (the instrumental or "social contract" stage) orientations toward the law. Ibid., p. 69.

8. Hess and Torney, *Development of Political Attitudes*, pp. 52, 53.

9. Ibid., pp. 46–50.

10. Ibid., p. 52.

11. David Easton and Jack Dennis, *Children in the Political System: Origins of Political Legitimacy* (New York: McGraw-Hill, 1969), pp. 278–79.

esting to note, the Court does not lose its image as a generally distant and unresponsive institution among the older children.[12] It is as if childhood fantasies about the absolute virtue and utter dependability of authority figures are shifted from immediate to more distant symbols—thus preserving the sanctity of the law while taking account of its manifest shortcomings in everyday events.

Taken together, childhood perceptions of the law and legal institutions evidence orientations which are generally consistent with the myth of rights—some of them distinctly American, others apparently quite widely shared. American children, like youngsters elsewhere, come to take rules both seriously and for granted as they grow older.[13] In contrast with other youngsters, Americans appear to have "more concern with individual freedoms." [14] Even more to the point, American children seem more likely to believe that their rulers are subject to the same laws as are ordinary citizens.[15] Developmental trends in the United States also reveal the emergence of a shared standard of fairness: children come to associate fairness in laws with equality of treatment.[16] Legal philosophers think of this particular standard of fairness as integrally linked to the very notion of rules—perhaps further substantiating the pervasive influence of rules.[17] Indeed, rules

12. Hess and Torney, pp. 40–41.
13. Tapp and Kohlberg, "Developing Senses of Law and Legal Justice," pp. 73–85. The other nations included in the study were Mexico, Taiwan, and Turkey.
14. Gallatin and Adelson, "Legal Guarantees of Individual Freedom," p. 104. The comparisons were among Germans, British, and Americans.
15. Fred I. Greenstein and Sidney Tarrow, "Political Orientations of Children: The Use of a Semi-Projective Technique in Three Nations," in Harry Eckstein and Ted Robert Gurr, eds., *Sage Professional Papers in Comparative Politics* (Beverly Hills, Calif.: Sage Publications, 1970), 1:520–29. In addition to American children, English and French children were interviewed.
16. Judith Y. Torney, "Socialization of Attitudes towards the Legal System," *Journal of Social Issues* (No. 2, 1971), p. 152. Younger children tend to think of fairness solely in terms of doing good and preventing evil.
17. See H. L. A. Hart, *The Concept of Law* (London: Oxford University Press, 1961), pp. 153–63.

become so much a part of social consciousness that the distinction between rules and laws loses its meaning.[18]

Some of the developmental trends are in less obvious harmony with the myth of rights but do lend themselves to an interpretation compatible with the myth. Indeed, they may even be seen as essential ingredients in a belief system hospitable to constitutional politics. Consider the more flexible vision of legal rules that emerges with age.[19] Consider, additionally, that although older children are more concerned with protecting individual rights, most of them end up with a highly contigent sense of what rights actually are. They are willing to suspend the guarantee of rights during emergencies or, to a lesser extent, in order to serve the welfare of the community.[20] Rights seem to take on an "abstract" or rhetorical cast, even among the older children: "Most children's attitudes toward rights of free expression for specific dissenting political groups depend more upon their attitude toward the groups than upon their acceptance of the general principle of free speech."[21] Similarly, age and education bring increasingly sophisticated and evasive attitudes toward obedience of the law. An absolute duty to obey is typical of primary school children, but middle schoolers are more inclined to adopt a "morality of circumstance." ("Well, it depends on what's going on. If it's a matter of life and death or, you know, something pretty important, then it's all right. But it should be followed as much as possible.") College students move toward the more sophisticated formulations of the "morality of rule"—with an integral place for disobedience. ("When the rule is immoral or unjust because I believe

18. Tapp and Kohlberg, "Developing Senses of Law and Legal Justice," pp. 73–85.

19. See Hess and Torney, *Development of Political Attitudes,* p. 52, and Gallatin and Adelson, "Legal Guarantees of Individual Freedom," p. 100, table 4.

20. Gallatin and Adelson, pp. 96–102.

21. Gail L. Zellman and David O. Sears, "Childhood Origins of Tolerance for Dissent," *Journal of Social Issues* (No. 2, 1971), p. 123.

that people are morally accountable for their actions, and this is above the law or rules.")[22] From one perspective, these wishy-washy attitudes might seem to cast doubt on just how serious a commitment we have to the law. A more realistic interpretation, in my judgment, would be to see this equivocation as perfectly in keeping with the curious ambiguities of the myth of rights itself—that is, its claims to nurture a form of politics that is an artful blend of expedience and principle, stability and change. Moreover, all this flexibility and voluntarism seem to be firmly embedded in enduring connotations of permanence and continuity.[23] Why else the elaborate rationales and transparent hypocrisies that the older children invoke in defense of departures from legal ideals?

On the basis of available evidence, it is difficult to determine which, if any, of the images that take root during childhood endure among adults. Nor is it possible to tell whether trends set in motion early in life progress in a linear fashion into and through later years. Researchers claim that adherence to the most basic legal values seems to have considerable staying power. "There are some changes with age . . . but norms about the justice of law and necessity for conformity are established at an early age." [24] More to the point, children obviously do not create their orientations; they must, of course, pick them up somewhere in the adult world. One study which included teachers as well as their pupils revealed teacher attitudes that appeared to be reasonable projections of developmental trends among the children:

Teachers' ratings of the importance of various topics clearly indicate that the strongest emphasis is placed upon compliance to law, authority, and school regulations.

22. Tapp and Kohlberg, "Developing Senses of Law and Legal Justice," pp. 82–83.
23. Hess and Torney, *Development of Political Attitudes,* p. 261, fig. D.02.
24. Ibid., p. 215.

Indeed, it seems likely that much of what is called citizenship training in the public schools . . . is an attempt to teach regard for the rules and standards of conduct of the school.[25]

For our purposes, it is not necessary to determine whether the schools, the family, or forms of public ritual are responsible for the belief system that emerges among children. Whatever its exact source, it seems safe to assume that the developmental trends observed in children reflect, at least in a general sense, values that permeate the American ethos.

The most substantial body of adult data, while bearing on the Supreme Court alone, does provide a useful perspective on the developmental trends. What appears once again is that curiously ambiguous commitment to legal values that emerged among the older children. On the one hand, the cynicism that creeps into orientations toward the police and the president in adolescence apparently overtakes the Court in later years. In comparison with the Congress and the president, respondents have relatively less confidence in the Court and, in addition, doubt that it is doing particularly important things.[26] Moreover, there seems to be very little reluctance to express opposition to individual decisions of the Court.[27] All this despite the fact that people are very poorly informed. Even those with the most information, numbering just 12 percent of the total sample, displayed only a rudimentary familiarity with the Court—that is, the capability to

25. Ibid., p. 218.
26. Kenneth M. Dolbeare, "The Public Views the Supreme Court," in Herbert Jacob, *Law, Politics, and the Federal Courts* (Boston: Little, Brown, 1967), pp. 196–97.
27. Walter F. Murphy and Joseph Tanenhaus, *The Study of Public Law* (New York: Random House, 1972), pp. 42 and 43. This same research is reported elsewhere in more detail. See, in particular, Walter F. Murphy and Joseph Tanenhaus, "Public Opinion and the United States Supreme Court: A Preliminary Mapping of Some Prerequisites for Court Legitimation of Regime Changes," *Law and Society Review* 2 (May 1968):357–84.

identify individual judges or to indicate specific likes and dislikes in open-ended questioning.[28]

On the other hand, the Court does seem to strike positive, if latent, chords among significant numbers of Americans. Murphy and Tanenhaus detect "a reservoir of good will" which the Court can call upon:

> Fewer than half of those who criticized the Court on particular issues were prepared to say that on the whole it was not doing a good job. Altogether, those unhappy about the Court's overall performance constituted only slightly more than one-third of those who assessed the kind of job the Court was doing. Even among white Southerners, the single group most hostile to the Court, people who felt that the Court was not doing its job very well comprised no more than 40 percent of those who responded to the job-assessment question.[29]

Furthermore, almost 40 percent of a national sample indicated in open-ended questioning that they understood that the Supreme Court had a constitutional role, that is, some responsibility "for defining and maintaining the basic rules of the game." [30] The Court's public image is, then, of a visible but distant governmental institution closely associated with legal and constitutional norms. As such, it would seem to be

28. Ibid., p. 42. Dolbeare also finds very little information about the work of the Court. Dolbeare, "The Public Views the Supreme Court," pp. 198–201.

29. Murphy and Tanenhaus, *The Study of Public Law*, p. 43. The authors point out that: "Since only people who could respond to a prior open-ended question about the nature of the Court's work were asked how well it was doing its job, those who believed that the Court was not doing a very good job make up less than one-sixth of all people interviewed, and those who thought the Court was performing very well constitute only 35 percent of the sample." For a less sanguine interpretation of the Murphy and Tanenhaus data, see Sheldon Goldman and Thomas P. Jahnige, *The Federal Courts as a Political System* (New York: Harper and Row, 1971), pp. 135–48. They find it "rather ironic that much of the Court's net positive support was attributed to members of the public who were least aware of its activities. To know the Court was not necessarily to love it." Ibid., p. 142.

30. Murphy and Tanenhaus, "Public Opinion and the United States Supreme Court," p. 365.

our most palpable symbol of the law and thus a probable heir to our faith in the indispensability of legal rules to social ordering. In short, the Supreme Court projects an image altogether in harmony with the myth of rights and the workings of constitutional politics.

CLEAVAGE AND CONFLICT

To this point, public perceptions of the law have been cumulated. It has been argued that the ostensible anomalies in these perceptions could be taken as signs of a social milieu that would be responsive to the cross-cutting claims of the myth of rights. If, however, distinctive patterns of perception tend to congeal around existing cleavages in the society, the anomalies might be sources or symptoms of dangerous social tensions. Reflect, for example, on the fundamental tendency among older children to see the law as a necessary condition of social interaction. Despite this marked developmental trend, significant numbers of respondents, up to and including those of college age, continue to associate the law with power and prohibition.[31] What have we here? Is it discord over ideals, which is easily reconciled in practice and in fact is suggestive of a resilient society open to alternative formulations? Or are we faced with mutually exclusive concepts of law, which give rise to sharply divergent expectations about legal processes, and perhaps reinforce social cleavages that divide Americans from one another? It is to this second possibility that we now turn.

The data indicate important and consistent differences

31. Tapp and Kohlberg, "Developing Senses of Law and Legal Justice," pp. 76–77, table 2. A study among adults in Texas, using somewhat different categories of analysis, concluded that essentially negative images of the law actually predominate. "The results convey a picture of the law in the minds of these citizens as a coercive force to prevent social evil in the sense of regression from the status quo rather than as a constructive force for the enhancement of their ideas of social good." Martha Williams and Jay Hall, "Knowledge of the Law in Texas: Socioeconomic and Ethnic Differences," *Law and Society Review* 7 (Fall 1972):108–09.

among Americans along class, race, and sex lines, but reveal some common ground as well, particularly when set in a cross-national context. Far and away the most striking divergences are among the races. Sex and class differences seem to account for very little of the variation and in fact mostly accentuate racial cleavage. The common ground among the races has to do primarily with ideals rather than with empirical perceptions. There is, in other words, more agreement on the way things should be than on the way they are. Whether this means that we are working within a single legal culture or are coming apart at the seams is a question to be dealt with at the end of this section.

The most distinct class and sex cleavages emerge from the data concerning the police—that is, lower status children and girls tend to esteem the police more highly. In comparison with boys, girls both like the police better and perceive the police as more authoritative.[32] Similar preferences appear among lower status children.[33] The relationship between status and esteem for the police, however, appears to be not linear but curvilinear. There is greater esteem among lower middle class youngsters than within either the upper middle or lower class.[34] A study of adult attitudes toward the police in Milwaukee also tends to confound the linear hypothesis. "Middle-class whites generally gave more favorable ratings to the police than whites in the working-class neighborhood." [35] If we are to make inferences about adult data on the basis of these developmental trends among children, it is the "middle-America" hypothesis that seems most consistent with the meager data available and that conforms most closely to political intuitions. The socialization data were gathered in

32. Easton and Dennis, *Children in the Political System,* pp. 374–76, and Torney, "Socialization of Attitudes," p. 148.
33. Hess and Torney, *Development of Political Attitudes,* pp. 140–44.
34. Torney, "Socialization," p. 147.
35. Herbert Jacob, "Black and White Perceptions of Justice in the City," *Law and Society Review* 6 (August 1971):73.

the early 1960s, and this leads understandably to speculations about trends that emerged late in the decade: "There were some data which could be interpreted as indicating glorification of police authority by lower-middle class children (tested in 1962). The late 1960s saw a rise in concern for law and order among adults in precisely the same social class." [36] But the links between police and the lower middle class may well transcend the traumas of the 1960s. Whereas the lower class child is likely to have conflict-ridden experiences with the police and the upper middle class child is led to think of the policeman as a social inferior, the lower middle class child probably tends to view the policeman as "an occupational model and hears glorification of authority and authority roles from his parents." [37] As for glorification, can we take as typical the following affirmation by the wife of a filling station owner?

> The police and firemen in the country have the worst time, worse than anyone else. They're the finest people we have, but they don't make the money they should, and they're insulted every day. What's the use of risking your life if you don't get any respect for it—and no thanks, and no appreciation? The same goes for all workingmen. [38]

It does seem to be true that police recruits are drawn primarily from the lower middle class; that they tend to be upwardly mobile; and that they think of the police career as a step in the right direction. [39]

The racial cleavages relating to the police are sharper, more intense, and less problematic. Nor need we work for infer-

36. Torney, "Socialization," p. 153.
37. Ibid., p. 148.
38. Robert Coles, *The Middle Americans: Proud and Uncertain* (Boston: Little, Brown, 1971), p. 105.
39. John H. McNamara, "Uncertainties in Police Work: The Relevance of Police Recruits' Backgrounds and Training," in David J. Bordua, ed., *The Police: Six Sociological Essays* (New York: John Wiley, 1967), pp. 193-99.

ences based on socialization research. There is a great deal of
data indicating that black people in particular have strongly
negative images of the police: "Blacks perceive the police as
more corrupt, more unfair, more excitable, more harsh,
tougher, weaker, lazier, less intelligent, less friendly, more
cruel, and more on the bad than on the good side than white
respondents." [40] What is true of blacks in Milwaukee seems to
be equally true of both black and Chicano minorities in
Denver: "There is no doubt at all that minorities in Denver
hold the police in less favorable regard than does the
dominant community." [41] Ethnicity thus turns out to be a
better predictor of attitudes toward the police than does
class—or, presumably, sex.[42] Not surprisingly, the police are
well aware of this hostility: "Very few people know what it's
like to have radicals shouting at you from one direction and
the Negro people in the slums looking at you as if you hate
each and every one of them." [43] Note the self-conscious
quality of these anti-police vibrations that the policeman
senses within the black community. His impressions seem to
be pretty much the same as those which black writers have
been pressing upon us for many, many years:

> The police are the armed guardians of the social order.
> The blacks are the chief domestic victims of the American

40. Jacob, "Black and White Perceptions," p. 73. See also The President's
Commission on Law Enforcement and Administration of Justice, *Task Force
Report: The Police* (Washington: Government Printing Office, 1967), pp.
145–48.

41. David H. Bayley and Harold Mendelsohn, *Minorities and the Police:
Confrontation in America* (New York: Free Press, 1968), p. 110. On Chicanos
and Puerto Ricans, see *Task Force Report: The Police*, p. 149.

42. Ibid., p. 42.

43. Coles, *The Middle Americans*, p. 57. This police sergeant's perceptions
are, it should be underscored, more complex and ambivalent than the above
quotation would suggest. He detects approval of the police among all of the
"good people, real people," including the "average" Negroes. "You go and
ask the average Negro in a Negro neighborhood about the police, and he
won't talk the way the civil rights people do. They call us all the time,
Negroes do." Ibid., p. 58.

social order. A conflict of interest exists, therefore, between the blacks and the police.[44]

He [the policeman] moves through Harlem, therefore, like an occupying soldier in a bitterly hostile country; which is precisely what, and where he is, and is the reason he walks in twos and threes.[45]

In other words, blacks do not simply respond more negatively to the police than do whites; they also perceive that they get treated worse than whites and believe that they are mistreated *because they are black.*[46]

Perceptions of the police are associated, in some cases rather closely, with attitudes toward the law and legal processes. Police and judges seem to be linked with one another in peoples' minds—particularly among blacks and working class whites—but distinguished from other local officials like teachers, welfare workers, and mailmen.[47] Negative assessments of the police spill over into distrust of judges and, according to a Detroit study, to the laws themselves.

Perhaps even more importantly, however, the overwhelming criticism of law enforcement that flourished in this ghetto also apparently extended to other facets of the legal system . . . Persons who accepted a conventional faith in the impartiality of the law and its administration formed a small and nearly imperceptible minority in the

44. Eldridge Cleaver, *Soul on Ice* (New York: McGraw-Hill, 1968), p. 134.
45. James Baldwin, *Nobody Knows My Name* (New York: Dell, 1962), p. 67. Similar sentiments can be found in the works of Richard Wright and many other black writers. As the commission pointed out: "Surveys may not accurately reflect the full extent of minority group dissatisfaction with the police. In-depth interviews with members of minority groups frequently lead to strong statements of hostility, replacing the neutral or even favorable statements which began the interview." *Task Force Report: The Police,* p. 147.
46. Harlan Hahn, "Ghetto Assessments of Police Protection and Authority," in *Law and Society Review* 6 (November 1971): 187 "Apparently, most ghetto residents tended to regard inequities in the provision of police protection primarily in racial terms."
47. Jacob, "Black and White Perceptions," p. 85.

ghetto. . . . While 89 percent of the respondents were
convinced that "most Detroit policemen" did not display
total honesty in the performance of their duties, 88 percent
also believe that "most judges in local courts break the
rules for personal gain or favors." [48]

There is a somewhat weaker companion tendency for support
of the police to extend to other features of the legal system.
"Social class differences are less pronounced than IQ differences, but—quite consistently—lower and lower-middle
class children are more inclined to rate law as fair. Girls as
well are more positive in their evaluation of law." [49] Once
again, images of middle America provide intuitive confirmation for a rather meager data base. There is reason to believe
that the sharp social divisions concerning the police are
symptomatic of deeper cleavages resonating through, although not necessarily beyond, legal matters.

While the cleavages are manifest there is evidence suggesting that, on values at least, there is a good deal of common
ground. One study found great similarity among Americans
on a wide range of values. More to the point, where there
were differences, white and black Americans tended to have
more in common with one another than with the police
respondents.[50] On legal values, specifically, there appears to
be quite a solid consensus: "Blacks, working class whites, and
middle class whites have the same expectations about how
perfect policemen and perfect judges should behave." [51]

48. Hahn, "Ghetto Assessments," p. 185.
49. Torney, "Socialization of Attitudes," p. 152. See also Hess and Torney,
Development of Political Attitudes, pp. 139–40, 179–82. I.Q., which turned out
to be an important explanatory variable, has not been considered in this
analysis, although "Social class and intelligence have been found to be
positively correlated in groups of children." Torney, p. 143. See also Jacob, p.
84.
50. Milton Rokeach, Martin G. Miller, and John A. Snyder, "The Value
Gap between Police and Policed," *Journal of Social Issues* (No. 2, 1971), pp.
160–63.
51. Jacob, p. 86. The Detroit study comes to roughly the same conclusion

There are even overlapping perceptions of the actual functioning of legal institutions:

> Not all blacks in the ghetto feel themselves the victims of injustice and not all whites are recipients of what they feel is just treatment. Considerable elements of the entire population indicated a gap between what they consider would be the ideal situation and reality as they perceive it. Middle-class whites—who have the fewest unfavorable experiences—perceive the smallest gap, but a substantial portion of even that sample indicated a sizeable gap between their expectations and the reality they perceived.[52]

Color and class lines thus seem to blur significantly when the *hopes* of Americans are included in the investigation.

Ideological polarization could reach the point where it would transcend and, in effect, neutralize our shared ideals. Signs of just such a polarization have already begun to appear in research findings. The same Milwaukee study which discloses common aspirations and dissatisfactions also indicates that distrust of the police is so high among blacks that it is essentially independent of police behavior. "The general

—albeit on what strikes me as a questionable interpretation of the data. Hahn argues that since blacks in the Detroit ghetto in a period just after the 1967 civil disorder continued to support such constitutional guarantees as the right to talk to a lawyer or to have a "quick and fair trial," we are justified in inferring "a strong faith in the fundamental principles that govern the process of adjudicating guilt or innocence in the society." This position is anchored in the premise that civil disorder would normally give rise to insistent demands for restoration of the public peace and a willingness "to sacrifice established civil liberties for the sake of restoring order and tranquility in the neighborhood." Hahn, "Ghetto Assessments," p. 186. But what if, as we have reason to believe, substantial numbers of blacks supported or were at least in sympathy with the protests? Is it not reasonable to see the support for civil liberties as no more or less than a reflection of the typical ghetto resident's fear and distrust of the established order? On black support—latent and overt—for the militants, see R. M. Fogelson and R. B. Hill, "Who Riots? A Study of Participation in the 1967 Riots," in *Supplemental Studies for the National Advisory Commission on Civil Disorders* (Washington: Government Printing Office, 1968).

52. Jacob, "Black and White Perceptions," p. 87.

reputation of the police in the black neighborhood has
become so bad that good experiences do not bring about
correspondingly good evaluations." [53] How is this seemingly
irrational response to be explained? Once blacks and other
deprived minorities believe that they are regularly and
systematically denied decent treatment, perhaps they come to
perceive good experiences as exceptions that prove the rule.
This kind of total disenchantment is symptomatic of ideological division and means that a new standard of rationality is
emerging. In such a setting the concept of rights, for example,
would be more likely to divide us than to unite us. For whites
the term would continue to be associated with equality of
individuals under the law. For blacks it would be just another
way of characterizing the privileges and disabilities of race
and/or class. While we should not make too much out of one
bit of data, given the severe tensions between minority groups
and the dominant whites, it would be wrong to assume that
our common aspirations will be enough to hold the society
together.

Clearly the image of the myth of rights as a unifying force
is weakened by these findings. They corroborate a variety of
other signals from the black community indicating a progressive loss of faith in the criminal justice system and in those
processes of constitutional politics that catalyzed civil rights
forces in the 1950s and 1960s. More fundamentally, the
cleavages alert us to the variety of images evoked by the myth
of rights—ranging from the law-and-order themes of middle
America to the egalitarian aspirations of beleaguered minorities. Responses to the myth of rights thus inevitably reflect the
diversity and complexity of our society.

While the myth of rights cannot transcend our differences,
it does exercise a compelling influence on many Americans

53. Ibid., pp. 78–79.

and provides shared ideals for the great majority. It was, recall, the intensity of commitment to law that accounted for the sex and class cleavages revealed in the data. Even otherwise alienated minorities are receptive to the values associated with legal ordering. In short, while we may respond to the myth of rights as groups—distinguished by age, color, sex, and perhaps other traits as well—most of us apparently do respond.

The political relevance of the myth of rights is, therefore, in no way called into question by these data. Indeed, when taken together with the work of the law writers and the prominence of legal rhetoric in political discourse, the survey data surely underscore the salience of the myth of rights. The problem that remains, however, is how to assess the political consequences of this ideological presence. Generally speaking, the impact of the myth of rights is most usefully looked upon as a complex and continuing dialectic between legal values and political action. The essential task of the remainder of this book will be to trace out this ideological imprint on American politics.

Part Two

THE POLITICS OF RIGHTS

6. RIGHTS AS RESOURCES

The politics of rights is a term to describe the forms of political activity made possible by the presence of rights in American society. Only insofar as we understand the politics of rights is it possible to realistically assess the political significance of the myth of rights.

As a starting point we must accept the ideological character of the myth of rights. To acknowledge the myth of rights as an ideology is not to downgrade its importance to American politics nor to deny the political significance of rights. It is simply to shift the focus of inquiry to the myth of rights as a belief system which impinges on American politics in a subtle, complex, and altogether problematic fashion.

At the same time, the descriptive accuracy of the myth of rights is immediately called into question. Ideologies alter perceptions and therefore influence description. An examination of the available empirical research will provide a more balanced view of the political status of legal rights than can possibly be glimpsed through the focusing devices of the myth of rights.

With the myth of rights in political perspective, it becomes possible to look directly at the politics of rights as it focuses attention on three manifestations of rights in the American political system. The myth of rights provides political *ideals*. These ideals are reflected in the formal *rules* which structure American institutions. Finally, the ideals and rules influence the *behavior* of governmental officials and private citizens. The politics of rights is, in short, concerned with the interplay between ideology and action in American politics. In this complex process, the impact of the myth of rights will be elusive and perhaps subliminal. While ideals are seldom if ever decisive, they are nevertheless among the most important determinants of political behavior.

A rethinking of the political relevance of litigation will be the third step in this introductory look at the politics of rights. If the status of rights is problematic, doubts are automatically raised about the political importance of judicial decisions. Surely judicial guarantees can no longer be thought of as politically conclusive. On the other hand, the politics of rights does suggest some far-reaching opportunities which stem from the connotations of legitimacy attaching to legal rights. The politics of rights, in other words, points towards a conception of rights as political resources. The further implication is that the value of rights resides less in the political power that backs them than in their close association with social justice in the minds of Americans. If so, doubt is cast upon the direct payoff of litigation but new possibilities are suggested—possibilities that can be realized by playing on the gap between existing patterns of politics and our cherished ideals.

This chapter will deal with these three introductory themes: (1) the political status of legal rights, (2) the interplay between political values and political behavior, and (3) the opportunities and limitations of litigation as a political tactic.

THE POLITICAL STATUS OF LEGAL RIGHTS: THE MYTH RECONSIDERED

The myth of rights leads us to believe that American political institutions are regularly responsive to constitutional values. The political world is seen as a reasonable approximation of legal and constitutional ideals. The assumption is that our rights are reflected in, protected by, and consistent with the basic tendencies of American politics—allowing, of course, for some inevitable slippage between reality and aspiration. Litigation is, in this view, an effective tool because it provides access to the substantial political power of the courts. Quite typically, Joseph L. Sax argues that litigation is preferable to "independent councils of experts, ombudsmen, negotiators, and so on," which "fail because they do not change the balance of *power*—precisely what the development of a scheme of enforceable legal rights, backed by judicial power can do." [1] Litigation is pictured as an effective way to redress the mistakes and deal with the shortcomings of American politics that result in denial of rights and neglect of constitutional values. Litigation, in short, is said to provide for more or less direct delivery of constitutional promises.

A sober assessment of the status of rights in American politics raises serious doubts about the capabilities of legal and constitutional processes for neutralizing power relationships. The authoritative declaration of a right is perhaps best viewed as the beginning of a political process in which power relationships loom large and immediate. Our rights are even at risk within the sheltered confines of governmental institutions, which are subjected to the rule of law and to a variety of control mechanisms designed to insure the integrity of legal processes. Let us consider briefly the inertial tendencies that underscore the primacy of power in the American political system.

There is no need to look any further than school desegregation problems to realize that the declaration of rights does not purge political conflict of its power dimensions. Neither irate parents nor intransigent southern congressmen have seen desegregation decisions as an invitation to employ reason and principle in search of truth.

> The unwarranted decision of the Supreme Court in the public school cases is now bearing the fruit always produced when men substitute naked power for established law. . . .

1. Joseph L. Sax, *Defending the Environment: A Strategy for Citizen Action* (New York: Knopf, 1971), p. 83. Italics in the original.

We pledge ourselves to use all lawful means to bring about a reversal of this decision which is contrary to the Constitution and to prevent the use of force in its implementation.[2]

Both the tone of this Southern Manifesto and subsequent developments belie optimistic impressions about the persuasive capabilities of legal principles.

It is, moreover, not only on segregation issues that the influence of judicial decisions has proven to be problematic. The same tendencies are apparent in other matters such as school prayers, defendants' rights, and reapportionment.[3] Suffice it to say, then, that when legal rights run counter to prevailing power relationships, it surely cannot be taken for granted that these rights will be redeemed on demand. It is not even clear that they will serve as the base line for reasoned discourse.[4]

A convincing and continually growing body of evidence demonstrates further that constitutional values are hardly paramount within our governmental institutions. Innumerable studies of the criminal justice system, for example, indicate not only that neglect of rights is common, but that this neglect is rooted in demands that the system itself makes on policemen, prosecutors, judges, and even on defense counsel.[5] More broadly, the work of Ralph Nader and others

2. "The Southern Manifesto: Declaration of Constitutional Principles," reprinted in Hubert H. Humphrey, ed., *School Desegregation: Documents and Commentaries* (New York: Thomas Y. Crowell, 1964), pp. 32–35.

3. For general summaries of compliance problems, see Theodore L. Becker and Malcolm M. Feeley, eds., *The Impact of Supreme Court Decisions* (2nd ed. New York: Oxford University Press, 1973), and Stephen L. Wasby, *The Impact of the United States Supreme Court: Some Perspectives* (Homewood, Illinois: Dorsey, 1970).

4. For a more systematic consideration of the impact of judicial decisions and a more careful look at the compliance literature, see Chapter 8 *infra*.

5. I find three studies particularly useful for demonstrating just how deeply these abuses of authority are ingrained in our criminal law enforcement apparatus. Jerome H. Skolnick, *Justice Without Trial: Law Enforcement in Democratic Society* (New York: John Wiley, 1966); Abraham S. Blumberg,

has sensitized us to the tendencies toward "lawlessness" in our governmental agencies and the inadequacy of the available machinery for maintaining legal accountability. The clear message is that institutional arrangements in this nation of ours are at least as likely to undermine rights as to nurture and sustain them.[6]

Nor are the courts immune from these insistent political pressures that tend to undermine legal rights. At each stage of the judicial process and at each level of the judicial system, the correspondences between political and legal forms are striking. Political rather than legal criteria ordinarily determine which of the more than 375,000 American lawyers are chosen and which are passed over in the process of judicial selection. While partially insulated once in office, lower court judges in particular remain linked to political processes. Career aspirations, for example, provide ample incentives for maintaining cordial relationships—both personal and professional—with influential politicos. Finally, research on judicial behavior indicates the unmistakable impact of personal policy preferences on judicial decisions. While this is no place to present a detailed analysis of judicial policy-making, some elaboration and documentation are clearly in order.

Judges are chosen for office in fundamentally the same fashion as other officials. Beneath superficial variations, recruitment patterns to public office are remarkably alike. Federal and state judges, elected and appointed judges, the Chief Justice of the United States and the lowly justice of the

Criminal Justice (Chicago: Quadrangle, 1970); and Herbert L. Packer, The Limits of the Criminal Sanction (Stanford: Stanford University Press, 1968), particularly pp. 149–246.

6. For a first-rate and comprehensive analysis of the political pressures on legal procedures, see James Eisenstein, Politics and the Legal Process (New York: Harper and Row, 1973). Published after work on this chapter was completed, Eisenstein's study could be profitably consulted in connection with the following discussion. On "lawlessness," see Theodore L. Becker and Vernon G. Murray, eds., Government Lawlessness in America (New York: Oxford University Press, 1971), and Jethro K. Lieberman, How the Government Breaks the Law (New York: Stein and Day, 1972).

peace are all products of the political system. At the federal level, the American Bar Association's Standing Committee on the Federal Judiciary does perhaps exercise a certain degree of quality control, and there are roughly comparable mechanisms in some state jurisdictions.[7] Screening procedures may weaken the worst forms of cronyism and patronage but they do not substantially restrict the opportunities for appointing judges who belong to the right party, are committed to the "proper" values and policies, and (when deemed advisable) are drawn from a particular social background, race, or religion. Election of judges may make for a slightly more politicized recruitment process, but it is difficult to take the distinction between election and appointment too seriously. Because the public tends to be apathetic about judgeships, vote-getting pressures are normally reduced. Political leaders are, however, fully engaged, and they are at the core of both modes of selection. "Whether judges have arrived on the bench through merit or elective procedures, in the last analysis someone has to pick who runs, who is appointed, and ultimately who will be *ratified* by the voters."[8] In some places, it is apparently not at all unusual to simply purchase judicial positions. Rumor has it that federal judgeships in New York have gone for $80,000, with lesser local positions available at lower prices.[9] But whether purchased for money or for service, judicial appointments are made more in accordance with political than with legal criteria.

Once in office, just how do these political appointees

7. Joel B. Grossman, *Lawyers and Judges* (New York: John Wiley, 1965).

8. Martin and Susan Tolchin, *To the Victor: Political Patronage from the Clubhouse to the White House* (New York: Vintage, 1972), p. 179. Italics added.

9. Ibid., p. 146, taken from Wallace S. Sayre and Herbert Kaufman, *Governing New York City* (New York: Russell Sage Foundation, 1960), chap. 14. For a more balanced discussion of recruitment to the federal judiciary, see Richard J. Richardson and Kenneth N. Vines, *The Politics of the Federal Courts: Lower Courts in the United States* (Boston: Little, Brown, 1970), pp. 56–79.

behave? In the first place, they seem to emerge from the recruitment process with their personal values—if not necessarily their independence—very much intact. "It is beyond serious question today that the judges of the Supreme Court have their own conceptions of public policy and that their attitudes and values affect the thrust of decision making." [10] Labels like civil libertarian or economic conservative are probably no less misleading when applied to judicial behavior than when attached to other political actors. What is true of the Supreme Court is, in all likelihood, applicable elsewhere along the line although there is admittedly less information about other judicial bodies. A careful analysis of urban trial courts in the New York City area, for example, concludes on an altogether compatible note:

> All the evidence developed in this study points to individualized, value- and attitude-based decision-making by these trial judges—quite distinct for each judge, clearly value-based and preferential rather than "legal" only, but particular to the individual and unrelated to obvious party or ethno-religious "determinants." [11]

Beyond these individual idiosyncrasies, there are undoubtedly systemic pressures which shape judicial outcomes in a manner generally consistent with predominant political tendencies. Criminal court judges, for example, are apparently laced into a set of relationships with prosecutors, police, and defense attorneys. The resultant structures tend to be responsive to bureaucratic pressure for efficient processing of

10. Sheldon Goldman and Thomas P. Jahnige, *The Federal Courts as a Political System* (New York: Harper and Row, 1971), p. 157. The factors influencing judicial decision-making have been the focus of extensive scholarly research. Goldman and Jahnige provide a systematic review of this work, pp. 149–200. See also Walter F. Murphy and Joseph Tanenhaus, *The Study of Public Law* (New York: Random House, 1972), pp. 116–78.

11. Kenneth M. Dolbeare, *Trial Courts in Urban Politics: State Court Policy Impact and Functions in a Local Political System* (New York: John Wiley, 1967), p. 78.

cases—often at the expense of legal values—and the judge, as a participant in this ongoing social process is forced to "play ball." [12] Systematic analysis of the lower federal court system reveals comparable although perhaps less explicit linkages between judges and other agencies of the political order.[13] To draw the only possible conclusion as modestly as possible, such judges can hardly be counted upon to transcend issues of power and influence. They are, after all is said and done, men who have learned to get along and to stay in step with those in power.

THE POLITICS OF RIGHTS

The descriptive shortcomings of the myth of rights in no way impugn its standing as a major American political ideology. What it contributes, in words borrowed from Judith Shklar, are "the standards of organization and the operative ideals" of American political life.[14] The principal impact of the myth of rights is on cognition and, more specifically, on perceptions of legitimacy. Its influence can also be found in the formal rules and accepted procedures of most American institutions. For our purposes, this institutional influence can be treated as a derivative concern. The formal rules are, in the final analysis, hostage to the political and cognitive pressures impinging on those responsible for their application and interpretation. But still it is necessary to determine just how, in which ways, and to what effect the standards and ideals of the myth of rights influence the course of politics in the United States.

Constitutional Values and Political Legitimacy

Once we begin to think about symbols and values, the myth of rights becomes altogether real. Political behavior is

12. Blumberg, *Criminal Justice*, chap. 6.
13. Richardson and Vines, *The Politics of the Federal Courts*.
14. Judith Shklar, *Legalism* (Cambridge, Mass.: Harvard University Press, 1964), p. 1.

regularly cued and shaped by perception. Belief in the law, acceptance of constitutional values, respect for legal institutions—these all become political facts, albeit with contradictory implications.

The myth of rights may work in behalf of change, but its dominant tendency is surely to reinforce the status quo. As the Watergate experience has so graphically demonstrated, legal ideals furnish standards for evaluating the performance of officials and institutions and thus can lay a foundation for protest. "The awareness of the discrepancy between the actual and the possible . . . helps to make the adolescent a rebel. He is always comparing the possible and the actual and discovering that the actual is flagrantly wanting." [15] The energizing consequences of such discrepancies cannot be taken for granted. Dissatisfaction with the police may, for instance, lead to community-organized schemes for mutual protection or to armed reprisals against law enforcement officials. Conversely, it has also been shown that perceptions of unfairness in the way police deal with crime can lead to acquiescence—to a willingness to "ignore it or wait around." [16] Beyond acquiescence, the myth of rights can generate support for the political system by legitimating the existing order. That is to say, it reassures us that the institutions of American politics will respond to just claims and that any mistakes that occur are not only aberrational but subject to the self-correcting devices built into the constitutional system.[17]

15. D. Elkind, "Adolescent Cognitive Development," in J. F. Adams, ed., *Understanding Adolescence* (Boston: Allyn and Bacon, 1968) as quoted in Judith Gallatin and Joseph Adelson, "Legal Guarantees of Individual Freedom: A Cross-National Study of the Development of Political Thought," in *Journal of Social Issues* (No. 2, 1971), p. 104.

16. Harlan Hahn, "Ghetto Assessments of Police Protection and Authority" in *Law and Society Review* 6 (November 1971):191.

17. This is a theme developed most authoritatively by Murray Edelman in *The Symbolic Uses of Politics* (Urbana: University of Illinois Press, 1967).

Fundamental among the many factors that determine the behavioral consequences of standards of perfection is the tendency of normative expectations to alter empirical perceptions. Whether departures from legal standards are dismissed as aberrations or taken as a cause for concern depends to a significant degree on the extent to which one is caught up in and distracted by the web of beliefs that make up the myth of rights. Depending on perspective, performance which is generally consistent with ideals may satisfy expectations and result in quiescence or, by projecting the image of responsive institutions, may escalate expectations and action. Similarly, disaffection may energize or enervate depending on personality and circumstance, the availability of leadership, the opportunities for action, and so on. Finally, it is important to remain sensitive to the net effect of cognitive influences. Symbols which cue the hopes of some members of the polity may evoke the fears of others. Thus, for each action in support of change that may be sparked by the myth of rights, there could be a powerful reaction in support of the status quo. The impact of the myth of rights on political events is therefore difficult to assess but incontestable.

Constitutional Values and Political Institutions

Constitutional values are of course infused into the formal rules and organizational procedures of virtually all governmental institutions, but they are not, as the myth of rights would have us believe, the controlling feature of governmental institutions. The beneficence of these values, moreover, cannot be taken for granted as the myth of rights implies. The politics of rights suggests that the influence of constitutional values on political institutions is hard to gauge, sometimes perverse, and surely not to be taken at face value, but nonetheless too important to neglect.

The courts are most directly implicated in the network of attitudes, practices, and rituals associated with the myth of rights, and the judges are generally conceded to have primary official responsibility for maintaining the constitutional integrity of the political system. For these reasons, this inquiry into the nature and extent of the impact of constitutional values on political institutions will be confined to the courts. Courts are nowhere near as well insulated from established configurations of power as the myth of rights leads us to believe, and there is little doubt that rules are bent and broken by judges who can be "corrupted" by personal preference as well as by more tangible inducements. On the other hand, judicial decisions do upon occasion run counter to the ostensible lines of political power. Moreover, only in the judicial system do professional training and role conceptions—rooted, of course, in the myth of rights—reinforce political independence.[18] The primary institutional influence of constitutional values is, therefore, heavily dependent on whatever tribute, beyond hypocrisy, judges are willing to pay to legal virtue.

But just how seriously do judges take constitutional values? This question can never be answered with great precision, because there is too much variation among judges and circumstances. Research suggests that constitutional values may have a residual influence on judicial decisions, but judges surely do not move inevitably toward constitutional values. Judicial decision-making studies tell us, at most, that some judges, some of the time, subordinate their personal preferences to what they sense as their obligations as judges.[19] More generally, as noted above, judicial decisions do not ordinarily run counter to the ostensible lines of power. On

18. In the other branches of government, the lines of responsibility to the electorate and hence to various manifestations of political power tend to compete in theory and overwhelm in practice adherence to constitutional principle—beyond, of course, certain accepted minimum rules of the game. For an effort to develop a theory of governance which meshes the interplay of pluralist forms of political power more closely and consistently with constitutional values, see Theodore J. Lowi, *The End of Liberalism: Ideology, Policy, and the Crisis of Public Authority* (New York: Norton, 1969), particularly Chapter 10, "Toward Juridical Democracy."

19. Murphy and Tanenhaus, *The Study of Public Law*, pp. 140–44.

those occasions when judges do take independent stands, constitutional values may serve as the inspiration and/or provide the rationale.

Let us briefly reconsider the nature of constitutional values. The myth of rights encourages us to associate these values with social justice and therefore to assume that there are satisfying constitutional solutions for all of society's problems. A more skeptical perspective suggested by the politics of rights leads toward a limited notion of constitutional values and to reservations about the adaptive claims of the myth of rights.

By way of illustration, consider the political struggles that had to be fought before the reform measures of contemporary welfare capitalism were deemed constitutionally acceptable. The Constitution was updated quite literally over the dead bodies of a goodly number of judges. It is all too common these days to dismiss this judicial intransigence as an effort by the court to overreach its legitimate area of authority. We ought to remember, however, that the new conceptions of private property and corporate responsibility that became the hallmark of the New Deal put significant pressure on traditional formulations of constitutional values. Whether as reason or rationale, these values provided an obvious line of resistance against novel and unwelcome changes. To put it another way, the changes brought on by welfare capitalism were unwelcome, at least in part, because they seemed to threaten cherished values.

An inquiry into the nature and limits of constitutional values will be the main task of the next chapter. My purpose at this point is to encourage a more critical perspective. To the extent that constitutional values are taken seriously, it must be understood that they imply constraints as well as opportunities. The more fundamental the changes sought, the more reasonable it is to think of constitutional values as problems that must be overcome rather than as solutions always at hand.

LITIGATION AND POLITICAL CHANGE

There is, these days, some ambivalence about litigation. The civil rights experience has made us all skeptics. Two decades after the *Brown* decision, we are still struggling inconclusively with school desegregation. Yet litigation is regularly used by, or on behalf of, a great diversity of groups seeking change: environmentalists, welfare mothers, prisoners, women, and so forth. The continued vitality of litigation may be read as a triumph of myth over reality—as a lesson in false consciousness. Or perhaps it is symptomatic of the willingness of middle class lawyers to settle for half a loaf—at least for their clients. Either way, litigation emerges as a strategy of desperation rather than hope.

The politics of rights, however, provides a more optimistic perspective on the persistence of litigative strategies for change. It suggests that the problem with litigative approaches may be less with the strategy than with the strategists. They are misled by the myth of rights toward a fundamental misunderstanding of the politics of change and, more specifically, toward exaggerated expectations about the political impact of judicial decisions. Ironically, this preoccupation with courts also leads strategists of litigation to ignore the opportunities that flow from the saturation of our culture with legal symbols. It is possible, therefore, to interpret the continuing interest in litigation as the product of an instinctive, if inchoate, understanding of the political importance of law in a society which associates legal values so closely with political legitimacy.

The next three chapters will assess the political utility of litigation from the perspective afforded by the politics of rights. This assessment will entail a reevaluation and reorganization of research findings that can be traced back to the first systematic efforts to understand "law as a political instrument" and to investigate "litigation as a form of pressure group activity." [20] It will in addition be necessary to integrate some quite different kinds of research material which provide an understanding of the links among litigation, cognition, and political action. Chapter 7 sets the stage by considering how much policy innovation can realistically be expected from judges. Chapter 8 considers the direct impact of judicial decisions in the manner suggested by the myth of rights. Not surprisingly, it turns out that there are formidable obstacles to using courts for the implementation of public policy. And Chapter 9 shows that litigation can be used as a catalyst of political mobilization. Because the strategists of litigation, for reasons firmly anchored in the myth of rights, have consistently passed up opportunities to use their legal skills in behalf of political mobilization, such results as there are to report have come as the unintended and unwelcome consequences of more traditional plans of action. Nonetheless, the results have come, and they strongly suggest that litigation can make an important, if ancillary, contribution to political change.

20. See Victor G. Rosenblum, *Law as a Political Instrument*, Studies in Political Science, PS/16 (New York: Random House, 1955), and Clement E. Vose, "Litigation as a Form of Pressure Group Activity," in *The Annals of the American Academy of Political and Social Science*, vol. 319 (September 1958), as reprinted in the Bobbs-Merrill Reprint Series in the Social Sciences, PS-290 (1958). See also Clement E. Vose, *Caucasians Only: The Supreme Court, the NAACP, and the Restrictive Covenant Cases* (Berkeley: University of California Press, 1967), and Jack W. Peltason, *Federal Courts in the Political Process*, Studies in Political Science, PS/25 (New York: Random House, 1955).

7. CONSTITUTIONAL VALUES AND POLITICAL GOALS

A consideration of the relevance of constitutional values to political goals will be a two-pronged exercise—concerned on the one hand with the policy implications of constitutional values and on the other with the role of constitutional values in judicial decision-making. Both facets are highly speculative. The character of judicial decision-making varies enormously from judge to judge, court to court, and time to time, and the amorphous nature of constitutional values further complicates matters. Despite the ambiguity some inchoate patterns do emerge, providing a useful starting point for an investigation of the policy opportunities associated with the politics of rights.

Judges do not regularly take independent stands on matters having to do with goals for the polity, but they are from time to time to be found out on the end of public policy limbs. There is no reliable way to forecast the occasions of judicial independence, since there are such great variations among judges and according to circumstances. It is, however, fair to say that courts are unlikely to take the lead on behalf of goals that are not firmly rooted in constitutional values, although they may be fully prepared to discount or disregard these standards when they are swimming with the political tide. Lacking a persuasive constitutional rationale, however, the chances for coaxing most judges into the front lines would seem to be rather slim. Constitutional values, then, will usually define the boundaries of judicial independence—

whether on behalf of new goals, for extension of accepted goals to new groups, or in defense of old goals that are under pressure elsewhere in the system.

Constitutional values are the patterns of preferences and practice that are rooted in the U.S. Constitution—values which have already been identified with the myth of rights. Insofar as judges take these values seriously, their response to policy problems will be influenced in three significant ways. *Policy directions* will reflect the liberal-capitalist bias of the Constitution. The pace of policy change will take on incremental *tempos.* And, finally, the character of judicial independence will be restricted by legal *forms.* Just as the meaning of the Constitution can never be established indisputably, the policy implications of constitutional values will always remain a matter of controversy. The wording of the Constitution supplies evidence of the values and visions of its framers, elaborated in commentaries like the *Federalist,* but visions and values are too nebulous to be captured and frozen in written provisions. The brevity of the Constitution and the social changes that have occurred since it was written lend a further note of ambiguity. Nonetheless, on the general issues of policy direction, tempo, and form, some patterns do emerge. These patterns provide a basis for significantly scaling down the message of unqualified constitutional beneficence conveyed by the myth of rights.

LIBERAL-CAPITALIST DIRECTIONS

The United States Constitution is based loosely on the familiar premise that the government is best which governs least. Government intervention that restricts personal choice or burdens private property is to be the exception, and all such interventions are subjected to standards designed to protect the citizenry against abuse of power by the government. These standards are found principally in the Bill of

Rights, but they are contained in other provisions of the Constitution as well. Taken together, they seem to add up to two essential guarantees beyond the basic commitment to minimum intervention. Intrusions into social and economic matters shall be both reasonable and equitable. Intrusions shall be reasonable in the sense that they are the product of careful deliberation, which is supposed to guard against arbitrary action by promoting consideration of the relevant facts and attention to the relationship between means and ends. Intrusions are to be equitable in that everyone is supposed to be treated equally before the law. As will become apparent, this question of equality before the law is much more complicated than may appear at first glance. While difficult to apply, it remains nonetheless an important constitutional standard. In sum, constitutional values imply minimum government intervention subjected to the standards of due process and equal protection of the laws.

There was a time when the Constitution could reasonably have been thought of as a charter for change, but that time is long past. The goals expressed and implied by the Constitution—a federal system, a national economy, a unified posture in foreign affairs, a viable military establishment—have all been achieved. Indeed, with respect to these goals we have as a nation been constitutional overachievers. Nowadays constitutional values are as likely to be obstacles to change as they are to facilitate change. It is this ambivalence that must be understood.

The notion of limited government stands as an obstacle to the assumption of new governmental responsibilities in economic and social matters likely to impinge on personal and property rights. Such programs as are undertaken are subjected to the often cumbersome requirements of equal protection and due process of law. The result is that in environmental matters, for example, constitutional values tend to insulate corporate enterprise from regulatory schemes and thus stand in the way of policy change. Of course these same Bill of Rights provisions have been exceedingly useful in developing new standards for protecting citizens in their contacts with the police, prosecutors, and criminal courts. Similarly, constitutional values tend to work against those who, in an effort to avert change, would subvert the electoral process by such measures as diluting the vote or restricting political expression. Since we have most decidedly not been overachievers on Bill of Rights matters, it stands as a fertile, but far from unlimited, source of new directions for American public policy. Constitutional values have their own built-in boundaries and their ambivalent impact on policy change emerges particularly well in matters having to do with racial justice.

School Desegregation

In the two decades since 1954 the articulated goals of public policy on racial matters have been completely transformed and litigation has, in effect, led the way. Prior to the *Brown* decision in that year, it would be reasonable to say that in the South the goal of public policy was segregation of the races in virtually all phases of life—schools, public accommodations, jails, housing, marriage. What was de jure in the South was accomplished in the North pretty much without the assistance of laws, which were largely silent. If it is not entirely fair to say that we were a segregated society altogether as a matter of public policy, it does not miss the mark by more than the margin of malign neglect in the North. By the 1970s all that had changed. The entire country and virtually all of its public institutions are now officially identified with desegregation as a goal of public policy, and litigation has spearheaded these sweeping changes.[1] It has

1. For a comprehensive and systematic presentation, see Harrell R. Rodgers, Jr., and Charles S. Bullock, III, *Law and Social Change: Civil Rights Laws and Their Consequences* (New York: McGraw-Hill, 1972).

not been a simple matter of cause and effect and these goals have not as yet been realized, but the nation has officially taken a new path and its first steps were by way of litigation.

This movement has, of course, been based on a good deal of judicial innovation—either overturning well-established lines of precedent or simply creatively adaptating existing doctrine. In its final rejection of the white primary in 1944, for example, the Supreme Court turned its back on the then accepted notion that primaries were not part of the regular election process.[2] Restrictive covenants were outlawed in 1948 by a novel interpretation of the state action doctrine— just the first of many new looks at this crucial concept.[3] And of course the *Brown* decision itself required rejection of the "separate but equal" doctrine which had stood as the law of the land for more than half a century.

While the Supreme Court has been willing to adopt new directions, it has remained firmly if somewhat ambiguously anchored in constitutional provisions and values. It is entirely in keeping with the initial premises of the Bill of Rights for the courts to provide protection against arbitrary action by state governments which deny the people their basic rights. Once blacks were admitted to the political community after the Civil War, it was a legal anomaly to continue to deny them equal treatment under the laws. Charles Black's fundamental defense of the *Brown* decision makes the constitutional case against segregation simply and directly:

I think they [the school cases] were rightly decided, by the overwhelming weight of reason, and I intend here to say why I hold this belief.

My liminal difficulty is rhetorical—or, perhaps more

2. Smith v. Allwright, 321 U.S. 649 (1944).
3. Shelley v. Kraemer, 334 U.S. 1 (1948).

accurately, one of fashion. Simplicity is out of fashion, and
the basic scheme of reasoning on which these cases can be
justified is awkwardly simple. First, the equal protection
clause of the fourteenth amendment should be read as
saying that the Negro race, as such, is not to be significantly disadvantaged by the laws of the states. Secondly,
segregation is a massive intentional disadvantaging of the
Negro race, as such, by state law. No subtlety at all. Yet I
cannot disabuse myself of the idea that that is really all
there is to the segregation cases.[4]

Needless to say, other views can be and have been expressed,
but it is difficult to escape the conclusion that in moving
against segregation—quite irrespective of the legal obstacles
—those nine justices were identifying themselves with basic,
if often neglected, liberal democratic values.[5]

Desegregation is, however, only the first step on the road to
racial justice, and most judges have been more reluctant to
take the lead at subsequent points along the way. Perhaps the
major watershed was the movement from desegregation to
integration—that is, from removing legal barriers blocking an
interracial society to taking affirmative action in pursuit of
that goal. Given the presence of both individual and institutional racism, integration clearly calls for government action
to prevent groups of citizens from discriminating against one

4. Charles L. Black, "The Lawfulness of the Segregation Decisions" in
Hubert H. Humphrey, ed., *School Desegregation: Documents and Commentaries* (New York: Thomas Y. Crowell, 1964), pp. 60–61.

5. Louis Hartz, *The Liberal Tradition in America: An Interpretation of
American Political Thought Since the Revolution* (New York: Harcourt, Brace,
1955), p. 167. Hartz traces the central tension to its roots in slavery, noting
that "in order to keep democracy for the whites, it was essential to develop a
theory of separate races for the blacks, and so the retention of a part of
liberalism grounded itself on one of the most vicious and antiliberal doctrines
of modern times." That is to say, blacks could be excluded from full
participation in a polity which adhereed to the tenets of classic liberalism
only so long as they were perceived as less than human.

another.[6] Similarly, given centuries of oppression, compensatory programs designed to right previous wrongs and accelerate the pace of change have been seen as a necessary step toward integration. In both respects, integration implies serious tensions with constitutional values. Attempts to prevent discrimination among citizens necessarily involve limitations on personal choice. Moreover, compensatory programs imply differential standards which run counter to the notion of equality under the law; they involve a kind of reverse discrimination.

Courts have not been altogether useless in promoting integration, but the judges have been reluctant to cross this threshold and have, therefore, supported integration in only a guarded fashion. Consider, by way of illustration, school busing programs—an important and controversial tool of integrated education. Whatever one's policy preferences, it is clear that busing does entail affirmative action by governments, forcing parents and children to behave in a manner deemed consistent with an interracial society. The Supreme Court has, not surprisingly, responded to busing with "reserve." The Court has never taken the lead in ordering busing and has been willing to approve it only where the need for transfer plans can be traced to earlier attempts by state governments to evade desegregation decisions.

> Absent a constitutional violation there would be no basis for judicially ordering assignment of students on a racial basis. All things being equal, with no history of discrimination, it might well be desirable to assign pupils to schools nearest their homes. But all things are not equal in a system that has been deliberately constructed and maintained to enforce racial segregation. The remedy for such segregation may be administratively awkward, inconvenient and even

6. On the distinction between individual and institutional racism, see Stokely Carmichael and Charles V. Hamilton, *Black Power: The Politics of Liberation in America* (New York: Vintage, 1967), pp. 3–6.

bizarre in some situations and may impose burdens on
some; but all awkwardness and inconvenience cannot be
avoided in the interim period when remedial adjustments
are being made to eliminate the dual school system.[7]

The Supreme Court has, in other words, shown an inclination
to move ahead with integration only when societal racism
could be imputed to historical patterns of governmental
racism. Working within this restriction it has been much more
difficult but not impossible to justify intervention in the
North than in the South.[8] More generally, it would seem
unrealistic to expect judges to take a leading role in positing
goals consistent with rooting out those elements of racism
which are buried deep within our social fabric.

Poverty Policy

Poverty policy offers further indications of constitutional
opportunities and sticking points. This nation's traditional
approach to poverty has been to ignore it officially and
stigmatize it socially—apparently on the dual assumption
that so long as being poor is taken as a sign of individual
failure, the fear of poverty will serve as an inducement to
hard work and the degradation of poverty will induce
political quiescence.[9] In the 1960s things changed a bit. The
president and Congress recognized poverty as a permanent
condition of our society—a problem that transcends business
cycles and temporary setbacks to individual families. The
declaration of war on poverty was at least a tacit admission
that poverty is transmitted from generation to generation;
that it affects a substantial portion of the population (20 to 40

7. Swann v. Charlotte-Mecklenburg Board of Education, 28 L. Ed. 2d. 55,
at 573 (1971). The judges were, in this case, passing on an integration plan
worked out by the local school board in conjunction with the Department of
Health, Education and Welfare.

8. Keyes v. Denver School District, 413 U.S. 189 (1973).

9. See Dorothy B. James, *Poverty, Politics and Change* (Englewood Cliffs,
N.J.: Prentice-Hall, 1972), chap. 2.

percent, depending on the baseline chosen); and that, for those millions, it makes a lie out of the myth of equal opportunity. There were, of course, two wars launched in the 1960s, but as John C. Donovan points out, poverty was "the war that did not escalate." [10] Indeed, there really has been no war against poverty, but instead a tentative effort to deal in a piecemeal fashion with some of the symptoms of poverty. What has been provided might best be termed survival assistance. A war on poverty would call for an entirely new perspective. In this perspective the poor would be thought of as victims and poverty considered a consequence of our system. These premises would necessarily lead to programs aimed at providing a decent life for the poor, rather than bare subsistence, and further to steps which altered the system to do away with the causes of poverty.

With antipoverty energies in the executive and legislative branches having petered out for the time being, the obvious question (at least in this volume) is whether litigation can be expected to serve as the cutting edge of change. The experience so far suggests that the courts could perhaps be useful up to a point. Since there is, however, no economic bill of rights in the Constitution, the chances would seem slim for enlisting the support of many judges for the egalitarian values which are implicit in any serious commitment to end poverty in America. "Although the equality of each citizen before the law is the rock upon which the American Constitution rests, economic equality has never been an American ideal." [11] The Constitution is, if anything, an obstacle, since it tends to shelter private property as well as personal and corporate gain.

Litigation may, on the other hand, prove to be a useful tool for redefining the status of poor people in their relations with

10. John C. Donovan, *The Politics of Poverty* (New York: Pegasus, 1967), chap. 8.

11. Gore Vidal, "Homage to Daniel Shays," *The New York Review of Books,* August 10, 1972, p. 8.

public bureaucracies. What seems to be emerging is a modest willingness to recognize that poor people must be treated as citizens with rights rather than as supplicants. In 1970, for example, the Supreme Court declared that welfare benefits could not be cut off without hearings which conformed to the due process clause.[12] But substantive guarantees have not really begun to emerge—say, to an adequate level of benefits.[13] The procedural standards are themselves very much in flux, but important gains have been made. "All in all, then, the legal assault on welfare departments contributed to the collapse of restrictions, partly by overturning major exclusionary statutes, but perhaps more importantly by instituting procedural safeguards that hampered the arbitrary exercise of discretion by relief officials."[14] For the poor, who depend so heavily on public bureaucracies, the right to have rights is especially important. It is a necessary, although hardly a sufficient, condition of human dignity. And such minimum procedural protections for the poor are altogether consistent with the underlying premise of the Bill of Rights.

Litigation may also be useful in the long run for improving the legal status of poor people in commercial dealings, where they are peculiarly vulnerable to exploitation.[15] However, the advantages of landlords and creditors are deeply rooted in common law, and the Constitution is of only limited assistance. Recently, for example, the Supreme Court refused to overturn an Oregon eviction statute which was heavily weighted in favor of the landlord. In this case, the tenant withheld rent because the landlord had taken such poor care

12. Goldberg v. Kelly, 397 U.S. 254 (1970).
13. Samuel Krislov, "The OEO Lawyers Fail to Constitutionalize a Right to Welfare: A Study in the Uses and Limits of the Judicial Process," *Minnesota Law Review* 58 (December 1973): 211–45.
14. Frances Fox Piven and Richard A. Cloward, *Regulating the Poor: The Functions of Public Welfare* (New York: Vintage, 1972), p. 314.
15. See Jerome E. Carlin, Jan Howard, and Sheldon L. Messinger, "Civil Justice and the Poor: Issues for Sociological Research," in *Law and Society Review* 1 (November 1966): 12–28.

of the dwelling that the city had declared it "unfit for habitation." The statute prohibited the tenant from raising such violations of the building code in the eviction suit, but the Court held for the landlord: "We do not denigrate the importance of decent, safe, and sanitary housing. But the Constitution does not provide judicial remedies for every social and economic ill. . . . Nor should we forget that the Constitution expressly protects confiscation of private property or income therefrom." [16] Nevertheless, it seems within the boundaries of reasonable (if somewhat distant) expectations to use litigation to do away with legal inequities in the commercial sphere. In the Oregon case itself, the Supreme Court invalidated a provision that required an appeal against eviction to be accompanied by a bond in *twice* the amount of the rent that would be paid during the period of appeal.[17] At least in the long run, judges are likely to be sensitive to appeals grounded in the traditional notion of equality before the law.

INCREMENTAL TEMPOS

Whatever innovation comes from the courts is virtually certain to take the form of small and erratic advances. Resistance to change is built into the judicial process in a number of ways. In the first place, judges are encouraged to take precedent seriously and to make changes in the halting kind of way that tends to mask change with the appearance of stability or at least of continuity. Moreover, resistance to change tends to increase at the thresholds derived from legal and constitutional values. When, whether, and to what extent judges will cross (and remain across) the thresholds is

16. Lindsey v. Normet, 92 S. Ct. 862 (1972), 874. The Court also rested its decision partly on grounds having to do with the federal system. "The Constitution has not federalized the substantive law of landlord-tenant relations."

17. Ibid., pp. 874–77.

ordinarily anybody's guess. And once a threshold is crossed or a precedent eroded, it is difficult to know whether a new line of precedent will emerge or whether there will be a retreat to higher ground. Finally, judges have regularly indicated that they are sensitive to the counter-majoritarian character of their own position and hence reluctant to engage in dramatic policy departures.[18] If the resultant tempo is characterized as incremental, let us recognize that incrementalism should not be thought of as the inevitable and orderly march toward progressive reform that is alluded to by the ideologists of the myth of rights. All these built-in frictions insure, instead, that if there is progress its tempo will be halting and thus unpredictable.

What opponents often seek to discredit as dramatic changes in course by courts usually appear on closer examination to be the abandonment of precedents already weakened by earlier decisions. The separate but equal doctrine was only a hollow shell when it was finally swept away in 1954. By that time a whole series of decisions had made it clear that separate educational facilities were unequal in ways that could be corrected only by ending separation. In a 1950 decision rejecting a black law school in Texas, for example, the Supreme Court put insurmountable obstacles in the path of the state by pointing out that the new law school would be smaller, less prestigious, and therefore unacceptable:

> Whether the University of Texas Law School is compared with the original or the new law school for Negroes, we cannot find substantial equality in the educational opportunities offered white and Negro law students by the State. In terms of number of the faculty, variety of courses and opportunity for specialization, size of the student body, scope of the library, availability of law review and similar

18. Alexander M. Bickel makes this a central theme of his work—most systematically presented in *The Least Dangerous Branch: The Supreme Court at the Bar of Politics* (Indianapolis: Bobbs-Merrill, 1962).

activities, the University of Texas Law School is superior. *What is more important,* the University of Texas Law School possesses to a far greater degree those qualities which are *incapable of objective measurement* but which make for greatness in a law school.[19]

By the time of *Brown,* then, all that the new Warren Court had to do was make the connection between higher education and primary education.

In the retelling, the progress of precedent in a particular line of cases tends to take on a misleading gloss of certainty. But the ways of judges are inscrutable and the progress of litigation is necessarily clouded by doubts. Is precedent being eroded or are exceptions being made which, in effect, evidence a judicial inclination to cling to the existing rule? Even when movement is unmistakable, there is no way of knowing how far along the new path judges are prepared to venture. In all likelihood there is no judicial consensus on the answers to these questions. Individual courts or judges may have clear positions, but the system will ordinarily remain in flux until a collective response emerges.

In important matters, the period of indeterminacy is ordinarily long and of course exceedingly trying for those who are counting on the courts. To welfare rights organizations and consumer groups, the only thing certain about the leads provided by judicial decisions is that they are ambiguous. Precedent provides a cover beneath which the judges seem to grope through the infinite variety of fact, doctrine, and value—perhaps toward new goals for the polity, perhaps toward a reaffirmation of the status quo.

The waters are further muddied by the political uncertainty that attaches to even the most forthright judicial declarations. Characteristically, there is not a single authoritatively articulated goal for each sector of public policy. There are instead a number of goals. Organs of government differ from one

19. Sweatt v. Painter, 339 U.S. 629 (1950), 633–34. Italics added.

another and, as has already been suggested, internal disputes may lead to purposefully ambivalent formulations. This study is in part directed at determining just how the courts influence whatever inchoate consensus may emerge. At the moment, however, it is important simply to understand that the process of ironing out differences among the branches results in a period of pulling and hauling that inevitably slows the pace and obscures the direction of change.

THE INTRUSIVE LOGIC OF LEGAL FORM

A further consideration impinges on the likelihood of judicial leadership and should therefore be taken into account. The logic inherent in rules is manifest in the procedures that structure judicial decision-making as well as in the habits of mind inculcated in law school and regularly defended, among other places, in the published opinions of American courts. As is the case with constitutional values themselves, it is easier to identify the procedures and to trace their logic and policy implications than to determine their actual influence on individual judges or on the court system generally. Once again it is best to think of residual concerns that set the context of judicial independence.

Formalization of new goals into legal rules may, to begin with, complicate rather than facilitate solutions to problems of public policy. Legal rules have an absolute quality insofar as they specify rights and obligations that are applicable immediately and indefinitely. "It is just this tendency toward the absolute that constitutes the essential meaning of 'a right,' whether it be legal or moral." [20] It is true that implementation can be deferred, that exceptions can be made, and that the open texture of legal rules offers opportunities for hedging. Nevertheless, once the rule has been formulated, expectations

20. Lon L. Fuller, *The Morality of Law* (New Haven: Yale University Press, 1964), p. 29.

are created and patterns of interests emerge. Thus the courts cannot treat their commitments lightly without incurring costs. Particularly in the early stages of policy development it may prove exceedingly cumbersome—and judges may understandably be reluctant—to lock themselves into a legally specified course of action.

Beyond the question of timing, however, there is a more general obstacle to judicial innovation in certain kinds of policy arenas—particularly those involving the allocation of economic resources. These matters are most appropriately dealt with by marginal utility calculations, which *focus on the consequences* of individual decisions. In contrast, judges tend to be tied to the procedural absolutes which are bound up in a regime of rules with its attendant emphasis on vindicating rights and enforcing obligations *irrespective of the consequences.* Lon Fuller, who has devoted a good deal of attention to this point, puts it as follows:

> To act wisely, the economic manager must take into account every circumstance relevant to his decision and must himself assume the initiative in discovering what circumstances are relevant. His decisions must be subject to reversal or change as conditions alter. The judge, on the other hand, acts upon those facts that are in advance deemed relevant under declared principles of decision. His decision does not simply direct resources and energies; it declares rights, and rights to be meaningful must in some measure stand firm through changing circumstances.[21]

Needless to say, analytic distinctions of this sort do not necessarily direct behavior in the real world. They are, however, suggestive of basic tensions that may well inhibit judicial activism.

To make these speculations more concrete let us look at the pollution problem. Throughout our history the prevailing

21. Ibid., p. 172.

theory seems to have been that our natural resources are there to be exploited for fun, profit, and progress. There are those who are influential in the environmental movement who believe that litigation can be instrumental in turning the nation around. Joseph L. Sax, for example, claims that the courts can lead the way toward official recognition that the environment is, in effect, a "public trust" and that private rights to exploit the environment should be counterbalanced by a "new charter of environmental rights":

> The idea of a public trusteeship rests upon three related principles. First, that certain interests—like the air and the sea—have such importance to the citizenry as a whole that it would be unwise to make them the subject of private ownership. Second, that they partake so much of the bounty of nature, rather than of individual enterprise, that they should be made freely available to the entire citizenry without regard to economic status. And, finally, that it is a principle [*sic*] purpose of government to promote the interests of the general public rather than to redistribute public goods from broad public uses to restricted private benefit.[22]

This appeal is both sober and persuasive. Professor Sax has identified crucial issues and chosen his words carefully so as to avoid empty rhetoric. Courts could probably work within this framework of national priorities, were it established elsewhere in the system, without any major overhaul of important legal doctrine. Is it, however, reasonable to expect judges to seize the initiative? I think not.

It is not only marginal utility calculations that stand in the way of judicial leadership in environmental policy matters. There are, in addition, the problems of standing, which currently limit access to courts on environmental matters,

22. Joseph L. Sax, *Defending the Environment: A Strategy for Citizen Action* (New York: Knopf, 1970), p. 165.

and of finding an environmental mandate among the provisions of the Constitution. It is difficult to get standing because
the interest of private parties in environmental degradation is
often not sufficiently individual and concrete to establish
legal standing to sue. When property values are jeopardized,
that is a different matter. Legally speaking, however, air and
water quality are everyone's problem, and, therefore, nobody's. All of this seems to be changing—in part, through the
efforts of Professor Sax who successfully promoted a bill in
the Michigan legislature which permits citizens to bring suit
against anyone who is seriously degrading the environment.
Senators McGovern and Hart introduced a similar bill into
Congress.[23] Moreover, as mentioned earlier, the Supreme
Court has indicated that it may be willing to recognize
damage to the environment as a justiciable interest—apart
from a demonstration of reduced property values.[24] The
constitutional obstacles to judicial leadership appear to be a
bit more formidable and enduring. The Constitution is after
all the product of a different era and, more specifically, the
work of exploiters of the environment and defenders of
private enterprise. Constitutional values tend therefore to
work against concerted governmental action. Even the cautious phrasing of the Sax plea reveals the obstacles to
forthright action in the environmental field that are posed by
basic American values. We must cease thinking of our natural
resources as generally available opportunities for "individual
enterprise" and "private benefit." Instead, we must look upon
them as "public goods" which are "freely available." The
lawyer who persuasively teases this abrupt about-face out of
the Constitution will qualify not simply as a legal virtuoso but
as a wizard. There is, of course, a familiar ring to all this, but
pollution also has its novel aspect.

23. *Common Cause,* 1 (April 1971): 9. The Michigan law is printed in the
Appendix to Sax, *Defending the Environment,* pp. 247–52.
24. Sierra Club v. Morton, 92 S. Ct. 1361 (1972), 1366–69. See, more
recently, Zahn v. International Paper 42 *Law Week* 4087 (1973).

Pollution is the unavoidable consequence of human behavior—the necessary by-product of even the most primitive technology. The rhetoric of environmental groups sometimes implies that our ultimate goal should be to eliminate pollution, but that is of course nonsense. Nor is it really feasible to establish some across-the-board level by which air and water pollution should be reduced. Considered more realistically, pollution control is a matter for marginal utility calculations:

> Pollution control is for lots of things: breathing comfortably, enjoying mountains, swimming in water, for health, beauty, and the general delectation. But so are many other things, like good food and wine, comfortable housing and fast transportation. The question is not which of these desirable things we should have, but rather what combination is most desirable.[25]

Given these premises, it is difficult to see just how litigation could serve as the cutting edge of major new departures in environmental policy-making.

In short, pollution control cannot really partake of legal absolutes and thus raises problems that many judges may see as fundamentally different from other policy arenas in which courts have taken the lead. What is to be the environmental counterpart of the "right to counsel"; to "one man, one vote"; or to "equal protection" in civil rights matters? These are all absolutes—at least as matters of principle. Whatever the delays and imperfections in implementation, these ideals have served as standards that judges can persistently employ in evaluating conduct. In contrast, environmental action involves the establishment of priorities among goals and then the assessment and reassessment of trade-offs. It is in this sense that pollution control and economic allocations generally are less amenable to judicial policy initiatives.

25. Larry E. Ruff, "The Economic Common Sense of Pollution," *The Public Interest* 19 (Spring 1970): 74.

All this is not to say that litigation cannot be useful in matters entailing economic allocation. It is rather to question the character and quality of judicial leadership that is likely to emerge. The crucial distinction is between a procedural role, which the courts can reasonably be expected to play, and a substantive role, which they are likely to avoid. The National Environmental Policy Act of 1969, for example, requires an "environmental impact statement" prior to all acts of the federal government "significantly affecting the quality of the human environment."[26] The courts have already shown a willingness to defend and develop standards of procedural regularity so as to assure serious investigation of the environmental hazards of new projects.[27] Of course, procedural regularity is as likely to protect as to prevent corporate incursions on the environment, since due process requirements tend to shield private property and corporate initiative from government regulation. In any case, these procedural delays and interstitial intrusions are a far cry from the kind of leadership role that judges have assumed in civil rights, law enforcement, and other matters more suitable for legal absolutes.

Courts generally and the Supreme Court in particular have from time to time taken the lead in formulating new directions and purposes for the polity. Despite ambiguity and variation it is possible to identify certain concerns, rooted in constitutional values and legal forms, which seem regularly to influence, if not necessarily to determine, the limits of judicial independence. There is good reason to believe that litigation

26. Frank P. Grad, *Environmental Law: Sources and Problems* (New York: Matthew Bender, 1971), chap. 13, p. 3.
27. Wilderness Society v. Hickel, 325 F. Supp. 422 (1970). Calvert Cliffs' Coordinating Committee Inc. v. U.S. Atomic Energy Commission, 449 F.2d. 1109 (1971). At the Supreme Court level these citations tend to appear primarily in Justice Douglas's dissenting opinions. See Committee for Nuclear Responsibility, Inc. v. Schlesinger, 407 U.S. 917 (1971).

can play a significant role in advancing new goals of public policy and enough evidence to suggest the character and limitations of that role.

But what political benefits derive from a judicial declaration of new political goals? Courts are only one of many authoritative agencies of government in a position to articulate goals for the polity. Judicial victories are often isolated triumphs. They may not even be taken up by the entire court system, much less be adopted by the other branches. Moreover, how important in the great scheme of things are political goals anyhow? What impact, whether direct or indirect, do they have on the course of public policy? These are the crucial questions and the acid test of the politics of rights; they will be taken up in the next two chapters.

8. THE IMPLEMENTATION OF PUBLIC POLICY

The enunciation of new goals of public policy results in a rearrangement of legal rights and obligations, but does not guarantee behavior in the real world that is consistent with the rearrangement. The myth of rights leads us to believe that litigation is an obvious and effective answer to any footdragging by opponents of the new order. The burden of this chapter, however, will be to indicate that direct deployment of legal rights in the implementation of public policy will not work very well, given any significant opposition. Litigation may be helpful to individuals who have the resources and determination to pursue remedies through the court system. But courts cannot be relied upon to secure rights more generally in the society for reasons rooted in legal policy and political power.

Using courts to make things happen in the real world ultimately pits the victorious litigant with a court order against those who are inclined to resist—meaning both the losing party and others who are similarly situated and therefore implicated in the judgment. Just how widely the net extends is always a matter for conjecture, although legal procedures and the apparent preferences of most judges ordinarily combine to particularize the legal import of judicial decisions. The practical impact is similarly restricted —in part as a consequence of the ambiguous and particularized legal situation, which provides endless opportunities for evasion and delay. More fundamentally, the impact is restricted by post-judgment power relationships. These power relationships vary a good deal from situation to situation with only a single constant: the judiciary's modest reservoir of coercive resources.

Lawyers might take strong exception to this pessimistic assessment—particularly when coupled with my relatively optimistic evaluation of litigation as a tool for altering the goals of public policy. The average lawyer would probably come to just the opposite conclusions, since judicial policy initiatives emerge erratically and unpredictably, while the lawyer can feel reasonably confident about using litigation to force delivery on existing legal commitments. But the lawyer's view is derived largely from experience with individual litigants. Whether corporate or private parties does not matter, because the courts are ordinarily both willing and able to act effectively in behalf of the individual litigant. On a social scale, things are different. Precisely because litigation is structured to serve individual needs, it tends to fragment problems by breaking them down into a multiplicity of discrete transactions. This distinction between the particular and the general is the key to the following discussion.

It is important to note that litigation is cumbersome as an instrument of compliance irrespective of what is being complied with. Legislation, executive orders, judicial decisions are all equally difficult to enforce if the coercive resources of the government are not made available. By the same token, distinctions between legal and constitutional rights are of little practical significance. The exalted status of a constitutional right does not ease the burden of litigation one bit. The analysis which follows is thus generally applicable to litigation as a tool for closing the gap between the promises and the reality of American public policy—regardless of whether that promise is of constitutional status or is a lesser enactment.

LEGAL PROCEDURES AND JUDICIAL PREFERENCE

Litigation is structured by procedures which fragment and particularize compliance. These procedures can be, and often are, stretched and shaped by judges who are sensitive to the importance of prompt and uniform implementation of the law. Particularization does, nonetheless, inhere in the judicial process as we know it. Moreover, particularization seems to be consistent with the preferences of most judges. Judicial preference is no doubt largely a product of training and socialization in the common law tradition, but particularization can also be seen as the rational choice of judges who wish to shield themselves from responsibilities that courts are not well equipped to assume. The consequence is to break compliance down into a series of one-on-one confrontations that play into the hands of those who oppose the rules promulgated by the judges.

It is all but inevitable that litigation will fragment and particularize the compliance process whenever there is a significant measure of resistance. If the norm in question is a court order, it is legally binding only on the parties to the original suit. But even when the norm is more generally applicable—statutes, class action court orders, or administrative regulations—there is always a certain amount of ambiguity concerning its precise scope and meaning. Those who are inclined to resist can build a legally defensible position.

The practical roots of this process of legal evasion were observed by Dolbeare and Hammond in their study of local resistance to the Supreme Court's patently general decision against school prayers: "We saw that this inertia was rationalized in at least two major ways: by 'misunderstanding' the requirements of the Court rulings so as to permit teacher discretion, and by resisting knowledge about the extent and character of prayers and other religious observances in the schools." [1] So long as litigation is the tool of compliance, the defensive positions established by those in resistance will have to be probed and tested in a series of separate legal encounters—each calling for painstaking accu-

1. Kenneth M. Dolbeare and Phillip E. Hammond, *The School Prayer Decisions: From Court Policy to Local Practice* (Chicago: University of Chicago Press, 1971), p. 148.

mulation of evidence, searching out of witnesses, preparation
of legal briefs, and generally dogged and expensive persistence through trials, delays, and appeals. The costs in time and
money can be enormous.[2] Former Senator Paul Douglas
reported that a New Orleans suit filed in 1952 required nine
years of litigation, five Circuit Court appeals, and seven
proceedings before the Supreme Court. The result was that
twelve blacks out of 55,000 in the parish were "integrated"
into white schools, and the total cost was $96,000 or $8,000
per child.[3] Indeed, where litigation is the only weapon against
administrative inertia, the process can be self-defeating—as it
seemed to be in Alabama after a great Supreme Court victory
which "restored" the vote to blacks in Tuskegee who had
been gerrymandered out of an electoral voice in city politics.
Subsequent to the decision, however, registrars made themselves so unavailable that only thirty blacks per year were
able to make application for registration, many fewer than
the number of registered voters lost through death. Accordingly, one black leader informed the governor that "if our
losses continue at sixty-four per year, there will be no Negro
voters in this county by 2017 A.D."[4]

The obvious alternative to the erratic and largely ineffectual judicial intervention just described would be some
kind of continuing oversight and control. Ordinarily, these
qualities are associated with effective administration. The
courts do have some limited capabilities for systematic
intervention. Implementation of Supreme Court decisions on
school desegregation and reapportionment has been en-
trusted to the lower federal courts in a manner which involves

2. Frederick M. Wirt's discussion of the voter registration litigation of the
Justice Department in Mississippi offers convincing testimony to the heavy
burdens which must be shouldered by those seeking to litigate compliance.
*The Politics of Southern Equality: Law and Social Change in a Mississippi
County* (Chicago: Aldine, 1970), pp. 91–116.

3. *U.S. Congressional Record*, 88th Cong. 2d Sess., 1964, 110:6824–26.

4. Bernard Taper, *Gomillion versus Lightfood: Apartheid in Alabama* (New
York: McGraw-Hill, 1962), p. 57.

long-term supervision. In the school cases, the lower courts were instructed to "retain jurisdiction" through a complex "period of transition" in which the judges were expected, in effect, to monitor desegregation plans.[5] The courts could employ similar techniques against officials who failed to carry out their statutory or regulatory responsibilities. Environmentalists see citizen litigation as a potentially powerful tool for forcing reluctant administrators to implement the many antipollution laws that are on the books:

> Since the conventional formulation holds that mandamus lies to compel the performance of ministerial duties but not where the action involves discretion, superficial analysis might lead the courts to deny the writ in cases of nonenforcement of environmental protection statutes. . . .
>
> If judicial control of administrative action is to be effective, the concept of abuse of discretion must be applied to agency inaction as well as to agency action, to decisions whether to prosecute violators as well as to decisions defining substantive violations. A pattern of selective enforcement may deny equal protection of the laws and . . . persons who lose the protection of a statute enacted for their benefit ought to have a judicial remedy of selective nonenforcement as a denial of equal protection.[6]

The record indicates that judges are inclined to allow prosecutors a great deal of leeway in both civil and criminal matters. Instead of mandamus, which implies a commitment to administrative supervision, the judges are much more likely to grant damages or perhaps enjoin a particular

5. Brown v. Board of Education of Topeka, 349 U.S. 294 (1955).
6. John C. Esposito, "Air and Water Pollution: What to do While Waiting for Washington," reprinted in Norman J. Landau and Paul D. Rheingold, *The Environmental Law Handbook* (New York: Ballantine, 1971), pp. 113, 114–15. A provision authorizing citizen suits against inaction has been written into the Federal Water Pollution Control Act. Frank P. Grad, *Environmental Law: Sources and Problems, Supplement* (New York: Matthew Bender, 1971), pp. 98–100.

practice. They are, in other words, generally prepared to live with the sputtering course of public policy and to content themselves with occasional interventions which right the most obvious and grievous wrongs.[7]

Surely this is the pattern to date in the environmental field. *The Environmental Law Handbook* tells us that the courts have closed "a million dollar pulp mill"; shut down a dump; held polluters accountable under a theory of "strict liability" for injuries, and so forth.[8] The courts' only apparent inclination to take on more supervisory functions is quite predictably confined to procedural matters. Statutes are, of course, full of procedural requirements—like the environmental impact statements mentioned earlier—which supplement the basic constitutional commitment to due process. The courts are, moreover, normally willing to force procedural restraints on administrators. Recently the federal courts ordered the Federal Power Commission to withdraw a license it had granted to the Consolidated Edison Company of New York for construction of a dam on the Hudson River at Storm King. The FPC was ordered to hold more thorough hearings and, in particular, to listen to the testimony of environmental groups that opposed the dam. The procedural nature of the "victory" is underscored by the results of the second hearing—a reaffirmation of the decision to authorize the dam.[9] Similarly, a requirement to take the environmental impact statement seriously can do no more than force administrators to consider—or at least receive—all of the factors. The final decision remains theirs, and the work of the courts is thus confined to opening the administrative process and/or delay-

7. For a critical analysis of the excesses of administrative discretion in America and a proposal for "cutting back unnecessary discretionary power," see Kenneth Culp Davis, *Discretionary Justice: A Preliminary Inquiry* (Baton Rouge: Louisiana State University Press, 1969), citation from p. 217.

8. See Chapter 4, "What the Courts May Have Done," pp. 155–214.

9. See discussion in the dissent of Justice Douglas, Scenic Hudson Preservation Conference v. Federal Power Commission, 407 U.S. 926 (1972).

ing the inevitable. In sum, the tendency toward discrete and episodic interventions is patently clear.

All this does not mean that courts will never intrude more systematically into the enforcement process, but merely that the odds are against it. The reluctance of the judges to take on administrative burdens is certainly understandable. Court procedures are primarily designed to cope with the stop-action components of the typical legal controversy: the application of a prior rule to a conflict between adversaries at a given time. The judges do not have at their disposal, among other things, the independent investigatory and fact-finding capabilities of the efficient administrative apparatus. Indeed, they do not really have the time to function simultaneously as administrators and judges—except upon occasion. Finally, and perhaps most fundamentally, they do not have an array of coercive resources adequate to cope with the power structures and vested interests that are inevitably engaged in the compliance process when it bears on important matters of public policy.

THE COMPLIANCE CALCULATION

Rights are declared as absolutes, but they ripple out into the real world in an exceedingly conditional fashion. The declaration of rights is ordinarily the prelude to a political struggle, and according to the evidence that struggle is primarily coercive. When it comes to getting large numbers of people to conform to norms they oppose, power is indispensable; it is necessary although it may not be sufficient. Frederick M. Wirt seems to have moved reluctantly to this conclusion in a detailed and perceptive investigation of the impact of law upon racial justice in Panola County, Mississippi. "There is a clear lesson drawn from this book. In civil rights matters, southerners move very little toward the goals of equality unless under direct federal pressures which threaten specific, injurious sanctions." [10] To think about compliance in terms of power and coercion is to take the first step—but only the first step—toward understanding both the problems of compliance and the unwillingness of the judges to become heavily engaged in enforcement processes.

With all that said, there are significant variations in the compliance calculation depending on the circumstances. Although the coercive resources of the judges are uniformly meager, the capacity to resist does vary a good deal. My interpretation of the considerable body of available research on compliance indicates that compliance is usually related to three characteristics of the target groups: their accessibility, resources, and determination. An investigation of these pivotal factors reveals the obstacles that must be overcome if litigation is to have a real impact; or, to put it more positively, will reveal the circumstances most conducive to compliance.

Accessibility

Both logic and evidence suggest public bureaucracies are more accessible than corporations or individuals and are therefore more amenable to judicial enforcement. The evidence is, however, circumstantial and the issue is clouded by alternative or complementary explanations. In civil rights matters, for example, progress on voting rights—a matter dependent in the first instance on state officials—has come much more easily than has open housing or equal opportunity employment. Moreover, measurable albeit modest progress on voting occurred during the period that litigation was the major tool of enforcement. Still, the major progress followed the political mobilization of the Freedom Summer of 1964 and the intrusive federal presence authorized by the Voting Rights Act of 1965. [11] Research on compliance with

10. Wirt, *The Politics of Southern Equality,* p. 290.

11. See Ibid., pp. 72–116 for an investigation of the impact of litigation alone and in combination with other enforcement mechanisms. See also Harrell R. Rodgers, Jr., and Charles S. Bullock, III, *Law and Social Change:*

the Supreme Court's school prayer decisions also suggests that accessibility is one of the important factors: "The more clearly the obligation to respond is focused upon a few identifiable public officials, and the more available are enforcement agencies . . . the more limited is the range of discretion on the part of post-policy forces and people." [12] While the evidentiary base is slim, the logic of accessibility is clear and persuasive.

The problem of using litigation against entrenched private interests is, in part, numerical. There are simply fewer voting officials to control than there are employers or landlords and, given the one-on-one tendencies of litigation, the capacity to resist will tend to vary with the numbers that must be brought into line. More basic is the accountability of public officials. Their actions are both visible and a matter of public record. Individual behavior is, in contrast, inaccessible. When a landlord refuses to rent to a member of a minority group, there are no public documents that might expose his racist impulses. The great preponderance of these transactions never even come to light. There is no corps of newsmen covering landlord-tenant relations. There is very little publicity, and the whole process is so diffuse as to be, in effect, invisible. The corporate world is somewhat different, since large corporations are at least much more visible. Their impact on events is too significant to escape attention, and some of their vital statistics are on record. Still, their inner workings can ordinarily be kept in the shadows if not altogether hidden, and smaller businesses are virtually indistinguishable from individuals when it comes to accessibility.

The issue of bureaucracy cuts across the distinction between public and private, with bureaucratic organization generally being more amenable to litigative techniques. Bureaucracies are structured by internal policies which are

---

Civil Rights Laws and Their Consequences (New York: McGraw-Hill, 1972), pp. 15–54.

12. Dolbeare and Hammond, *The School Prayer Decisions,* p. 146.

applicable throughout the system. These policies establish the lines of responsibility, making it likely that compliance orders, once they are accepted at the top, will work their way throughout the system. Accepting this line of argument does not necessitate taking the rational bureaucratic model at face value. Individual bureaucrats can and do escape the constraints of hierarchy and are perfectly capable of frustrating the intent of virtually any policy order. But in contrast to the ordinary impact of litigation, the compliance forces set in motion within the bureaucracy have a general impetus; it is the resisting forces which must swim against the tide. Moreover, bureaucracies affect the lives of large numbers of people. For example, it is estimated that federal court decisions striking down various state restrictions on welfare payments, like residency requirements, made an additional 100,000 people eligible for assistance. There are no figures on the actual changes in welfare rolls although they are believed to be "considerable." [13] What is clear is that each state rule change—and they are, incidentally, relatively easy to monitor—added large numbers to the pool of eligible recipients. There is, in other words, a kind of multiplier effect built into compliance litigation against bureaucracies.

Resources

The impact of political resources on the compliance process is more clear-cut. Those who can afford continuous legal service will get the full benefits of due process. Haywood Burns puts it as follows: "The measure of due process protection is considerably lower when what is at stake is the right to public assistance benefits, the right to a public education or entry into public housing than it is when government is acting to substantially affect some business or commercial interest." [14] It could, of course, be argued that the

13. Frances Fox Piven and Richard A. Cloward, *Regulating the Poor: The Functions of Public Welfare* (New York: Vintage, 1972), pp. 306–9.
14. Haywood Burns, "Racism and American Law," in *Law Against the*

measure of due process should be higher in regulatory matters than when benefits are being dispensed, but that would miss the point. Business and commercial interests are simply in a better position to purchase the leverage of due process.

Environmental groups, it is true, have had some significant success in using litigation as a delaying tactic. The Wilderness Society, Friends of the Earth, and the Environmental Defense Fund, for example, were able to gain the support of the courts all the way to the Supreme Court in blocking the issuance of permits for the construction of the Trans-Alaskan oil pipeline.[15] As Joseph Sax points out, however, "money can always wait." [16] Within less than six months, Congress had legislated the Supreme Court out of the pipeline controversy.[17] In addition, the procedural guarantees in the law tend in the long run to work in behalf of the corporate polluters—in part because regulations which burden private property traditionally incorporate a high level of due process protection, and in part because the legal fees corporations pay and even the fines they incur can be readily absorbed as business expenses. The American Smelting and Refining Company has been fighting an order of the Puget Sound Air Pollution Control Agency since the summer of 1968 and the end of its procedural opportunities is not yet in sight. The litigation has, no doubt, been costly, and some fines have been levied, but the battle continues and so, too, does the noxious pollution of the Tacoma Smelter.[18]

People: Essays to Demystify Law, Order and the Courts (New York: Vintage, 1971), p. 53.

15. *The New York Times* (bylined Warren Weaver, Jr.), 3 April 1973. P. 1.

16. Joseph Sax, *Defending the Environment: A Strategy for Citizen Action* (New York: Knopf, 1970), p. 51.

17. For details see, *Environmental Reporter: Current Developments* (Washington, D.C.: Bureau of National Affairs), pp. 457–58 and 587.

18. See Landau and Rheingold, *The Environmental Handbook*, pp. 256–67. Due process, it should be noted, provides not only the protection of hearings, appeals, etc., but also offers a way of attacking the antipollution standards

More generally, scholars who have studied the compliance process have found that the political balance has a direct impact on the officials who are ultimately charged with responsibility for implementing legal mandates. With respect to noncompliance with the school prayer decisions, Dolbeare and Hammond point out that local opposition had an obvious and altogether understandable effect:

> All state and local power holders—both official and private—had what seemed to them good reasons for not taking the actions and suffering the probable costs necessary to carry out the Court's mandates. Given their priorities, and their perceptions of their political contexts, it was simply not worth the trouble.[19]

In a more pluralistic context, the results of the school prayer decisions were different, since the distribution of resources between the opponents and supporters of the school prayer ban were considerably more equal.[20] Wirt's study of civil rights in Panola County also underscores the relevance of political resources: "The more cohesive the group to be regulated, the more compliance is hindered. Agreement by Mississippians on racial attitudes was very high." [21] The distribution of political resources thus provides an index of capabilities which have an important bearing on compliance.

Determination

The third factor in the compliance calculation is the will to resist. Put most simply, when the stakes are high, conflict is

---

themselves. It can be and has been argued that a 90 percent reduction in emissions as ordered by the Puget Sound Air Pollution Control Agency is arbitrary and hence contrary to due process.

19. Dolbeare and Hammond, *The School Prayer Decisions,* p. 148.

20. William K. Muir, Jr., *Prayer in the Public Schools: Law and Attitude Change* (Chicago: University of Chicago Press, 1967). Muir's fundamental concern is with the political psychology of compliance, and his conclusions will be given a fuller airing in the next chapter.

21. Wirt, *Politics of Southern Equality,* p. 282.

likely to be the most intense and the loser's will to resist likely to be at its strongest. The stakes are probably highest when the rights at issue are inelastic—that is, when victory is directly and totally at the expense of the loser.[22]

The economic and objective connotations of the concept of elasticity are perhaps a bit misleading. At times, the matter is that simple: "Votes brought to blacks by law took little from whites . . . but a job brought to a Negro by law means one less available for a white." [23] More often, the determinants of elasticity are a complex combination of reason and emotion. The police officer who resists extensions of the rights of the accused is responding to careerist incentives built into most police organizations, to perceived threats to his personal safety, and to ideological images of law and order.[24]

By and large the emotional issues tend to be the most inelastic, since they are the most difficult to compromise. Whatever can be translated into dollars and cents can be subdivided and bargained. Jobs were "inelastic" in Panola County, but an expanding economy or a significant flow of federal funds can quickly add a measure of elasticity to the job market. The fears and distrust bred by bigotry are more persistent and concessions more painful; the will to resist is most efficiently fueled by deprivations that jeopardize self-esteem or touch latent fears.

22. Ibid., pp. 310–11. The same notion is conveyed by game theory, which posits the zero-sum game as potentially the most conflictive.

23. Ibid., p. 310.

24. Due process guarantees amount, in the words of Herbert L. Packer, to an "obstacle course," which interferes with arrest and conviction procedures. See Herbert L. Packer, *The Limits of the Criminal Sanction* (Stanford: Stanford University Press, 1968), pp. 163–73, in particular. The result is, of course, to make the policeman's life more difficult. It is more difficult for him to "produce" in terms of the standards ordinarily used as the basis of promotion; he perceives that he is endangered in his confrontations with often desperate persons; and if convictions are thwarted by procedural niceties his work tends to lose meaning, since criminals remain free. On due process and the working life of the police officer, the best single source, in my judgment, remains Jerome Skolnick, *Justice Without Trial* (New York: Wiley, 1967).

Courts can, then, be of some use in implementing policies that apply principally to government agencies—particularly those policies relating to procedural matters turning on questions of due process. The deeper that it is necessary to penetrate into society, however, the more undependable courts become. These difficulties can be traced directly to judicial procedures and to the constitutional values in which they are rooted. Our government was set up so as to limit official intervention into society and, more specifically, into the lives of individual citizens. Active and effectual individuals were seen at once as a means to and as an end for the good society. It is therefore understandable and consistent that the judicial mechanisms for insuring rights were premised on individual initiative in defense of what were conceived of as individual freedoms. Be all that as it may, the consequence is to sharply restrict the effective range of courts in the implementation of public policy.

Within or beyond their effective range courts are further handicapped when the stakes of implementation are high. The obstacles to be overcome on important and controversial issues are so great, the coercive resources of the courts so meager, and the path of litigation so halting that reliance on judges would seem ill-advised. Acting alone, they are unable to force compliance and are therefore ordinarily unwilling to become integrally involved in the compliance process. Acting together with the dominant forces in society, their role becomes ancillary at best—nudging a few individuals into line. Without support of the real power holders, then, litigation is ineffectual and at times counterproductive. With that support, litigation is unnecessary. While this conclusion indicates that the *direct* impact of litigation on implementation is likely to be minimal, it does not exclude the possibility of *indirect* influence—in particular, the use of litigation as a means of altering the balance of power. It is this opportunity that will be considered next.

9. *LEGAL RIGHTS AND POLITICAL MOBILIZATION*

Regardless of the problems of implementation, rights can be useful political tools. It is possible to capitalize on the perceptions of entitlement associated with rights to initiate and to nurture political mobilization—a dual process of *activating* a quiescent citizenry and *organizing* groups into effective political units. Political mobilization can in this fashion build support for interests that have been excluded from existing allocations of values and thus promote a *realignment* of political forces. These three themes, activation, organization, and realignment, will structure this chapter.

It might seem odd, even paradoxical, to think of a legal strategy in connection with such a wide range of political activities. If courts cannot effectively insure the general application of acknowledged legal rights, what contribution can legal rights and legal institutions make to political mobilization—and in what manner?

Since rights carry with them connotations of entitlement, a declaration of rights tends to politicize needs by changing the way people think about their discontents. "One of the most successful elementary forms of mobilization of otherwise unacculturated sections on the periphery of society is the claim for the return of rights believed to have been illegally removed or denied." [1] The point is, of course, that the concept of rights evokes images of something "unjustly or

1. J. P. Nettl, *Political Mobilization: A Sociological Analysis of Methods and Concepts* (New York: Basic Books, 1967), p. 247. Nettl is writing of national integration of newly emerging nation states.

illegally taken away" and therefore of "a return to some
previous *status quo*." [2] What counts is not whether the court
order actually leads to a redistribution of values, but rather
the impact of the judicial decision on cognition. Insofar as
court decisions can legitimate claims and cue expectations,
litigation can contribute to both activation and organization;
to the building of new coalitions; and, in the long run, to a
realignment of forces within the political arena.

POLITICAL ACTIVATION

One of the primary obstacles to social change is the
acquiescence of the oppressed. It is, at least at first glance,
puzzling that people can learn to accept as normal that which
the detached observer perceives as severe deprivation. The
fact remains, however, that we learn to adapt—to endure
the trials that life imposes on us and to harden ourselves to
the burdens that others must bear. All this is the despair of
reformers who can work much more effectively in an
atmosphere of indignation at one's own deprivations and
compassion for the deprivations of others.

If we tend to accept the existing order as inevitable, it is at
least partly because it is the only reality that we know and
therefore the only reality that we can fully comprehend. Our
identity—that is to say, our expectations and our aspirations
as well—is a "gift" of the society in which we live. John Stuart
Mill pointed out more than a century ago that conceptions of
self are shaped and perhaps determined by social forces.

> All women are brought up from the very earliest years in
> the belief that their ideal of character is the very opposite to
> that of men; not self-control, but submission, and yielding
> to the control of others. All the moralities tell them that it is
> the duty of women, and all the current sentimentalities that
> it is their nature to live for others; to make complete

2. Ibid.

abnegation of themselves, and to have no life but in their affections.[3]

Similarly, it seems clear to at least some black people today that their oppression has its roots in the identity that society imposes upon them.

They are oppressed initially in the subtle psychological confrontations of child and society. Living in a society where prominent authority figures are white, and where black men are featured as incompetent and foolish, black children at an early age become aware that theirs is an inferior social status and do not develop the level of self-esteem that other children do. Their feelings of worthlessness are frequently nurtured and reinforced in their dealings with others: (1) inhumane treatment by public school teachers with responses warped by their inability to cope with the transition from the relatively tranquil middle class universities to what they perceive as the violence and instability of urban slums; (2) brutal treatment by policemen with strange conceptions of the difference between order and disorder; and (3) cruelty by parents whose aggressive impulses toward a hostile world are often displaced on their offspring. Even as children many American blacks are not likely to hope for anything—achievement, wealth, happiness, or long life.

Adolescent experiences build upon this childhood foundation, and the feelings of hopelessness and self-hatred are more firmly and elaborately woven into the fabric of personality.[4]

Murray Edelman puts the general proposition particularly well: "Perception of deprivation, then, like all perception, is a

3. John Stuart Mill, "The Subjection of Women," in *On Liberty, Representative Government, The Subjection of Women: Three Essays by John Stuart Mill* (London: Oxford University Press, 1971), p. 444.

4. William W. Ellis, *White Ethics and Black Power: The Emergence of the West Side Organization* (Chicago: Aldine, 1969), pp. 103–04.

function of social cues regarding what is to be expected and what exists; it does not correlate directly or simply with objective conditions or with any particular measure of them." [5] In any case, the status quo implication of these imposed political identities is clear: the patterns of subordination and superordination are accepted as natural by those on top and by those on the bottom as well.

Consider, for example, poverty in America. Is it a social problem? American values encourage us to accept poverty as a constant aspect of the human condition—even as a desirable stimulus to ambition.[6] If we are poor in a land of opportunity, society's signals tell us that we have only ourselves to blame. Less embarrassing, then, to suffer in silence than to call attention to our inadequacies. At the same time that this ideology of opportunity leads the disadvantaged to conceal their discontents, it also divides people from one another. Those who have not made it have failed and are not the responsibility of those who have succeeded. The simple truth is that whether discontents become political issues depends, at least in the first instance, on whether they are perceived as social problems—more a matter of cognition and values than of objective measures of deprivation, oppression, and injustice.

Lawyers are mediators between the individual and those with governmental and private power. They have ready access to important symbols of political legitimacy: the courts, the law, constitutional rights, and so forth. The attorney is therefore in a position to help cut through the

5. Murray Edelman, *Politics as Symbolic Action: Mass Arousal and Quiescence* (Chicago: Markham, 1971), p. 107. In an earlier volume Edelman made a similar point: "The very question of what man *is,* let alone what he wants, is in part a product of the political system, and in turn conditions the system." *The Symbolic Uses of Politics* (Urbana: University of Illinois Press, 1967), pp. 19–20. Italics in the original.

6. This argument is developed in detail in Dorothy B. James, *Poverty, Politics, and Change* (Englewood Cliffs, N.J.: Prentice-Hall, 1972). See, in particular, Chapter 2.

debilitating pall of acquiescence by transforming individual discontents into political demands. More specifically, adequate legal service can aid in altering self-conceptions by imparting to the client a sense of "legal competence"—confidence in his efficacy in dealings with others.[7] In addition, litigation undertaken on behalf of the client tends to bring him into direct and effectual contact with the courts, which are important organs of governmental authority. Like other governmental acts, court orders are, in the words of Murray Edelman, "powerful shapers of perceptions."[8] Note that neither of these steps in the direction of personal and political efficacy is dependent in any way on the modest store of coercive resources that is at the disposal of the judges nor upon any *unique* powers of legitimation attributed to courts by the myth of rights.

Let us first consider the attorney-client relationship. The contrast between the assertive attorney and the discontented but acquiescent citizen could hardly be sharper. Attorneys are taught to take rights seriously and to believe that their professional skills are useful for asserting rights, even against imposing aggregations of political and economic power. If some of the assertiveness of the typical attorney rubs off on his client—if the attorney can significantly increase the client's capacity for indignation—then access to legal services may ultimately serve the cause of social change in important ways.

The competent subject will have a sense of himself as a *possessor of rights,* and in seeking to validate and implement these rights through law he will be concerned with holding *authorities accountable to law.* . . . We suggest that the legally competent subject does more than appeal to the

7. Jerome E. Carlin, Jan Howard, and Sheldon L. Messinger, "Civil Justice and the Poor: Issues for Sociological Research," in *Law and Society Review* 1 (November 1966): 60–62.
8. Edelman, *Politics as Symbolic Action*, p. 101.

considerateness of officials; he insists that official actions and decisions be consistent with authoritative rules.[9]

That changes in this general direction are possible is the conclusion of a study made of one Connecticut legal services project: "The most striking change which we have discerned is in the amount of legal knowledge acquired by clients in the program. . . . Post-service interviews show an increased willingness to use the services of lawyers and to differentiate those situations in which referral to the legal process would be of little value." [10] Whether or not people actually learn their rights from attorneys is less important than that they begin to believe that they have rights. What counts is that they cease sublimating their grievances and begin to seek redress.

Litigation can further advance the process of activation, since the courts share the symbols of legitimacy with other authoritative governmental agencies. At the very least, a judicial decision—even if it is unfavorable—indicates that the problem is no longer solely a private matter. Its existence has been officially acknowledged, thus implying that solutions are not solely a matter of individual responsibility. Secondly, judicial decisions create legal rights and carry with them connotations of entitlement. The judicial decision may not effectively redistribute any resources or influence but it will in all likelihood cue expectations of redistribution. The connotations of entitlement may also be reasonably seen as a contribution to self-esteem: deprivations that formerly might have been viewed as symptoms of personal inadequacy can henceforth be seen as unpaid governmental debts. Finally, the general character of legal enactments can lay the basis for a collective political identity, since the entitlements provide a

9. Carlin, Howard, and Messinger, "Civil Justice and the Poor," p. 70. Italics in the original.

10. George F. Cole, "Clients of a Legal Services Project," paper prepared for delivery at the 1971 Annual Meeting of the American Political Science Association, p. 15.

joint stake and the deprivations a mutual cause. In sum, litigation can politicize individual discontents and in so doing activate a constituency, thus lending initial impetus to a movement for change.

To be more concrete, consider the message conveyed by the Supreme Court's declaration in *Brown* v. *Board of Education* that "separate educational facilities are inherently unequal." Surely black people did not have to be told that their schools were inferior, nor for that matter was this news to most whites. Moreover, the judgment did not bear witness to that inequality in any particularly dramatic fashion—a matter on which the decision and the judges have been often criticized.[11] It was, nonetheless, read as a signal that changes were on the way, and surely it gave rise to anticipations which set the tone, established the direction, and influenced the outcome of a political controversy that continues to press upon us.

While blacks were, of course, conscious of the commonality of their grievances without the assistance of the Supreme Court, judicial intervention did lend political significance to those grievances—in the first instance, simply by *officially* acknowledging their existence. More specifically, the *Brown* decision can be seen as one of the earliest and most noteworthy of a long string of official enactments which made it clear as a matter of public policy that the deprived conditions of black people were a consequence of handicaps imposed both de jure and de facto by the established forces of the society. Surely hopes were kindled by these enactments. Is it not also reasonable to believe that a sense of a collective political destiny was extended and reinforced?

11. Moderate criticism on these grounds has come from the ranks of the law professors. See, for example, Louis H. Pollak, "Racial Discrimination and Judicial Integrity: A Reply to Professor Wechsler," *University of Pennsylvania Law Review* 108 (November 1959): 24–31. A more strident version of the same theme can be seen in Howard Moore, Jr., "The Court and Black Liberation," in Robert Lefcourt, ed., *Law Against the People* (New York: Vintage, 1971), p. 58.

If litigation has been useful in mobilizing blacks, it could be at least as useful—and perhaps more useful—for mobilizing other disadvantaged groups in the society. The courts could hardly convey anything to blacks about their blackness, but the judges were in a position to demonstrate the political relevance of being black. Much the same would hold true for the poor, for women, for prisoners, and for other self-conscious and reasonably cohesive groups. The stakes of litigation are higher in cases where intrinsic unity is less evident. Among consumers, environmentalists, debtors, and other inchoate interests both the collective identity and its political relevance must be demonstrated. Those interests which we all share to some degree, and which, therefore, do not distinguish us from one another, have traditionally been the most difficult to organize.[12] So long as these problems are perceived as our common lot, a pall of fatalistic acceptance makes for quiescence. To the extent that litigation can demonstrate that individuals are not isolated in their discontents and that these discontents have a status in the law, legal tactics can help to establish a collective political identity.

POLITICAL ORGANIZATION

Activation and the establishment of a collective political identity are only the initial steps along the path toward

12. One study of public opinion on pollution tends to bear out this inclination to think of such problems as someone else's. In Durham, North Carolina, 83 percent of the respondents saw pollution as a serious national problem; 62 percent saw it as a serious problem in Durham; and 31 percent saw it as a neighborhood problem which was serious. Since air pollution in Durham is above the national average and since the neighborhood reaction was the same in all sections of the city, it would seem that most people in Durham have learned to live with pollution. Arvin W. Murch, "Public Concern for Environmental Pollution," *Public Opinion Quarterly*, 35 (Spring 1971): 101. Clearly, the problem of pollution tends to emerge so slowly, gradually and imperceptibly that adaptation precedes awareness: Are "those lazy, hazy, crazy days of summer" the cue for nostalgia and reverie or the smoggy harbinger of environmental decline?

effective action. Political demands do not automatically become political issues.[13] If they are to be taken seriously, political demands must be pressed by effective political organizations. Once again, lawyers and litigation can be useful although hardly decisive.

For political organizations to take root and become effective, members must take themselves seriously and must be taken seriously by others. These are significant obstacles to overcome in a society dominated by powerful and seemingly impervious bureaucratic structures. In order for a group to take itself seriously and begin attracting supporters, it must believe not only in its cause but also in its capabilities. In these difficult early stages, lawyers are in a position to lend organizing impetus to the group by enhancing its sense of efficacy. The same traits and skills that make lawyers helpful in the early stages can, however, make them unreliable strategists over the long haul.

What the lawyers provide at the outset are organizing skills and resources together with a credible strategy. Their technical skills can be useful in dealing with the details of establishment such as drafting a charter, working out the legal status of the organization for fund raising and tax purposes, and making contractual arrangements on administrative matters. More generally, the lawyer's presence at an organizational meeting can, in a society responsive to the myth of rights, lend an air of importance and legitimacy to what is often a meager group of citizens with very little political experience. Most important, lawyers have at their disposal litigation and its credible promise of tangible and proximate results in the form of courtroom victories and legal leverage to be used against stubborn and powerful opponents.

The growth of the National Welfare Rights Organization in the late 1960s indicates the kind of contribution that a legal

13. On the distinction between demands and issues, see David Easton, *A Systems Analysis of Political Life* (New York: John Wiley, 1965), pp. 140–49.

strategy can make to political organizing. Welfare agencies often fail to provide the full range of benefits to which the poor are entitled according to the law. The poor are ordinarily not aware of all of their entitlements, they are generally not very aggressive in making claims, and they are easily intimidated by agencies upon which they are heavily dependent. In short, the poor lack legal competence.[14] As Richard Cloward and Frances Piven pointed out in an influential article in *The Nation*, this situation created opportunities for an effective strategy of political organization.

> The strategy is based on the fact that a vast discrepancy exists between the benefits to which people are entitled under public welfare programs and the sums which they actually receive. . . .
>
> Movements that depend on involving masses of poor people have generally failed in America. Why would the proposed strategy to engage the poor succeed?
>
> First, this promises immediate economic benefits. . . .
>
> Second, for this strategy to succeed, one need not ask more of most of the poor than that they claim lawful benefits. . . .
>
> Third, the prospects for mass influence are enhanced because this plan provides a practical basis for coalition between poor whites and poor Negroes.[15]

It seems fair to say that these legal entitlements played an important part in the organizing efforts of welfare rights leaders,[16] and that the gap between what the law promises and what it delivers implies similar organizing opportunities in other issue areas.

14. Carlin, Howard, and Messinger, "Civil Justice and the Poor," pp. 42–52 and 69–84.

15. Richard A. Cloward and Frances Fox Piven, "The Weight of the Poor: A Strategy to End Poverty," *The Nation*, 202 (May 2, 1966): 510, 513–14.

16. Frances Fox Piven and Richard A. Cloward, *Regulating the Poor: The Functions of Public Welfare* (New York: Vintage, 1972), pp. 320–30.

Once the organization takes root legal tactics can continue to be useful, but lawyers may become unreliable tails unwilling to give up wagging the dog.[17] The lawyer can provide useful counsel on tactics at virtually all stages of organizational growth and development, since the organization must face up to the legal consequences of various tactics. If it decides to employ litigation, the attorney can counsel organizational leaders on how to behave so as to maximize chances of bringing a successful test case—that is, one in which the major issues are taken up by the courts. Similarly, the attorney can assess the likelihood and character of criminal and civil liability that is implied by various courses of action. When conflicts with the law do develop, the lawyer automatically becomes the vital defense arm of the organization—protecting leadership from the criminal justice system and other organization resources from the bailiff. On the other hand, lawyers are by training, socialization, and expertise inclined to exclusive use of litigation and negotiation. They tend to find politics somewhat distasteful and ordinarily try to steer away from militant confrontations.

At some point, the attorney's caution is likely to run counter to deeply felt needs of the membership or of constituency groups. For example, most civil rights organizations experienced strains of this sort during the 1960s as blacks grew increasingly militant. The role and attitude of

17. As Cloward and Piven point out, legal tactics are not the exclusive province of lawyers—at least, not where the entitlements are spelled out clearly and unequivocally as in welfare regulations. "Organizers will have to become advocates in order to deal effectively with improper rejections and terminations. . . . In some cases, it will be necessary to contest decisions by requesting a 'fair hearing' before the appropriate state supervisory agency; it may occasionally be necessary to sue for redress in courts. Hearings and court actions will require lawyers . . . However, most cases will not require expert knowledge of law, but only of welfare regulations; the rules can be learned by laymen, including welfare recipients themselves (who can help man 'information and advocacy' centers)." "Weight of the Poor," p. 512. While others can admittedly be trained to perform legal functions, lawyers, understandably, play pivotal roles when legal tactics are employed.

lawyers in a recent organizing effort of home owners in two
ghetto areas of Chicago are also illustrative.[18] These people
had been led either by desperation or misrepresentation to
purchase homes on contracts under terms which were much
less favorable than ordinary mortgage arrangements.

> The terms of the contracts . . . allow the purchaser to
> take immediate possession of the property, but give him no
> equity or title until the full contract price is paid. . . . Also,
> like the restrictive terms of a conditional sales contract, the
> seller has the right to reclaim the property and to keep all
> past payments if a single payment is missed. And while the
> buyer is obliged to pay for insurance, taxes, and all repairs
> on the property, the seller usually selects the insurance
> company and can collect all claims for damages to the
> property.[19]

In the beginning, the lawyers by initiating suits lent hope and
purpose to the organization. Subsequently, when the members turned to direct action in the form of a payment-with-
holding strike, the lawyers objected strenuously—arguing in
part that their litigation might be jeopardized. For the
membership, however, the strike was a way of bringing
economic pressure to bear on the sellers, of reinforcing
organizational cohesiveness, and of using the mass evictions
that were bound to follow as a way of creating a political
issue. Without making any definitive assessment of the
balance sheet, it seems clear that strike action did temporarily
increase organizational enthusiasm and, moreover, brought
Mayor Daley directly into the conflict. There were problems
as well, but the point is that lawyers tend to resist a range of
options that seems altogether reasonable in the context of
grass roots or even pluralistic politics.

18. The following information is taken from James Alan McPherson, " 'In
My Father's House There Are Many Mansions, and I'm Going to Get Me
Some of Them Too!' The Story of the Contract Buyers' League," *The
Atlantic* (April 1972), pp. 51–82.
19. Ibid., p. 53.

POLITICAL REALIGNMENT

Even successful efforts at activation and organization are threatened by countermobilization, but legal tactics do have some built-in capabilities for increasing *net* support. In working from rights established by law or derived from constitutional values, legal tactics evoke images of entitlements not only among the direct beneficiaries but within the ranks of all Americans who are responsive to the myth of rights. Of course it is unlikely that very many of those immediately and directly threatened will become supporters, but the mass of those who are not involved in the conflict could be either neutralized or persuaded by legal symbols. In short, a legal approach tends to be self-legitimating and thus increases the likelihood of a favorable political realignment.

The civil rights movement reveals the opportunities for altering the balance of political forces. The most immediate and decisive reaction to the *Brown* decision was the unequivocal and united opposition of the powerful southern bloc in Congress. Other Americans reacted more slowly—perhaps in part because that decision and subsequent litigation tended to confirm their faith in the progressive and beneficent character of the political system. By the mid-sixties, however, segregationists had been sufficiently isolated and discredited to permit the passage of increasingly strong civil rights legislation as well as more and more insistent implementation of desegregation policies by the executive branch.[20] In retrospect it seems fair to say that the withholding of officially acknowledged rights contributed significantly to the legitimacy of the civil rights movement and to the adoption of its program.[21]

20. See Harrell R. Rodgers and Charles S. Bullock, III, *Law and Social Change: Civil Rights Laws and Their Consequences* (New York: McGraw-Hill, 1972), for a comprehensive survey of the stages of implementation in a wide variety of civil rights matters.

21. For personal statements which bear witness to the tendency of support for the movement to build in reaction to denial of legal rights by southern officials, see William M. Kunstler, *Deep in My Heart* (New York: William

There are those who see the civil rights experience as confirmation of the theory of change associated with the myth of rights. Litigation is, in this perspective, viewed as a tool which prompted government agencies to rethink the goals of public policies while isolating the segregationist opposition. It is thus possible to view the civil rights era as a time of "colloquy" among judges, legislators, and administrators, a colloquy which was fruitful precisely in the measure that segregationist politics had been discredited by judicial initiative. The judge's function was, in other words, to call attention to the enduring principles of American politics—to what I have termed constitutional values—and in this way to demonstrate the dangers inherent in the expedient compromises that are the inevitable consequence of political bargaining.[22] Not surprisingly, the same theory has been applied to other matters. Joseph Sax advocates similar tactics as a way of "making democracy work" in behalf of the environment.

> Courts are not to be used as substitutes for the legislative process—to usurp policies made by elected representatives —but as a means of providing realistic access to legislatures so that the theoretical processes of democracy can be made to work more effectively in practice. Citizen initiatives in the courts can be used to bring important matters to legislative attention, to force them upon the agendas of reluctant and busy representatives.[23]

Morrow, 1966), and Howard Zinn, *SNCC: The New Abolitionists* (Boston: Beacon Press, 1968).

22. For an early and, I would say, definitive development of this position, see Alexander M. Bickel, *The Least Dangerous Branch: The Supreme Court at the Bar of Politics* (Indianapolis: Bobbs-Merrill, 1962), particularly Chapter 6 in which the general theory is applied to the politics of school desegregation. In a subsequent study devoted solely to school desegregation, the focus tends to shift from the workings of constitutional politics to a more conventional attack on judicial activism. Alexander M. Bickel, *The Supreme Court and the Idea of Progress* (New York: Harper and Row, 1970).

23. Joseph L. Sax, *Defending the Environment: A Strategy for Citizen Action* (New York: Knopf, 1970), p. xviii.

Note that making democracy work does not, for Sax, entail the travail of participatory politics any more than it did for the civil rights leadership of the 1960s. Participation is confined, at most, to "citizen initiative" in behalf of litigation —meaning that participation is filtered through lawyers who shape issues and, in effect, resolve them in concert with the duly constituted political authorities.

There is another way of viewing the civil rights era which calls into question the lawyers' vision of change without pain. Legal and constitutional values may have temporarily neutralized some of the opposition to desegregation and at least initially channeled political activity into institutional processes. In the long run, however, such changes as did occur were accompanied by more or less the full range of political conflict. Mobilization of blacks escalated well beyond the boundaries of constitutional values and processes. Moreover, mobilization led to countermobilization once the stakes of the conflict became clear. If there is a lesson to be learned from the 1960s, it is that the politics of rights is no different—and ultimately no less conflictive—than conventional politics. Its distinguishing trait is simply that it *may* work on behalf of groups ordinarily excluded from conventional politics.

Could it be any other way? The law can hardly transcend the conflicts of the political system in which it is embedded. In the first place, enough ambiguity attaches to legal and constitutional values so that ordinarily neither side has a corner on the symbols of legitimacy. The Southern Manifesto calling for massive resistance to the *Brown* decision was characteristically couched in terms altogether consistent with the myth of rights, for it pledged the use of "all lawful means to bring about a reversal of this decision which is contrary to the Constitution." [24] And, of course, the inertial tendencies built into the legal process made it a useful tool for the

24. In Hubert H. Humphrey, ed., *School Desegregation: Documents and Commentaries* (New York: Crowell, 1964), p. 34.

well-entrenched forces of segregation. Since the law could be used to slow the process of change to a snail's pace, it is understandable that newly mobilized blacks were easily disillusioned with judicial processes, and the pace of change seemed to quicken only when "busy and reluctant" Congressmen and executive officials were prodded—often by extralegal action. Once the impact of change became more concrete, opposition began to mount. Many of those who had been attracted to the civil rights movement or neutralized by its uncertain implications joined the opposition as the costs of change manifested themselves in affirmative action hiring, fair housing plans, school busing, civil disorder, and so forth. In short, the fallacy of consensual change quickly became clear.

While consensual change may be an illusion, the impact of law on political attitudes, and therefore on the political arena, is not. William K. Muir's study of compliance with the Supreme Court's decision outlawing prayer in the public schools provides some insight into the variety of ways that changes in the law can be reflected in political attitudes.[25] At the extremes, changes in the law may convert some while being taken as a provocation by others. Changes in the law may also moderate attitudes; there were those in Muir's study whose favorable attitudes toward school house religion were softened but not transformed by the Supreme Court's decision.[26] Muir characterizes the range of responses as follows:

> Within any single discrete organization of individuals whose behavior lawmakers intend to affect, the reaction to the law is never monolithic within the group but varies from person to person. The responses do not move in the same direction, nor with the same intensity, nor with respect to the same objects. It was this varied range of

25. William K. Muir, *Prayer in the Public Schools: Law and Attitude Change* (Chicago: University of Chicago Press, 1967).
26. On these moderating tendencies see in particular ibid., pp. 100–08.

response which was the most important result of my study, and explanation of these variabilities is my most important task.[27]

Among the more important cognitive factors identified by Muir are the effectiveness of political leaders and the cues of reference groups.[28] What stands out in this welter of ambiguous signals, however, is that all but a small minority of the respondents were ascertainably influenced by the judgment.[29] Legal norms may not induce acquiescence; they may not be self-authenticating; but they do seem capable of exercising an independent influence on political attitudes. A legal strategy may therefore contribute to the processes of political realignment but in a more unpredictable and inconclusive way than is implied by the myth of rights.

It follows from the preceding evidence that a legal strategy can contribute to political mobilization and in this way to political change. The mobilizing potential of the legal approach to change stems from the role of courts as articulators of public policy goals and from their demonstrated willingness to validate departures from existing practice. Given the responsiveness of most Americans to legal symbols, declarations of rights by courts tend to alter political perceptions.

27. Ibid., p. 81.
28. For a complete list of "concluding hypotheses," see Ibid., pp. 132–34. Robert L. Crain comes to complementary conclusions in his study of school desegregation, *The Politics of School Desegregation: Comparative Case Studies of Community Structure and Policy-Making* (Chicago: Aldine, 1968).
29. It should be noted, however, that Muir's study involved only officials who were in some way immediately affected by the decision. The effects on others were surely weaker and perhaps different in kind. Dolbeare and Hammond's work suggests that one cannot count on the law's influence even on the relevant actors. They were, however, more concerned with behavior than with cognition. *The School Prayer Decisions: From Court Policy to Local Practice* (Chicago: University of Chicago Press, 1971). Muir does, in any case, give us plausible hypotheses, based on psychological constructs, for further investigation.

Even less authoritative evocations of rights—as, for example, by attorneys or community leaders—can cue the hopes and expectations so important to successful mobilization.

To think of the law and of legal rights in this fashion entails a significant break with the myth of rights tradition. According to that tradition, rights are entitlements to be secured either by litigation which forces compliance with court orders or by consensual processes associated with constitutional politics. Rights are also viewed as ethical imperatives anchored in liberal democratic values and adding, as well, a note of continuity to the erratic world of politics. Our constitutional order is viewed as providing equitable, rational, progressive, and hence desirable procedures for resolving political conflict. By the same token, liberal democratic values are identified with a just society and are taken as adequate guides to public policy.

In contrast, I have argued that rights are most sensibly thought of as agents of political mobilization rather than as ends in themselves. This is an argument primarily based on pragmatic considerations. The evidence suggests that litigation may be useful for providing remedies for individuals but that its impact on social policy is open to question. The implementation of social policy by court orders is likely to be slow, costly, and perhaps self-defeating. The utility of constitutional politics is similarly suspect. There is very little reason to believe that legal and constitutional values are directly persuasive to the elites who are most immediately responsible for making decisions for the polity. These elites are, however, likely to respond to effectively organized interests, and legal symbols can be usefully employed in behalf of political mobilization. The politics of rights, therefore, involves the manipulation of rights rather than their realization. Rights are treated as contingent resources which impact on public policy indirectly—in the measure, that is, that they can aid in altering the balance of political forces.

Part Three

THE STRATEGISTS OF RIGHTS

10. LEGAL EDUCATION AND PROFESSIONAL SOCIALIZATION: THE MYTH OF RIGHTS REVISITED

The basic message of the politics of rights to lawyers interested in altering the status quo is simple. They are directed to turn their attention, at least in part, to the mobilizing potential of litigation. But lawyers are likely to resist the message of mobilization. Their legal training and professional experiences predispose them to think about litigation more conventionally, to internalize the myth of rights.

An investigation of the socializing experiences of American lawyers is therefore an essential precondition to understanding the policy roles that they will be inclined to play and the strategic counsel that they will provide to political organizations. These are important matters, since lawyers are bound to play a prominent role in any strategy of change that relies on legal tactics. Neither legal education nor professional experiences are likely to alter the politics of lawyers in the more obvious ways. Party preferences will not change, nor will radicals be changed into conservatives. The influence is more subtle. It is the influence of ideology on behavior.

Chapter 11 will focus directly on the priorities and preferences of the small "activist" minority of the American bar whose members serve as strategists of rights for groups interested in change. While a great many differences will emerge among these lawyers, none of them entirely transcend their educational and professional experiences. An examination of these background experiences will, therefore, help explain the causes and character of resistance among lawyers to the politics of rights.

Three factors will be considered: (1) the basic skills learned in law school; (2) the world view imparted as those skills are learned; and (3) the role expectations thrust upon the lawyer by his profession. The first and third factors have a familiar ring. The second is more novel and requires an introduction.

My argument is that a distinctive approach to problem solving is imparted in law school, and that this approach influences the way lawyers think about societal issues more generally. A world view is implicit in legal analysis and tends to come along as a kind of silent partner in legal education. To oversimplify a point that will be developed in the third part of this chapter, the lawyer is encouraged to engage in what might be termed rule-mongering, and this preoccupation tends to narrow his vision.[1] Whatever may be the implications of rule-mongering for the ordinary practitioner, it has a disabling impact on activist lawyers who are rummaging around for causes and tactics.

The following discussion—an interpretive essay on legal education—will concentrate on only a few salient features, since available research on legal education does not deal directly with the problems that concern me. This is not at all surprising, since even the more zealous reformers are under the influence of the myth of rights and thus not prepared to ask any really fundamental questions about the political implications of law school training. Reform proposals are directed only at doing better or quicker what is already done—or at extending the unquestioned benefits of legal education to the broader university community.[2] My purpose

1. See, once again, Judith Shklar, *Legalism* (Cambridge, Mass.: Harvard University Press, 1964) for the roots of this argument.

2. See, for example, the Carrington Report, reprinted in Herbert L. Packer and Thomas Ehrlich, with the assistance of Stephen Pepper, *New Directions in Legal Education* (New York: McGraw-Hill, 1972), pp. 95–162. For a more self-consciously political approach, which also neglects the issues raised here,

is, in any case, to make a point that has not previously been made rather than to provide a balanced critique of legal education.

LEGAL ANALYSIS

Because most people understand instinctively what legal analysis is all about, legal symbols are useful in political discourse. People grasp particularly well the *limitations* of the legal perspective. How natural it is to accept the pejorative connotations of the adjective "legalistic," for example. Is there any mystery about what Attorney General Mitchell meant when he asserted: "We face in the United States a situation where the discovery of guilt or innocence is in danger of drowning in a sea of legalisms." [3] Even without further elaboration, did we not realize that Mr. Mitchell was rejecting "the hydra of excess proceduralism, archaic formalisms, pretrial motions, appeals, postponements, continuances, collateral attacks, which can have the effect of dragging justice to death and stealing the very life out of the law." [4] Well, perhaps we did not understand about the collateral attacks, continuances, and pretrial motions, but we knew as soon as we saw the word legalism that Mr. Mitchell was concerned with archaic formalisms. When we accuse someone of being legalistic, we suggest an excessive zeal for purely formal details which becloud rather than clarify the *real* issue. The legalist is someone who is lost among the trees and cannot *or will not* consider the overall shape of the forest. So it is a sense of willful closure together with an obsession for procedure and minutiae that we associate with the law game. An unfair caricature? Perhaps. On the other hand, like all good caricatures, it reveals some important features.

see "The Rutgers Report: The White Law School and the Black Liberation Struggle," in Robert Lefcourt, ed., *Law Against the People: Essays to Demystify Law, Order, and the Courts* (New York: Vintage, 1971), pp. 232–52.
3. *The New York Times*, 17 July 1971, p. 1.
4. Ibid.

Consider the case method, which is the key to legal education in America. The case method focuses on the appellate opinion, and the student is taught to separate the opinion into its component parts—to parse a case. At one time, this meant teaching him to sift through the complex facts, competing claims, and judicial pronouncements in order to draw forth the controlling rule enunciated by the court and the reasons and doctrine linking the relevant facts to the rule. After three years of this it was assumed that the student now thought like a lawyer and could be certified with an LL.B. These days, we are assured, all this has changed—at least in the better law schools.

Legal realism has infiltrated legal education through the same Langdell case method which had been the object of its attack. But where Langdell used the appellate opinion as a way of finding the "true" rule of law, we now assume that task can be learned quickly and easily, that particularly after the first year our students can parse a case and tell us what is holding, what is dictum. Under pressure from the weight and dynamism of an ever-increasing body of law, we have shifted our emphasis and have made "the case" the occasion for a much broader inquiry—one which will enable the lawyer to capture the dynamic of a given field, to cope with the changing legal scene and to call into question the old rules.[5]

Students are, in other words, encouraged to think about the way in which precedent is eroded and doctrine changes. An increasingly "realistic" faculty sensitizes the student to the "extraneous" factors that may determine whether a given judge will be receptive to a particular argument—prejudice, dyspepsia, political debts, and so forth. The student may even

5. Abraham S. Goldstein, "The Unfulfilled Promise of Legal Education," in Geoffrey C. Hazzard, Jr., ed., *Law in a Changing America* (Englewood Cliffs, N.J.: Prentice-Hall, 1968), p. 159.

be asked to reflect upon the societal implications of a given opinion for a body of law.

Everything has changed. Or has it? Dean Goldstein's statement indicates clearly that parsing is still at the very least the point of departure for effective legal training. As such, it would seem capable of exerting a considerable influence; it is after all the initial common experience and the necessary preparation for broader inquiry. There is, however, reason to believe that parsing remains as much a keystone as a preface. First, no real alternative seems to have been developed.

> But because we are not clear which concepts or course of training should be made central, we tend to treat the appellate decision as if it were an all-purpose hypothetical problem leading in any direction the teacher chooses to travel—sometimes to a search for behavioral presuppositions, sometimes to an assessment of impact, sometimes to discerning the lines along which doctrine is likely to develop.[6]

In the absence of agreement on the new dimensions of legal education, law schools tend to fall into the inertial patterns of the traditional consensus, and the broader inquiry turns out to be pretty much of a series of random variations on the original theme. There are no structural changes, only a few decorative modifications: a reflecting pool, an observation deck, and so forth. But if law schools continue in well-worn tracks, it is because the old methods have proven serviceable if not altogether satisfactory. Even critical and self-conscious law students recognize the worth of the skills imparted by a legal education and associate them with "attributes highly prized by successful lawyers." [7] Legal skills may not be enough—at least not at Yale, which must live with its avant

6. Ibid.
7. Duncan Kennedy, "How the Law School Fails: A Polemic," in *Yale Review of Law and Social Action*, 1 (Spring 1970): 77.

garde reputation and with restless students who learn to parse in the first year. But the old quest for legal logic and analytical rigor goes on, and not simply as a preliminary but as a mood which sets the tone and in the end probably determines the boundaries of innovation.

Typically, then, the law student spends the better part of three years learning legal analysis. The case method teaches how to determine the controlling rule in a legal dispute: the student learns that there is a rule and that the job is to find it. Finding no longer has the sense of pure discovery that it once did. It is not taken for granted any longer that the rule as such is there, waiting for the judge or the attorney. The law student is sensitized both to the case law and to the "open texture" in the patterns of American law.[8] Rules change; what is settled today may be altered tomorrow. The ingenious lawyer must learn to capitalize on open texture and turn change in favor of the client. The good craftsman learns to provide a respectable legal rationale for the judge. Judges may not be persuaded by legal skills, but they find it difficult to act without a legal rationale. The average American judge simply prefers to deliver a decision which is either consistent with precedent or which yields a rule that can be lived with for a while.

It is, then, the quest for continuity that characterizes legal analysis—not the ad hoc solution but the general guideline. What the student must learn are the secrets of harmony and consistency; these are the rules of the law game. Like the rules of chess, or of any game, the rules of the law are based on an *internal* logic. The rules that endure tend to be those that allow the game to proceed as smoothly as possible. The law game is itself a game of rules: "subjecting human conduct to the governance of rules." [9] If that is to be done smoothly,

8. Goldstein, "The Unfulfilled Promise," p. 162.

9. Lon L. Fuller, *The Morality of Law* (New Haven: Yale University Press, 1964), p. 46.

there must be a reliable way of determining the applicable rule at all times and in all situations. Which institutions have jurisdiction? How can these institutions be activated? What are the accepted canons of interpretation? Are there guides for establishing precedence among relevant rules? Speaking more generally, even the lawyer as opportunist must come to understand or sense something of the logic and symmetry of a system of rules. To certain minds there is no doubt a fascination to this logic and symmetry. There is intellectual and even aesthetic satisfaction in coming to understand the internal logic of the system and real gratification in working out dependable doctrines which reconcile apparent contradictions among rules. But the law is not a parlor game, it is a social institution bound up with the most important dimensions of human freedom and oppression.[10] At the chess board, intellectual satisfaction may suffice. In the real world, however, the rule system is important primarily as it relates to societal goals; it is a means rather than an end. The preoccupation of legal education with the law game as such tends, therefore, to be confining:

> However much we talk the language of legal realism or of functionalism, we are doing so essentially from the inside view of the working lawyer, one which makes little effort to place law and legal institutions and legal decision-makers in a context which would enable us to learn what jobs can be done by law and what cannot.[11]

The student, in other words, learns not to raise the most troubling questions. For success in law school:

> The key element is control. . . . He accepts the "context," whatever it may be, and achieves above all a sort of "respectability." Getting directly to the point often means

10. Judith Shklar uses the same image to make a somewhat different point. See Shklar, *Legalism*, pp. 105–06.
11. Goldstein, "The Unfulfilled Promise," p. 161.

above all avoiding areas of ambiguity, "subjectivism,"
issues too large for him to understand or which may
provoke fundamental disagreement.[12]

These habits may make the student into a serviceable and
compliant tool of the client's interests but would also seem
likely to provide a world view that narrows the lawyer's
vision.

THE NARROWING VISION

It may seem a long and perhaps indefensible leap from the
professional skills imparted by a legal education to a general
world view. After all, doctors, engineers, and architects are
also prepared for their calling in university settings—indeed,
in semi-autonomous professional schools. Are we to assume
that they, too, come into the real world equipped not only
with basic skills but with a special perspective on the
problems of the world?

By asserting that there is a world view implicit in the
paradigm that structures legal education, I mean that the
student is provided with an approach which seems to both
explain and justify the working of the American system.
There is another way of making the same point. Legal
education imparts a sense of efficacy which extends beyond
the obvious skills learned in law school. Lawyers are effica-
cious not simply because they know how to activate institutions with injunctions, writs of habeas corpus, and the like.
Mastery of the mechanics of public institutions may be, in
fact, the most important skill that law students pick up, but
they are encouraged to believe more broadly in their competence. Chances are that they were already aware upon
entering law school of the disproportionate share of lawyers
among our appointive and elective officials. It is even more
likely that they knew of the traditional position of the

12. Kennedy, "How the Law School Fails," p. 77.

American lawyer as adviser to those in power in both business and government. Once in law school, students learn just why lawyers are so important; more specifically, they come to appreciate the general utility and analytic power of legal skills.

The image of the lawyer as the renaissance man of American public life is promoted and nurtured by a legal education in a number of ways which tend to distinguish law school from other professional educations. Most significantly, the law curriculum reflects virtually the full range of societal problems. As law students move through this curricular incarnation of American life, they become sensitive to the apparent efficacy of the legal process. Ironically, confidence as a lawyer may be advanced by degradation as a law student. Treated day after day to "the spectacle of the professor smiling quietly to himself as he prepares to lay your guts on the floor once again," [13] students no doubt come to see legal skills as synonymous with analytic power—the capacity to clarify complex problems and communicate to others the range of choice open to those in search of solutions. Moreover, students note that disputes are often effectively resolved by simply locating the controlling rule and determining who is obligated and who is entitled according to that rule. For each dispute there is either a rule or else a rule can be derived. The existing or potential rule becomes both the common denominator and the universal solvent of social conflict. The legal system takes on the trappings of a kind of overall regulator in that it assures us of a single authoritative rule for each dispute as well as an internally consistent system of rules. In sum, the students' professional concerns and training are indissolubly linked to the world around them, and the legal paradigm makes it possible to order and more generally to make sense out of what is to the uninitiated hopelessly amorphous.

13. Ibid., p. 80.

But even granting a world view, in what sense does it narrow the vision? Like all world views the legal paradigm is basically a focusing device. Rather like a complex of roads through the wilderness, it provides both guidance at a particular point along the way and a sense of confidence and understanding about the entire area. But like a road map the law game simplifies as it explains. The sense of mastery conveyed by the paradigm is at least partially an illusion, built as much on what is excluded from the analysis as upon the rigor and logic of the method. One could travel wilderness roads often enough to be able comfortably to dispense with a map and still not know the wilderness lying beyond the asphalt—the real wilderness, after all. Similarly, one could be thoroughly familiar with the overlay of rules which decorates the society and not be very wise in the ways of the world. It is important to recognize, for example, that in the world beyond the case book judicial decisions do not always resolve conflicts. Of course the focusing and simplification remain useful so long as rules and society—or asphalt and wilderness—are not confused. Unhappily, it is all too natural to mistake simplification for clarification and focusing for understanding. Legal education, for its part, seems likely to nurture the confusion.

There is a more fundamental aspect of the problem. The rules that the lawyer learns to read into social relations, it must be understood, are simply a point of view. Indeed, they are just *one* point of view and not a natural property of the world around us. There are many other points of view and each is arguably as persuasive as the law game. To Marxists, human behavior is of course economically determined. The positivist finds the crucial distinction between "is" and "ought." The legal view is no more narrowing than any other unidimensional explanation of the world, and legalists are not unlike other ideologues in their unwillingness to face up to the limitations of their paradigm. All ideologies tend to distort and narrow the vision.

What may make legalism a bit more deluding than some other world views is its covert character. Law professors and lawyers do not believe that they are either encumbered or enlightened by a special view of the world. They simply feel that their legal training has taught them to think logically. In a complex world, they have the intellectual tools to strip a problem, any problem, down to its essentials. They have picked up and are prepared to pass on to their students this instinct for the jugular. But covert or overt, it is a rare bird who shares Dean Goldstein's understanding that the case method simply makes "the lawyer especially skilled in showing the limits and inadequacies of what is proffered by others." [14] This is no mean feat, as generations of students who have had their guts spilled on the floor realize.[15] It is also useful, no doubt, in probing and testing matters of public and business policy. But what is actually nurtured in law school is the more imposing myth of a "lawyer-generalist": "a conceit which converts the accidental fact that the lawyer is an available social handyman, ready to take on a wide variety of complex assignments, into a basis for supposing he has a competence to deal with ever more complex phenomena." [16] Perceptive students can perhaps see through the facade and when they do their indictment is devastating. An instinct for the jugular is clearly evoked:

> But it is still shocking to hear professors dismiss all disciplines except the law as intellectually shoddy and

14. Goldstein, p. 160.

15. Sociologist David Riesman tells us that law professors do not just pick on students but can be every bit as tough on the visiting social scientist. "But, speaking for myself, I must say that the atmosphere of a law school is too abrasive, too cocky, to make an easy colleagueship on matters where the social scientist is apt to feel grave self-doubt—notably, at the frontiers of intellectual work." One cannot help but be reminded of Kennedy's remark about "control," by the remainder of the Riesman quote: ". . . if one is exploring rather new areas . . . then to meet constantly the really quite amiable needling of the skeptical lawman may be tiresome." David Riesman, "Law and Sociology: Recruitment, Training, and Colleagueship," in William M. Evan, ed., *Law and Sociology: Exploratory Essays* (New York: Free Press, 1962), pp. 25–26.

16. Goldstein, pp. 161, 163.

practitioners in other fields as a class of dolts. It is hard for the student not to wince at the air of magisterial self-satisfaction with which professors tend to approach questions *that they know little about.*[17]

The students may wince but apparently not even the discriminating few are immune from the call of the law, from its "great unifying threads—philosophic, moral, and intellectual —which draw apparently disparate areas together and give the law much of its fascination and much of its power."[18] It would seem that the believers still are able to convert the heathen to some measure of faith in the legal paradigm.

PROFESSIONAL RESPONSIBILITY

Just as law school imparts habits of mind which tend to narrow the lawyer's political vision, the accepted standards of professional conduct encourage modes of behavior that narrow the tactical choices open to activist lawyers. The *Code of Professional Responsibility* diverts activist urges away from deliberate, direct, and coordinated political action and channels them instead into piecemeal legal responses to perceived injustices. It is difficult to determine the effective impact of the Code, and I do not mean to impute to it a controlling influence on behavior. There are, however, costs that attach to the violation of professional ethics. Activist lawyers are particularly vulnerable since they are likely to be out of step with the powers-that-be in the profession—that is, with those normally charged with the responsibility for disciplinary proceedings. Moreover, the Code reflects both the fundamen-

17. Kennedy, "How the Law School Fails," p. 72, emphasis added. Again, Kennedy tends to come to conclusions very much like those of David Riesman, who noted, "a professional self-image of omnicompetence" which he attributed in part to the "lawyer's wish to maintain a pattern of practice and teaching in which he can play by ear." Riesman, "Law and Sociology," p. 24.
18. Kennedy, p. 76.

tal predispositions of the legal profession and myth of rights values as well. Practitioners, including activist lawyers, can be expected, therefore, to internalize its message in some measure. The relevant features of the Code for our purposes are: dedicated representation of clients, improving the level of professional skills, and protecting the market for legal services.[19]

Clearly, the lawyer's first and primary responsibility is to the client. The client's interests are to be represented to the best of the lawyer's ability, altogether irrespective of their social implications.[20] In this context, the prominent role of lawyers in the Watergate affair makes sense. As Richard Barnet, a Harvard Law School graduate himself, puts it: "Far from importing legal standards, lawyers who become national security managers are too ready to defer to their client, the state, and to ignore the law or make it up. A lawyer is paid to be a partisan." [21] The problem is compounded when the lawyers in question are without experience in the policy-making process and accustomed to functioning within the restraining influences exerted by the court system. It is not surprising that, to one inexperienced and working for the chief executor of the laws, zealous representation of a client might be difficult to distinguish from service to the law.[22]

19. The discussion which follows draws heavily on the position developed by Raymond Marks et al., *The Lawyer, the Public, and Professional Responsibility* (Chicago: American Bar Foundation, 1972). It is not intended to be a comprehensive analysis or balanced critique of the *Code of Professional Responsibility* but a limited investigation of selected aspects which are germane to the activist bar.

20. "A lawyer should represent a client zealously within the bounds of the law." Canon 7, *Code of Professional Responsibility*, p. 1159. Effective 1 January 1972 (Seattle: Washington State Bar Association). The sole focus of four of the nine canons is responsibility to clients.

21. Richard J. Barnet, *Roots of War: The Men and Institutions Behind U.S. Foreign Policy* (Baltimore: Penguin Books, 1973), p. 56. Barnet was writing well before Watergate about the part played by lawyers in the national security bureaucracy.

22. As two of Egil Krogh's former teachers at the University of Washington Law School wrote of his involvement in the burglary of Daniel Ellsberg's

The difficulty is compounded by the way in which the ordinary lawyer's world tends to be broken down into a multiplicity of individual concerns. The overriding obligation is to serve any parties who come along, provided only that competent service can be rendered, that there is no conflict of interest or illegality, and that the client can afford the lawyer's services. The nature and limits of professional responsibility are nicely conveyed by the following exchange between Anthony Lewis of *The New York Times* and President Nixon's impeachment inquiry lawyer, James D. St. Clair:

> Does a lawyer have a duty to appraise the facts of a case, independent of his client's views? Mr. St. Clair indicates yes. He is an officer of the court, and for example he can never properly use false evidence. But Mr. St. Clair adds, "If you mean his becoming judge and jury himself, obviously no." [23]

Relationships between lawyer and client are, moreover, sealed in discrete compartments by the canon of confidentiality.[24] It is not the lawyer's role to work out the links between the client's difficulties and broader social problems and certainly not the lawyer's role to use a client's case as the

---

psychiatrist: "We neither condone nor excuse what Krogh has done. But we view his situation as a prime example of the tragic case, too frequently found in Mr. Nixon's administration, of an eager and innocent young man corrupted and unsupervised by his superiors." *The Seattle Times*, 14 December 1973, p. A 12.

23. The background of the interview further enhances its relevance to this study. Mr. Lewis begins his column by reminding us that James St. Clair was associated with Joseph N. Welch's dramatic repudiation of Senator Joseph McCarthy during the Army-McCarthy hearings in 1954. "Some people who lived through those days are bewildered at the role Mr. St. Clair is playing now, as President Nixon's lawyer. They wonder how a lawyer who helped repair the American conscience at another bad time can lend his skills to the defense of a man whom they see as today's symbol of political lawlessness." Anthony Lewis, *The New York Times*, 21 February 1974, p. 33.

24. "A lawyer should preserve the confidence and secrets of a client." Canon 4, *Code of Professional Responsibility*, p. 1146.

occasion for dealing with these problems. To do so would
encourage the attorney to think of client needs as means
rather than as ends. If this threat sounds academic and
detached, ponder the common problem of a lawyer with the
choice of getting a client off on a legal technicality or of
fighting the case on an important but problematic point of
principle—like the constitutionality of conspiracy laws or the
limits of police discretion.

The tension between cause and client is a familiar one to
activist lawyers, and they are directed by the Code to look
first to the client's interest. Of course the waters are ordinarily
a good deal muddier than this discussion might suggest.
Activist lawyers can work for causes. The law even provides a
mechanism, the class action suit, which permits an attorney
to plead for a client and for all others in like circumstances. It
remains true, nevertheless, that the Code casts a shadow of
ambivalence over the work of the activist lawyer. The fact
that the lawyer is directed toward the particular and away
from the general inhibits fundamental social inquiry. The
ideal of loyalty to clients may not preclude a concern with
public responsibility or social policy, but it surely diverts
attention and energies.

Quality control of legal services was a central concern and
apparently the organizing animus for the bar: "In other
words, early professional organization in the United States
dealt with only one aspect of professionalism—the acquisi-
tion and improvement of the skill base." [25] What ultimately
emerged are uniform minimum standards, which have developed during the shift from an apprentice system to legal
education in accredited professional schools.[26] The case for
quality control is obvious and there is no need to belabor the
benefits that accrue to the public. Its inhibiting influence on

25. Marks, *The Lawyer, the Public, and Professional Responsibility*, p. 11.
26. For a succinct discussion, see Herbert Jacob, *Justice in America:
Courts, Lawyers, and the Judicial Process* (2nd ed. Boston: Little, Brown,
1972), pp. 43–74.

the activist lawyer is more subtle and indirect but nonetheless unmistakable.

The "pursuit of professional excellence" impinges on activist law in two distinct but related ways. The attention of lawyers is directed away from the profession's conservative implications—its service of precedent on the one hand and the "interests of corporations" on the other. They are instead encouraged to think of the contribution that high quality representation makes to the adversary process and to the legal system more generally. The emphasis on quality control thus feeds into or at least articulates well with the myth of neutrality: "The assumption was, and, we feel, to a large extent is, that the craft of law is employed in a neutral fashion and that it is available to the clients of a firm for whatever legitimate use they might want to make of it." [27] A second implication of the emphasis on professional excellence is that lawyers are likely to think of their capacity for public service entirely in terms of legal skills. Their skills are, at once, a source of expertise and the boundary line of legitimate professional behavior. The activist lawyer who partakes of this ethos is likely to approach problems of public policy in a rather unidimensional fashion—either opposed or insensitive to the full range of political/legal tactics.

Finally, we come to the market concerns of the bar, which cast a kind of entrepreneurial pall over the entire profession. The market is cared for through a series of practices that limit the supply of legal services and maintain their price well above the level that would be established by the free play of competition. Supply is kept in check through control of entry into the profession by way of law school accreditation and bar examinations. In addition, the code is biased against paraprofessionals who might handle routine but remunerative work like the processing of divorces.[28] The reason that such

27. Marks, pp. 252–53.
28. "A lawyer should assist in preventing the unauthorized practice of law." Canon 3, *Code of Professional Responsibility*, p. 1143.

work is remunerative is the minimum fee schedule, which establishes rates for legal services and prohibits price cutting as an unfair competitive practice. Of course, all of these measures are presented as necessary to maintain quality control: "The prohibition against the practice of law by a layman is grounded in the need of the public for integrity and competence of those who undertake to render legal services." [29] Yet it remains true that many more *qualified* students are applying for law school these days than are being admitted and the minimum fee concept is the product of trade association thinking, pure and simple.

> As a start toward internal regulation, the legal profession will have to drop the minimum fee and the self-aggrandizement evident in its definitions of and approach to the unauthorized practice of law. As long as there are clients and interests in need of service and representation, the profession is ill-advised to talk of protecting the public against inadequate representation. The profession's excuses for minimum fee and vigilance against unauthorized practice are weak in any case. The profession should attend to those receiving little or no service.[30]

In this context, the opposition of the American Trial Lawyers to no-fault automobile insurance is simply the latest chapter in the continuing saga of *the bar as trade association.*

There are a number of ways in which the trade association tendencies of the bar create pressures against activist law. Most simply put, lawyers are led to think of their services as a product which is sold rather than as a vital public necessity. Attention is focused on those services that pay rather than on the societal job that has to be done. To reach out to those

29. Canon 3, Ethical Consideration 1, *Code of Professional Responsibility*, p. 1144.

30. Marks, p. 292. See also Lester Brickman, "Expansion of the Lawyering Process through a New Delivery System: The Emergence and State of Legal Paraprofessionalism," *Columbia Law Review* 71 (November 1971): 1177–81.

who might need the "product" by cutting rates or by educating potential clients as to their rights and the opportunities for litigation is deemed unprofessional.[31] Indeed, lawyers who foment litigation are in some jurisdictions liable under barratry laws that were used against NAACP lawyers in the early days of the civil rights movement. The preoccupation with fees reinforces the strong ties between the legal profession and business and monied interests.

It is now time to reflect on this brief glimpse of legal education and professional standards. Our concern is not with the browbeaten student or aggressive professional who plays the game in order to "make it," nor with the professor who has an obvious interest in perpetuating the lawyer-generalist myth, but with the more general appeal of the legal approach and its impact on activism within the profession.

A consideration of the full range of professional socialization reveals two sets of forces working in part at cross purposes. The school experience tends to make lawyers *action-oriented.* They have confidence in their legal skills as tools of analysis and persuasion. These skills enable lawyers to focus complex problems, to defend solutions in a rational and tough-minded fashion, and also to evoke important symbols of legitimacy. Finally, professional life is largely occupied with "doing"—and in particular with making public authorities responsive to the clients' needs. At the same time there is a current of quiescence running through the profession which does not so much prevent activist law as divert and inhibit activist responses. Lawyers are, on the one hand, encouraged to think of the normal pursuit of their calling as tantamount to public service and, on the other, led to believe

31. Lawyers who serve causes and seek clients whose plight both typifies that cause and permits it to be litigated are vulnerable to prohibitions in the Code against solicitation or advertising. See Canon 2, Disciplinary Rules 101–104, *Code of Professional Responsibility,* pp. 1124, 1132.

that many of their activist urges are inappropriate and professionally demeaning. Most members of the profession seem to succumb to these pressures or at least to rationalize their prosperous private practices in professional terms. The remarks of John G. Laylin, a senior partner in Covington and Burling (one of the most powerful of the Washington D.C. law firms) can probably be taken as typical: "Hell, I'm a lawyer, not a reformer. *We* are lawyers. We act as counsel. . . . You know, some of these younger people don't seem to understand the proper role of a lawyer. We're not here to save the world, or to force our own ideas on someone else, but to represent clients." [32] Many lawyers have resisted the profession's call for political quiescence reasonably well, and it is these activist lawyers who concern us. But resistance among activists to professional constraints tends to vary in important and revealing ways. After all, each step away from the professional path carries with it unethical connotations. In the following chapter, the thresholds of professional reluctance will constitute the organizing theme for understanding the objectives, methods, and potential political utility of the activist bar.

32. Quoted in Joseph C. Goulden, *The Superlawyers: The Small and Powerful World of the Great Washington Law Firms* (New York: Weybright and Talley, 1972), p. 52. Italics in the original.

11. THE ACTIVIST BAR:
PROGRAMS AND PROSPECTS

Relatively few lawyers are interested in serving the cause of change. Those who are I refer to as the activist bar.[1] These activist lawyers do not comprise a homogeneous or even a distinct group. There is no consensus among activist lawyers on either methods or goals. Moreover, many who are included divide their time between activist work and conventional practices. To talk about an activist bar is, then, to employ an analytic tool which highlights some basic common ground and helps to explain some important differences.

Activist lawyers share a concern for public policy problems and a willingness to use their legal skills in policy-relevant ways. Generally speaking it can be said that the ordinary practitioner serves clients while the activist lawyer serves causes. The activist lawyer is seeking a new professional role.[2]

1. The lawyers whom I refer to as the activist bar are often characterized as public interest lawyers. There are three reasons that my term is more useful for the purposes of this study. In the first place, public interest lawyers are often, although not uniformly, thought of in relation to consumer, environmental, and poverty law, whereas my concern is with the full range of public policy. Secondly, it is my impression that activist lawyers are not so much guided by a concern with the public interest as by a sense of personal responsibility to act in furtherance of goals and values in which they believe. Finally, the major thrust of the work of these committed lawyers is to provide legal representation for hitherto unrepresented or underrepresented minorities, and whether this reinforcing of pluralist tendencies through support of *special interests* is, in fact, in the *public interest* remains, to my way of thinking, an open question. In short, the public interest characterization misses the point and is misleading as well. For an alternative way of looking at activist lawyers, see Jonathan D. Casper, *Lawyers Before the Warren Court: Civil Liberties and Civil Rights 1957–66* (Urbana: University of Illinois Press, 1973), pp. 71–89.

2. Raymond Marks with Kirk Leswing and Barbara A. Fortinsky, *The*

Activist lawyers tend to identify with and work for "constituencies" whose needs are "anticipated" and, in all likelihood, "shaped." It is, incidentally, in this latter sense that activist lawyers often emerge as *strategists* of rights.

Activist inclinations define important common ground within the activist bar. Three divergent tendencies are discernible, however, and they can be traced in large measure to different levels of involvement with the myth of rights. Traditional activists are most deeply influenced by the myth of rights and most responsive to its signals and values. At the other end of the spectrum are radical activists who ridicule constitutional procedures and generally disavow constitutional values as well. In between, the innovative activists tend to avoid questions of principle and accept or reject plans of action on the basis of a pragmatic assessment of situation and circumstance.

To choose any of the activist paths is to go directly against the grain of the legal profession's conception of professional responsibility. Lawyers, like doctors, have thought of professional responsibility in terms of the excellence of the service provided rather than in terms of who was being served. Clients are neither sought nor chosen. The true professional simply accepts those who come along and are in need of legal representation. Beyond clients, the lawyer's only obligation is to the law, but these obligations are hardly mutually exclusive:

> The traditional view of a lawyer's role . . . relies heavily on the adversary method. . . . He is an advocate. . . . He is interested solely in seeing to it that the interest of the party he represents is as ably advanced as is humanly possible. If this is done—on both sides of any adversary conflict—it follows . . . that the result will be both acceptable and just. . . . In short, the traditional lawyer has seen himself as

Lawyers, the Public and Professional Responsibility (Chicago: American Bar Foundation, 1972), p. 202.

serving the public interest by simply doing his daily job of representing only one side of a controversy. . . . It follows, of course, that no special effort is required to serve the public interest. Service to the public is necessarily a by-product of the adversary system.[3]

So long as lawyers are willing to close their eyes to the fact that the price mechanism of distributing legal services excludes many in the society from representation, they can continue to take comfort in their neutrality. A lawyer may reason "that if he does anything but serve the singular interests of his clients he is disserving the public interest." [4]

The policy preferences of activist lawyers are thus burdened by ideological considerations bound up in the myth of rights and by professional role expectations. All of the activists have escaped some of these constraints; some of them have escaped most of these constraints; but none have completely transcended the tensions between socialization and politically effective legal tactics. In part these pressures are self-imposed. They result from an internalization of values. It is this theme that will predominate in the survey of activist programs in the next section. On the other hand, activist lawyers are also subjected to external pressures. These pressures are generated within the legal profession and in the political system more generally. They are also associated with the myth of rights and with professional standards. As I shall demonstrate, external pressures result in a variety of resource problems that seriously cloud the prospects of the activist bar.

THE RANGE OF ACTIVIST PROGRAMS

The underlying theme of this survey of activist programs is to be found in the interplay of the myth of rights and activist impulses. Activist lawyers have opened their eyes to the

3. Ibid., pp. 9–10.
4. Ibid., p. 10.

inequities of the price system, they have seen through the illusions of neutrality, and they are eager to use their skills to advance their policy preferences. A substantial residue of professional socialization remains, however, even among the radicals. The result is to divert activist lawyers from programmatic, politically sensitive strategies into modes of behavior which bank on the sufficiency of legal tactics alone.

Traditional Activism

Traditional activists rely heavily on the leading case approach. Problems are litigated which provide particularly striking illustrations of either the shortcomings of current constitutional doctrine or else underscore the gap between constitutional doctrine and real world behavior. The hope of traditional activists is that cases will rise as high as possible in the judicial hierarchy. The ultimate goal is a definitive decision by the United States Supreme Court itself. Traditional activists invest in leading case tactics because they believe that authoritative pronouncements by the Supreme Court will alter patterns of behavior in the real world. They believe, in other words, that rights make an important difference—both ethically and politically.

Obviously, traditional activists are heavily caught up in the myth of rights and are well represented in the ranks of activist lawyers. There are two well-known organizations which typify traditional activism and the following discussion will draw exclusively on their experiences. The American Civil Liberties Union (ACLU) and the National Association for the Advancement of Colored People (NAACP) pioneered activist law.[5] Their campaigns have served both as models and as object lessons for others. They have provided the training ground for at least a couple of generations of activist lawyers.

5. See "Private Attorneys-General: Group Action in the Fight for Civil Liberties," *Yale Law Journal* 58 (1949): 574–98. This early effort to come to grips with activist law focuses on the ACLU, the NAACP, and also on the Commission on Law and Social Action of the American Jewish Congress.

They speak, moreover, to values which are deeply ingrained in the legal profession and in the polity as well. Finally, traditional activists still furnish a major portion of the dependable punch of the activist bar as it exists today.

A striking testimonial to the NAACP's commitment to the theory and practice of constitutionalism occurred in Alabama between 1956 and 1962.[6] In 1956 as part of the program of massive resistance to the NAACP's school desegregation victory, the state of Alabama enjoined the NAACP from operating in that state. The organization's response was typical; it battled in the courts. A 1958 victory in the Supreme Court was not enough and it was not until 1962 that legal conflict ended. In the intervening six years the NAACP had appeared before 21 judges in five courts, obtained 67 orders, and spent $25,000 in legal expenses. By the time of its victory the NAACP's Alabama membership had dropped from 27,309 to 29 and its estimated loss in revenue was $200,000. Who won? Was it the NAACP whose right to function was finally vindicated or the state of Alabama which was interested in immobilizing the NAACP during the years of massive resistance? In any case, if the NAACP's belief in the orderly processes of constitutional government was being tested, it could hardly have been found wanting.[7]

The ACLU has not been reluctant to proclaim its commitment to constitutional principles and practices nor to accept the connotations of political neutrality that go with its often-heard claim that "Our real client is the Bill of Rights." [8]

6. A number of studies could be consulted for a systematic consideration of the NAACP: Clement E. Vose, *Caucasians Only: The Supreme Court, the NAACP, and the Restrictive Covenant Cases* (Berkeley: University of California Press, 1967); Langston Hughes, *Fight for Freedom: The Story of the NAACP* (New York: Norton, 1962); and Randall W. Bland, *Private Pressure on Public Law: The Legal Career of Justice Thurgood Marshall* (Port Washington, N.Y.: Kennikat Press, 1973).

7. For details, see George R. Osborne, "The NAACP in Alabama," in C. Herman Pritchett and Alan Westin, *The Third Branch of Government* (New York: Harcourt, Brace, 1963), pp. 149–203.

8. The neutral, nonpolitical character of the ACLU can be best appreciated by leafing through *The Policy Guide of the American Civil Liberties Union*

The ACLU is, of course, often attacked for its left-wing tendencies, but the Union vigorously denies such charges. In response to recent allegations the ACLU published a chilling list of right-wing causes that it had defended during the previous year—including among others the Ku Klux Klan, the National Socialist White People's Party (identified as the Nazi Party of Virginia), and so on.[9] It is probably true, nonetheless, that the ACLU is more heavily engaged on the left. The explanation for this association with left-wing causes, however, in no way calls into question the Union's professed neutrality or its constitutional commitment. It is after all the left wing that is most likely to be harassed by those in power, most likely to require the free services of the ACLU, and most likely to turn toward the ACLU.

Consider by way of corroboration the ACLU's somewhat inconstant connections with the movement against the Vietnam War. Clashes between the "movement" and duly constituted authority have often involved police practices, prosecutorial methods, and statutes of dubious constitutional standing. In addition, our involvement in an undeclared war raises serious constitutional questions about the entire Vietnam venture and carries with it an obvious and more general

---

which was distributed in 1970. Predictably, the great bulk of the guide is devoted to particular constitutional problems. Two more general policies that are relevant to the points developed in this section are No. 515, "Definition of Legal Role and Policy," and No. 523, "Cooperation with Other Organizations." See also Charles Lam Markham, *The Noblest Cry: A History of the American Civil Liberties Union* (New York: St. Martins Press, 1965).

9. For the charges, see Joseph W. Bishop, Jr., "Politics and the ACLU," *Commentary*, December 1971, pp. 50–58. The ACLU's official reply was published in the organization's newsletter. See Nat Hentoff, "Commentary and Carbon Papers: Fantasizing the ACLU," *Civil Liberties*, March 1972, pp. 1 and 4. A book about the ACLU written in 1965 is quite typically dedicated "To those who have made the most significant contributions in the past quarter-century to the development of conscience in the United States . . . with ambivalent thanks." The ambivalence is understandable, given the names listed, which include: Richard M. Nixon, Senator Joseph McCarthy, George Lincoln Rockwell, Robert H. W. Welch, J. Edgar Hoover, and Father Coughlin. Markham, *The Noblest Cry*, p. vi.

threat to constitutional government per se. All this would seem to add up to a strong case for enthusiastic ACLU intervention. As antiwar protest began to spill over, however, into civil disobedience and/or deliberate renunciation of courts, freedom of speech, or constitutional government, serious reservations predictably emerged within the ranks of the ACLU. The result has been only limited and tentative support following intense and divisive internal debate.[10] Jessica Mitford sees the fainthearted support given by the ACLU in the Spock case as part of an historical pattern—a failing of political courage in situations of extreme controversy:

> The ACLU's schizophrenic behavior in the Spock case may come as no surprise to those familiar with the history of the organization over the past few decades. . . .
>
> In the simple old days before the sixties, . . . the main targets of political repression were Communists and their alleged fellow travelers. Some ACLU leaders today concede that all too often, in that critical period, the organization ducked the onerous task of providing legal defense for these controversial individuals.[11]

Perhaps Ms. Mitford is correct in her assessment of ACLU motives. It remains true, however, that theirs is the kind of erratic course on substantive policy matters that is built into the constitutional commitment of the traditional segment of the activist bar.

10. There was, for example, speculation that the resignation of the ACLU executive director, John de J. Pemberton, Jr., grew out of conflicts over the Union's "war policy." *The New York Times* (bylined Martin Arnold), 11 April 1970, p. 1.

11. Jessica Mitford, *The Trial of Dr. Spock* (New York: Knopf, 1969), pp. 269–72 (Appendix 6. "The Role of the American Civil Liberties Union in the Case of the Boston Five"). Just to keep the record straight, both Professor Bishop and Ms. Mitford admit that the ACLU, in the words of Ms. Mitford, "has had and will have periods of greatness as a champion of political freedoms." See also Marlise James, *The People's Lawyers* (New York: Holt, Rinehart and Winston, 1973), pp. 8–14.

In sum, the traditional activists engage in what might be termed partially programmatic litigation. It is litigation with a purpose that transcends the interests of individual clients and is in this way distinguished from normal bar practice. In pursuance of their purposes the traditional activists, moreover, seek clients with suitable cases and pick and choose among clients according to organizational priorities. They thus eschew the "neutrality" which makes money the primary determinant of client choice. Nonetheless, when measured by political rather than professional standards, the departure of traditional activists from conventional paths appears quite modest. They remain wedded in goals and methods to constitutional values and as a consequence engage in a form of political action in which means and ends tend to get equal weighting. The result is behavior which, at least in the short run, may be counterproductive. As a consequence, they often seem to their detractors like the proverbial liberals who know what must be done but whose principles prevent them from doing it. And indeed it seems altogether fair to conclude that they are more responsive to principle than to policy.

Radical Activists

It is often said that there is no such thing as a radical lawyer—that a radical lawyer is a contradiction in terms. Such observations can be taken at a number of levels. They are prescriptions: the radical should not pay the daily tribute to the status quo that is entailed in working among and according to the rules of the established order. They are predictions: the radical, demeaned and frustrated by ritual obeisance before the powers-that-be, will not be able to survive as a lawyer. They are suspicions: the lawyer's role compromises and coopts; the lawyer is by definition not a radical and not to be trusted. Whatever may be the ultimate truth on these matters, the doubts and tensions they imply seem to percolate destructively through the ethos of the many lawyers who are trying to make it as radicals.

In this context, the least costly form of radical legal action is defense of those seen as victims of repression: black radicals, prisoners, antiwar groups, and so on. Of all courses open to lawyers, no other seems less threatening to a radical role and image. In the first place, defense of "movement" notables serves to safeguard a scarce resource, leadership. Some even argue that since trials are so newsworthy, a properly orchestrated defense which plays up the repressive features of the system can be useful in channeling public consciousness and therefore in building a political movement. Victory thus protects leaders; defeat produces martyrs; and either way a politically sophisticated trial strategy pays off in heightened public awareness.

The trouble is that the whole argument can be turned around. If the court convicts, the movement has lost a scarce resource. If there is an acquittal, the public sense of the system's ultimate justness is reinforced. Such reflections cast a shadow over the life of the radical lawyer and probably account for defections from the ranks. In general, however, even radical lawyers are in defense work shielded by the pragmatic streak. The immediate courtroom need is too urgent; the contribution too obvious; and the schedule too crowded to permit immobilizing speculation on the radical purity of the lawyer's role.

Beyond defense work for political victims, radical lawyers seem to have developed no satisfactory legal agenda and in fact are probably not even trying very hard. Initially attracted to legal services programs, they have now generally concluded that "lawyers for the poor can't win": "The more independent and aggressive the neighborhood office, the more likely it is to alienate those very interests it needs to survive." [12] This conclusion is partially based on defeats and

12. Robert Lefcourt, "Lawyers for the Poor Can't Win," in Robert Lefcourt, ed., *Law Against the People: Essays to Demystify Law, Order, and the Courts* (New York: Vintage, 1971), p. 137. Other collections which provide information on radical activists are: Jonathan Black, ed., *Radical*

frustrations, but it stems as well from ideology and, to be more precise, from an unequivocal rejection of conventional views of law and change: "The law is a mechanism for governing which arises out of social contradictions in order to preserve the interests of one class in opposition to others." [13] Short-term gains and long-term failure are the most that they have come to expect from legal processes.

Moreover, legal strategies seem not only useless but positively dangerous. While they can never bring real change, they can produce the illusion of change in the form of momentary gratifications which buy off pressures for fundamental restructuring of the society. Individual problems may be dealt with or attenuated by legal reformers, but the underlying causes of injustice and inequity remain. In short, the radical lawyer tends to see legal strategies directed at social change as counterrevolutionary.

For the serious, self-conscious, and committed radical lawyer, the dilemmas are painful, endless, and inescapable. Beyond the obvious pitfalls of defense work, for example, radical lawyers must confront the risk differential, which tends to alienate them from their clients. It is the client's freedom and well-being that are on the line, not the attorney's. The radical lawyers who seek to share client perils—by joining in the client's disregard of established procedures, for example, or by encouraging the client to make crucial decisions on strategy and tactics—may be jeopardizing their effectiveness as lawyers and thus devaluing *the one unique contribution* they have to offer a political movement: legal skills. Systematic long-range efforts on behalf of prison reform, in defense of basic freedoms, or to ease the burdens

---

Lawyers: Their Role in the Movement and in the Courts (New York: Avon, 1971); Ann Fagan Ginger, ed., *The Relevant Lawyers: Conversations out of Court on Their Clients, Their Practices, Their Politics, Their Life Style* (New York: Simon and Schuster, 1972); and James, *The People's Lawyers.*

13. Kenneth Cloke, "The Economic Basis of Law and State," in Lefcourt, *Law Against the People,* p. 67.

of poverty are clearly out of the question, because they implicate radical lawyers deeply in the system to which they are opposed. The inclinations of the most dogmatic radical lawyers will thus inevitably take them beyond their legal skills.

More pragmatic radicals have learned to live with the contradictions of their professional situation. Arthur Kinoy, for example, urges radical lawyers to dwell less on the purity of their position.

> Is it not a total contradiction to be a "radical" teacher of law, a "radical" lawyer—a contradiction which can only be resolved by exculpatory proclamations that "law is illegal" or hortatory pronunciamentos that the "only struggle is in the streets?"
>
> To these earnest and deeply troubled lawyers I have but one reply. Yes, the "radical" teacher of law, the "radical" lawyer lives, functions, struggles, in the midst of contradictions; his or her life is itself a contradiction. But this should be no shock, no surprise.
>
> Every radical who has honestly attempted to study society, as one great student of society once remarked, not for the purpose of understanding it but for the purpose of changing it, knows that "there is nothing that does not contain contradiction; without contradiction there would be no world." [14]

Still, the only line of action that emerges is defense work which is clouded by the myth of rights.

Defending political clients "also permits the radical lawyer to emerge as the champion of people's liberties which the ruling class is abandoning. It provides a focus for the organizing of massive support among the broadest sections of the people, to whom the protection of the "right" of

14. Arthur Kinoy, "The Role of the Radical Lawyer and Teacher of Law," in Lefcourt, p. 277. The closing lines are from Mao Tse-tung, *On Contradictions.*

American citizens to liberty and justice remains an important question." [15] The myth of rights can be detected not only in the implicit tribute to constitutional values but in the assumption that Americans will respond in significant proportions to the spectacle of rights denied. All this is a far cry from the opportunities for political mobilization implied by the politics of rights. Indeed, they seem much more in line with certain features of "constitutional politics" as described and advocated by the ideologists of the myth of rights.

Of all components of the activist bar the radicals are, nonetheless, the most sensitive politically and the least inhibited professionally. If they cannot be expected to contribute much *as lawyers* to a sustained strategy for change, it is because of a paralyzing tension between their self-conceptions as radicals and the parts they must play as lawyers.

Innovative Activists

While there is a streak of pragmatism among the radical activists, pragmatism is virtually the defining characteristic of the innovators. They are short on theory and eager to act. They seem to have a healthy skepticism about the utility of legal processes and are sensitive to political factors like organization, access, and influence. Finally, they seem to be less preoccupied with professional conceptions of the lawyer's status and role. What is characteristic, then, is a frame of mind with practical, tactical inclinations. If a tactic seems to be working, nurture it; if not, discard it. If it is frowned upon

15. Ibid., p. 289. Professor Kinoy is, I should add, altogether typical of the more pragmatic radicals, who cannot see beyond defense work and are heavily influenced by the myth of rights. Consider William Kunstler's statement in the same volume: "The Anglo-American legal system is, in theory at least, a generally satisfactory institution. It contains all of the ingredients necessary to insure the equitable and egalitarian resolution of conflicts among citizens and between citizens and the state." William M. Kunstler, "Open Resistance: In Defense of the Movement," in Lefcourt, p. 271.

by the profession, so be it. If its long-term consequences are in doubt, that is a bridge to be crossed later. Most significantly, if there are political obstacles, confront them.

It can, of course, be argued that lawyers have always had a reputation for pragmatism, a taste for politics, and an inclination to exercise influence. To some extent, however, they tend to distinguish professional and political roles. Even the Washington law firm with virtually its entire practice focused on government policy and its partners and associates moving back and forth between positions in the bureaucracy and private practice is loath to think about its task as political. According to a partner in the well-known firm of Arnold and Porter: "Once a firm gets to be well established and institutionalized, proficiency is the thing that attracts clients—the notion that this firm can handle matters competently and effectively, regardless of the politics of the Administration." [16] Contrast this characteristic position with that of Gary Bellow, the co-founder of the California Rural Legal Assistance program: "The problem of unjust laws is almost invariably a problem of distribution of political and economic power; the rules merely reflect a series of choices made in response to these distributions. . . . "Rule" change, without a political base to support it, just doesn't produce any substantial result." [17] The target of Bellow's attack was the test case strategy of the NAACP, and his conclusion was that lawsuits should be treated as "vehicles for setting in motion other political processes and for building coalitions and alliances." [18] In sharp contrast, accepted practices call for maintenance of a line between the political and legal activities of the American lawyer. As Roy Wilkins, Executive

16. Quoted in Joseph C. Goulden, *The Superlawyers: The Small and Powerful World of the Great Washington Law Firms* (New York: Weybright and Talley, 1971), p. 143.

17. "The New Public Interest Lawyers," *Yale Law Journal* 79 (May 1970): 1077.

18. Ibid., p. 1087.

Director of the NAACP, put it recently, "Politics and civil rights don't mix." [19] Attorneys often run for office, and traditional activists use litigation to alter the course of public policy, but it is an innovation to construct an integrated campaign comprised of legal, electoral, and other political strategies—an innovation which those with traditional leanings are inclined to oppose.

Innovative programs are found most conspicuously among the ranks of public interest lawyers and within the Legal Services Program, which was a spinoff of the war against poverty.[20] In neither case is the work uniformly innovative. Environmental lawyers, as the work of Joseph Sax suggests, seem to lean heavily on the familiar leading case strategy. The overwhelming mass of legal services energy goes into legal assistance, which a former director, Terry Lenzner, described as follows: "Our philosophy is that we would operate like any other law firm and respond to the needs of the clients." [21] In legal assistance matters the attorney is passive; he does not seek clients and tends to accept those who arrive on a largely first-come, first-served basis. On the other hand, some legal services offices have adopted programs which are much more consistent with the implications of the politics of rights. Not surprisingly, Ralph Nader has been the most innovative of the public interest lawyers, but others have adopted and adapted his initiatives.[22]

Within legal services, law reform is one of the more promising programs. It involves legal assaults on practices

19. *The Seattle Times*, 8 July 1972, p. A 2.
20. The Legal Services Program is a diffuse combination of local, regional, and national components, including about 2,000 lawyers with a budget of roughly $50 million. These lawyers are permitted to serve only those Americans living at or beneath the poverty level and nonprofit groups and organizations. For a comprehensive and current account of the program, see Commerce Clearing House, *Poverty Law Reporter*, vol. 2. Section 8000 is devoted entirely to Legal Services and is kept constantly up to date.
21. *The New York Times*, 29 August 1969, p. 1.
22. "The New Public Interest Lawyers," pp. 1069–1152, particularly 1079–91.

and statuses that have been accepted by the legal world as far back as most people can remember. The twin targets of law reform are the problems of the poor as consumers in the commercial world and in their dependency relations with public bureaucracies. Traditionally, it is the poor who have the obligations and the bureaucrats, landlords, and collection agencies that have the rights and prerogatives.[23] The goals of law reform have been summarized by Cruz Reynoso of the California Rural Legal Assistance program: "We are giving poor people resources to fight their problems in a legal way." [24] Law reform thus gives promise of cumulating. It can, in the first place, convey a sense of efficacy and entitlement. Moreover, insofar as it focuses on public bureaucracies, there is some hope that the statuses gained in court can be translated into material benefits by litigation.

Group representation, another legal services innovation, is potentially the most far-reaching of all the innovative strategies. In its simplest form, however, it entails virtually no departures from conventional house counsel for corporate enterprise. All that is involved is putting legal services attorneys at the disposal of community groups, which they serve in a variety of ways like drafting legislative proposals, initiating litigation, checking contractual agreements, and so forth. This may not seem to be anything special. But such representation can easily blend into mobilization, since the presence of a lawyer lends weight and legitimacy to a community group struggling to establish itself. Legal skills become more like bait than like the tools of the trade as the attorney moves along the spectrum from "house counsel" to organizer. Departures from professional paths of this sort do not go unnoticed, and in the next section we shall consider the political repercussions of movement-building tendencies.

23. Jerome E. Carlin, Jan Howard, and Sheldon L. Messinger, "Civil Justice and the Poor," *Law and Society Review* 1 (November 1966): 9–89.
24. *The New York Times* (bylined Steven V. Roberts), 30 December 1970, p. 29.

Ralph Nader's contribution is best characterized as research and destroy, and it implies a strict policy orientation.
Clients are beside the point. The lawyer's job is to identify a
public policy problem, seek out its causes, and then bring
pressure to bear to solve it. There is not much that can be said
about the first two stages. Problem identification tends to be
absolutely ad hoc and varies widely from lawyer to lawyer
and from place to place. Public interest lawyers are too busy
acting in behalf of the public interest to worry a great deal
about how it is defined. As to seeking out causes, the
appropriate process is obvious: serious research into all
relevant factors, be they technical, political, or legal. Bringing
pressure to bear invites a whole series of tactics which are of
interest primarily because they tend to draw the lawyer into
the political arena. Nader has, of course, sought to mobilize
the public with his published research; his forces have
lobbied Congress and tried to monitor the administration of
federal programs; and there have even been efforts under his
aegis to set up public interest research groups working out of
college campuses.

Clearly, it is this innovative work which is most in keeping
with the message of the politics of rights. The efforts of the
innovators are more sustained than those of the radicals and
thus better suited to movement building. The innovators are,
on the other hand, more comfortable with politics than are
the traditional activists. Of course, politics of rights tendencies are not well developed, nor do they dominate the
behavior of any identifiable body of lawyers. More disheart-
ening than the embryonic character of these tendencies are
the pressures that impinge on all elements of the activist bar
to make the prospects of explicit politicization rather unen-
couraging.

THE PROSPECTS OF THE ACTIVIST BAR

Obviously the activist bar is in flux. Its methods, goals, and
priorities are in doubt and, in my judgment, its prospects are

uncertain. It faces a number of challenges that would be difficult to deal with even if it were more coherent and in better shape internally. In the first place, it is by no means clear that its numbers, which have grown significantly in recent years, will continue to increase or even stabilize. Secondly, there is some reason to believe that opposition, which to date has been modest and episodic, may pick up in the years ahead. Finally, the financial position of the activist bar which has always been precarious will surely be a continuing and probably an increasingly serious problem. All three of these difficulties are tied together in ways which suggest that the survival and political achievements of the activist bar may be inversely related. That is, in order to survive, activist lawyers may have to adopt approaches which will move them farther away from effective political action and will, in addition, make activist work less appealing to potential recruits.

Recruitment

Most observers would probably agree that in recent years the ranks of the activist bar have been swelled by a steadily increasing flow of new law graduates. There are, in addition, defections from the ranks of the established bar—including public figures like William Kunstler, who has of course joined the radical activists, and lesser known attorneys who have moved into public interest law after conventional practice with even the most prestigious firms.[25] Unfortunately, there are no systematic data on the growth of the activist bar.[26] All we know is that legal services and public defender programs

25. Goulden, *The Superlawyers*, chap. 10. Goulden reports on defectors like Charles Halpern and William Dobrivir. Halpern became Director of the Center for Law and Social Policy after having served as associate at Arnold and Porter (Abe Fortas's former firm). Dobrivir was with perhaps the premier Washington firm, Covington and Burling, before going into public interest law on his own.

26. At this writing, Joel F. Handler and Jack Ladinsky are completing a national study of activist lawyers.

have more applicants than they have positions, and that young lawyers seem to flock to Ralph Nader and other public interest opportunities. Even without figures, therefore, we can be sure that recruitment has not been a problem for the activist bar.

But will law schools continue to produce students whose activist inclinations take precedence over their professional aspirations? To what extent has the lure of activist law simply been a passing fashion—the law students' ephemeral response to turmoil elsewhere on the campus and in the society at large? Indeed, in the absence of reliable data, can we even speak with assurance of an upward trend? Similarly, we do not really know how deeply the activist urge has penetrated. The best graduates of the best law schools have been touched—at least according to the recruiters for the top law firms—but what about the other schools where the bulk of American lawyers are educated? Figures on Harvard, Yale, and Virginia do show sharp decreases in the number of students entering private practice in recent years. On the other hand, there are significant variations even among these three schools and as early as the class of 1970 a turn back toward private practice appeared.[27] Although no conclusions can be drawn either way, it would be prudent not to discount the curricular and professional pressures which may in the long run make the apparent activist trend of the late sixties seem like an aberration or at most a tiny tributary of the mainstream of American law.

And what of those who have already chosen and will in the

27. "Harvard dropped from 54 percent in 1964 to 41 percent in 1968; Yale from 41 percent in 1968 to 31 percent in 1969; and the University of Virginia, from 63 percent in 1968 to 54 percent in 1969. For the class of June 1970 these rates were reversed. At Harvard the percentage of students entering private practice rose dramatically." Marks, *The Lawyer, the Public and Professional Responsibility*, p. 206. See also Rita J. Simon, Frank Koziol, and Nancy Joselyn, "Have There Been Significant Changes in the Career Aspirations and Occupational Choices of Law School Graduates in the 1960's," *Law and Society Review* 8 (Fall 1973): 95–108.

future choose the activist path? How enduring a commitment is it reasonable to expect? According to Derek Bok, former dean of the Harvard Law School and now president of Harvard University, most of the activists will sooner or later drift back into the mainstream.

> I suspect that these later classes will not deviate very far from their predecessors when the time comes to choose a *permanent job*. Despite the sincere interest of many students in social service and the advocacy of unpopular causes, the alternatives to the law firm are unlikely to attract them in the end. . . .
>
> In the end I suspect that the impact of the current generation on the law firms will be useful and that it will occur with much less turmoil and unrest than most leading law schools have experienced. By the time students reach a firm they will be a bit older. Their probing and questioning will take place in an environment where the practical limits that the world imposes will be far more evident than they can be in school or classroom.[28]

Surely there are a number of temptations that the new lawyers must resist and a great many burdens they must bear. Perhaps the most sobering experience is the sheer drudgery of the routine work they must do and the depressing conditions in which they find themselves. "Guys coming out of law schools see it as a very romantic thing—to go out and change the world through litigation; and soon they find out, however, that it isn't so romantic. *It's just a lot of hard work.*"[29] There is, of course, some work which is intellectually challenging and personally enticing—most obviously, the political trial or the pioneering test case in which the attorney is "asserting

28. Derek Curtis Bok, "New Lawyers in Old Firms," *The New York Times*, 3 February 1971, p. 37. Italics added.

29. Anonymously quoted in Marks, *The Lawyer*, p. 211. Italics in the original.

rights that have never been asserted before." However, the
great preponderance of effort, at least in legal services, is in
"classic individual service" which accounts for "95 percent of
our caseload." There are satisfactions even in the routine: "It
has to do with knowing you aren't ripping off someone . . . it
is a very satisfying job in some ways." [30] On the other hand,
grinding out another divorce or dealing with a repossession is
not just routine, it also carries with it the frustrations of
Sisyphus. Life on a treadmill is not very rewarding—all the
less so when one is confronted with conditions which are
depressing in the extreme. Some may find themselves reacting
with hostility to their clients, like the young Chicago public
defender who began by pleading for a job: "Don't even pay
me. Give me a dollar a year. I just want to work." He ended
up hating his job, contemptuous of the criminal justice
system, despising his clients, and looking for a quiet practice
in Florida. "When I was a kid a guy would stick you up, take
the money and run. Now they'll *kill* you. Those f---ing kids
will kill you." [31] The Public Defender Program may be a
special problem, and Connie Xinos may be atypical. No
doubt there will be those who can endure and perhaps even
thrive, but how many—and for how long?

The most committed of the activists are likely to be
tempted by increasingly radical alternatives while less constant souls will be drawn back toward the profession. Among
the radical activists there is, of course, a momentum which
moves them toward the brink of law. For others, the
temptations of the profession are at least as strong. As a
matter of fact, most of those who comprise the activist bar are
only "internal emigrants," who have never really left the
mainstream. They remain as associates or partners in private

30. *The New York Times* (bylined Juan M. Vasquez), 6 July 1972, p. 17.
The quotes are, respectively, from Frank Duggan, Director of Operations for
the Federal Legal Services program; Robert G. Monroe, Director of the
Milwaukee program; and Jerome Morris of the Washington, D.C., office.
31. "Justice on Trial," *Newsweek*, 8 March 1971, pp. 28–32. Italics in the
original.

firms while volunteering time to the ACLU and to environmental organizations, or while working out of store front law offices and public interest departments set up by their firms. Indeed, many of the top firms in recent years have found it useful in recruiting to project an aggressive public interest image to new graduates. The most thorough and systematic study of public interest work among private firms, however, strikes a skeptical note:

> It is important to point out that rhetoric about public interest work is the basic currency of exchange between the students and the firms, but the actual level of public activity in the law firms, for both those who do the hiring and those who are hired, in many instances does not support the weight of the rhetoric.[32]

When everything is added up—the tentative commitment, the ambiance of the big firm, and the financial concerns of smaller firms—there would seem to be a strong likelihood that lawyers and firms will move quietly and almost imperceptibly out of activist roles.

Opposition

The "if you can't beat 'em, coopt 'em" tendencies just discussed will probably comprise the activist bar's greatest threat in the long run. Even the more overt opposition seems to be directed at forcing activist lawyers into conventional paths rather than putting them in direct jeopardy. Opponents tend to be restrained, whatever their underlying goals may be, by the partial immunity attaching to legal action.

The intensity of opposition is directly proportional to the unpopularity of the cause that is served, but opposition can be shaped and deflected by cautious and conventional action programs. Ralph Nader, who is attacking consumer exploitation by big industry, seems to enjoy backing by a "lopsided

32. Marks, *The Lawyer*, p. 208.

majority of the American people." [33] In contrast, the NAACP
was the target of enormous hostility, at least in the South.
Today, radicals take most of the heat. The ACLU presents a
somewhat different picture since it has ordinarily remained at
arm's length from the causes of its various clients and has
taken refuge in the neutrality of its permanent client, the Bill
of Rights. Since the ACLU defends dissidents it still has
opponents, but the opposition is muted and diffuse compared
to assaults of earlier decades on the NAACP and current
attacks on radicals. The radicals in particular invite intense
and unrefracted opposition by their uncompromising identification with the goals, methods (even extralegal), and life
styles of the "movement." And of course the radical lawyer
who participates fully in the "movement" is vulnerable to the
full range of sanctions imposed against those who are
perceived as enemies of the existing order.

The problems of the publicly funded Legal Services
Program are particularly interesting, because they reveal
quite clearly the pressures that can be effectively mounted
against both law reform and movement building—in short,
against the most promising signs of innovation. As Fred
Graham, former legal writer for *The New York Times*, put it:
"Many persons seem to cringe at the thought of the federal
government financing litigation against state and local governments—especially if the result is to raise the local tax bite
to support the poor." [34] Among those who have cringed are
former Governor Claude Kirk of Florida, former Vice
President Spiro T. Agnew, and California Governor Ronald
Reagan. Vice President Agnew claimed that he was not
against the program as such but objected because it had gone
"way beyond the idea of a governmentally funded program to
make legal remedies available to the indigent and now

33. "The Louis Harris Survey," in *The Seattle Times*, 29 March 1971, p. A
15.
34. *The New York Times* (bylined Fred P. Graham), 28 December 1969,
Section IV, p. 6.

expends much of its resources on efforts to change the law on behalf of one social class—the poor." [35] The altogether stirring list of opponents is no doubt something of a consolation to those like New York City Legal Services Program Director Lester Evens who "measure[s] our success by the amount of attacks on us." [36]

These attacks cannot, however, be laughed off, since they are taking their toll. The innovative features of legal services are being systematically cut back, so as to purposefully and, in my judgment, effectively rob the program of any potential it might have for political mobilization. In the middle of 1973 new guidelines were issued which virtually obliterated the innovative character of the program. Directors were instructed as follows:

1. "Law reform will no longer be a primary or separate goal of the program or the chief criterion in evaluating or refunding projects." [37]
2. Legal assistance to groups is to be on an ad hoc basis only and is not to include help in organizing. No legal assistance is to be provided for any groups involved in "political action, lobbying, violent or disorderly disobedience, or other unlawful or improper conduct." [38]
3. Educational activities are not to include programs "for the sole purpose of apprising eligible persons of their legal rights and obligations, and of the opportunities for legal assistance available . . . through the Legal Services Program." Nor are there to be any projects which "have as their purpose or probable result the organizing of groups for political action . . ." or a series of specified organizing activities like strikes or boycotts.[39]

35. *The New York Times* (bylined Juan M. Vasquez), 8 July 1972, p. 12.
36. *The New York Times* (bylined Juan M. Vasquez), 6 July 1972, p. 17.
37. *Poverty Law Reporter*, 2:9787.
38. Ibid., p. 9788.
39. Ibid., p. 9792.

Similar kinds of restrictions are included in a bill to establish a Corporation for Legal Services, which has been under consideration for a long time.[40]

Regardless of how the current legislative controversy ends, the handwriting is on the wall. Even those who defend the program tend to support it in rather conventional terms. Consider the response of *The New York Times* to an earlier legislative assault by California Senator Murphy against one of the most innovative projects, the California Rural Legal Assistance program: "The irony is that the 1800 lawyers in O.E.O. programs all over the United States are working not against but within the legal system. They have taught hundreds of thousands of indigent clients to take their grievances into the courts instead of the streets." [41] The line of argument taken by the *Times* implies that the program's best defense is not to be too offensive. The safest path is legal assistance and, more generally, tactics responsive to professional standards. Even in those somewhat brighter days the

40. H. R. 7824, *U.S. Congressional Record* (unbound), 93d Cong. 2d Sess., 1974, 120:H3787–96. See also American Bar Association, "The Corporation for Legal Services," Joint Information Report (unpublished), 131 pp.

41. *The New York Times* (editorial comment), 29 November 1969, p. 32.

42. The response of the legal profession to legal services has been mixed. The American Bar Association has consistently defended the program, but at the state and local levels there has been significant opposition—including law suits aimed at enjoining legal services from operating. See *Poverty Law Reporter*, 2:9151–68. It is understandable that the top and the bottom of the legal profession would not see eye to eye. The view from the top is in part conditioned by the improved public service image that the profession gains as the scales of justice are put in somewhat better balance. The small practitioner with his eye on the market would obviously prefer a "judicare" program which provided public money to indigents for legal service at rates consistent with the profession's minimum fee schedule. Legal services, in contrast, may be chipping away at the small practitioner's client base if those with some financial resources are served. The legal services attorney who is willing to work for modest wages is, in addition, undermining the price of legal skills. As a lawyer who was a member of the board of directors of one local program put it in an interview with a researcher: "Frankly, I'm getting a trifle 'fed up' with the amount of time I am being asked to consume relating to the history of an organization that has practically ruined the income base I

program ordinarily took that safe path. A commission set up to investigate charges against the CRLA concluded that "the function of the CRLA is to serve the rural poor, not as union organizers, advisors, or negotiators, but as a law firm concerned with legal matters." Commission recommendations looked a good deal like the mid-1973 guidelines.[43] To steer clear of the controversial may protect the program from extinction. But the political utility of the program will be severely curtailed and eventually the services, or at least the dedication, of the most committed young lawyers will certainly be lost.

Financing

Of all the threats to the growth and viability of the activist bar, none is so serious and immediate as its own precarious financial condition.[44] The activist bar is more or less uniformly functioning on behalf of those portions of the population without much money. Even if lawyers are willing to work for much less than the going rate, they still must support themselves and pay the costs of litigation. The cost of the NAACP's litigation program which culminated in the *Brown* decision is estimated at $200,000.[45] Court costs, support services in the law office, research, and travel are all essential parts of effective legal action and mean that a good firm cannot run on a shoestring. At least one commune found that it could not do first-rate work without capable legal

spent 15 years establishing." Harry P. Stumpf, "The Legal Profession and Legal Services: Explorations in Local Bar Politics," paper delivered at the Sixty-sixth Annual Meeting of the American Political Science Association, September 8–12, 1970, p. 13. See also Mark Soler, "Legal Assistance Is Dying in New Haven," *Yale Review of Law and Social Action* 3 (Fall 1972): 9–18.

43. *Poverty Law Reporter*, 2:9153–54.

44. The best discussion of this problem is in "The New Public Interest Lawyers," pp. 1105–19.

45. Samuel Krislov, *The Supreme Court in the Political Process* (New York: Macmillan, 1967), pp. 41–42.

secretaries and ended up paying the secretaries more than the attorneys.[46]

Membership dues and fund raising drives are the closest thing to a proven plan. The NAACP and the ACLU have supported their programs reasonably well over a long period of time by these methods, and solicitation will probably turn out to be the chief source of funds for environmental programs. The most obvious consequence of such methods is a kind of hand-to-mouth operation, which diverts an enormous and continuing amount of energy from substantive work. There is also reason to doubt that this model can be used "successfully" by the activist bar in general. All the successful groups have worked on behalf of a cause with which middle class liberals with money could identify. To achieve even the uncertain stability of the ACLU and the NAACP, in other words, requires permanent association with mainstream American values and aspirations and a willingness to avoid rocking the boat too vigorously. Middle class reformers may flirt with more militant options, but a reliable financial base calls for a more permanent grip on bourgeois affections.

Some activist lawyers look to self-supporting firms as a way of establishing independence and security, but the evidence to date indicates that there is an inadequate financial base for the more challenging opportunities. Small firms and individual practitioners can use a traditional practice to finance activist efforts, and if the new graduates do change the temper of the profession such efforts will become increasingly common. With the modest resources available to them, these lawyers may be able to provide "legal assistance." They will, however, hardly be in a position to take on major corporations, government bureaucracies, or settled judicial precedent in a sustained fashion.

46. "The New Public Interest Lawyers," p. 1118.

Only the big firms are in a position to provide support for systematic campaigns, but the pro bono effort of the established firms is suspect. Even these days when such work is fashionable, the big firms have not so much increased the effort as altered the delivery system. Instead of encouraging individual associates to work on their own, the firm now identifies itself with the pro bono work. Some fear that as the fashion passes even these modest efforts "will, over time, diminish." [47] Moreover, these firms are very cautious and tend to prefer low-profile legal assistance programs that do not endanger relationships with their corporate clients:

> The law firms scrutinize the public interest client in a more searching manner. Threats are seen, conflicts are imagined or manufactured. At the intake session the unseen regular client is a silent partner, a role he does not have in the usual course of business. [48]

Only Ralph Nader, apparently building on his successful damage suit against General Motors and his own reputation, has managed to finance large-scale operations. Nader's name and reputation are his own and carefully guarded. Others do, however, see some hope in extending the "GM technique" through litigation with opportunities to claim damages or attorney fees. Such possibilities exist in the consumer and environmental fields, for example, but they remain largely untested. [49]

Of course foundations do have the funds to support imposing programs, and at its best foundation funding can be a very attractive arrangement. Foundations have been receptive to innovation and ordinarily the money comes with relatively few strings attached. Unfortunately, foundations are not reliable over the long haul, and already there is evidence that activist legal programs are no longer in fashion.

47. Marks, *The Lawyer*, p. 265.
48. Ibid., p. 260.
49. "The New Public Interest Lawyers," p. 1118.

Moreover, the foundations see their function as launching social experiments rather than sustaining them for an indefinite period of time. As foundation funds dry up, the activist lawyer can find himself with a purpose and a program but no dependable income and no money-raising experience. Consider the Project for Corporate Responsibility, initiated by Nader money to take on corporate enterprise and particularly General Motors. After two unsuccessful efforts to enlist stockholders in the cause, the project—even with some supplemental grants from other foundations—ran out of money. The director, Phil Moore, remained optimistic about his program but not about financing: "But it's a war of attrition—think of it, $120,000 it would take us to put out one mailing to GM shareholders, and we have the rent due two days ago and I'll be damned if I know what we're going to do unless some foundation springs for bread." [50] Some foundations have been more dependable over the long haul. Midas International, for example, has been willing to sustain the successful and enterprising Chicago firm, Businessmen for the Public Interest.[51] Taken as a whole, however, the foundations seem an inconstant and decreasing resource.

Finally we come to public funding, which at least in relative terms is generous and predictable. The Legal Services Program has achieved in a few years a degree of apparent stability that it took the NAACP and the ACLU decades to build. Moreover, the intent and inertial tendencies of government programs suggest both staying power and potential for growth. The drawback of government funding is also obvious and has already been considered. When the government pays the bills, independence is limited by the strength and nature of the protective political coalition that can be mobilized. Programs must therefore be formulated and implemented with an eye on the political climate.

50. Quoted in Goulden, *The Superlawyers*, p. 372.
51. Marks, *The Lawyer*, pp. 161–63.

The future prospects for the activist bar appear to be decent but hardly stirring. None of the three indicators—recruitment, opposition, and financing—points in a clearly expansive direction. Taken individually, they suggest modest growth at best. Taken together, the reading is a less promising trade-off of quantity for quality. So long as the activists move in traditional paths, opposition will be checked and money will probably be available. With more enterprising activism, opposition is likely to increase and funds dwindle. Even this trade-off may not be possible, since in the long run the activist bar will be attractive to young lawyers only so long as it projects an image of vigorous accomplishment. Needless to say, as activist law begins to look like a treadmill or a dead end, those committed to change will gravitate elsewhere and those who follow the fashions will probably drift back into more conventional professional practices.[52]

Admittedly, these forecasts do not take into account the developing ethos of public responsibility that some observers sense in the profession. If such changes do occur they will probably be a long time in coming. They will be dependent on significant changes in legal education and will have to await the day when this new breed of lawyer is able to have a significant impact on the profession. To change a fundamental social institution like the law is necessarily a slow process, even under the best conditions.

Moreover, the ethos of public responsibility that I expect to develop will in all probability take a conventional tone. Its goal will be to make the adversary system work by providing more equal representation to all parties in legal disputes. If the center of gravity of the profession should shift even this

52. The frustrations of the poverty lawyer are nicely chronicled in Samuel Krislov, "The OEO Lawyers Fail to Constitutionalize a Right to Welfare: A Study in the Uses and Limits of the Judicial Process," *Minnesota Law Review* 58 (December 1973): 211–45.

far, there will no doubt be a spinoff of more radical ideas and energies. The climate would then prove more favorable to innovative activism. The difficulty with such projections—in addition to the fact that they take us into the distant future—is that they rest on a very ahistorical view of the legal profession.

This is not the first time that the winds of change have been detected. In the thirties legal education underwent a searching reexamination and young lawyers with a mission began to emerge from law schools. The profession was, however, equal to the challenge. Legal education continues to respond to cases and doctrines, and the new breed of the thirties are the "superlawyers" of the sixties and seventies. Will it be different this time? Clearly it can be, but in the absence of more persuasive evidence, I for one would be reluctant to bet against the resilience of the legal profession.

Epilogue

12. THE POLITICAL RELEVANCE OF LEGAL RIGHTS

The purpose here is to put the basic themes of the study into a broader political context in order to better understand the relationships between legal rights and political change. A brief review of the basic themes will be followed by consideration of the question implicit in this entire endeavor: Is it sensible to think about political change in terms of a *strategy* of rights?

Looking Back

Law in the United States has two realities. In its familiar form, the law is palpable; it appears as formal rules, official institutions, and the like. The ideological existence of the law is more elusive; it takes shape in the mind, and is a reflection of and a reaction to the law's more palpable presence. The political presence of the law is to be found in the interaction between these separate realities.

The myth of rights is, of course, the ideological manifestation of law. It encourages us to associate rights with social justice. The myth also suggests that rights are timeless and can thus serve as guides to change. Finally, according to the myth of rights, the legal processes of governance offer effective protection to the rights of Americans. We are, in sum, led to believe that legal processes deserve to play and do in fact play an important *independent* role in American politics.

Available research casts doubt on the descriptive validity of the myth of rights. At all points, law and politics are inextricably intertwined and in this combination politics is

the senior partner. Laws are delivered to us by the dominant
political coalition as are the judges and other officials
responsible for interpretation and implementation. As a
consequence our rights are always at risk in the political
arena and therefore provide very little independent leverage.

Law thus serves the status quo in a kind of dual capacity.
Legal processes are closely linked to the dominant configurations of power. At the same time, in its ideological incarnation, the law induces acquiescence in the established order by
suggesting that the political system is beneficent and adapta-
ble.

It is true, nonetheless, that there are some residual opportunities for change associated with the law. The politics of
rights indicates that the American system is responsive to
constitutional values—albeit imperfectly and circuitously.
Insofar as rights are respected, the system is relatively open
and subject to a degree of popular control. Litigation can,
moreover, be of some use in protecting these features of the
system. This scaled-down, defensive version of the myth of
rights is, however, only *one* thing that the politics of rights has
to tell us. The more general message of the politics of rights
has to do with political mobilization.

Looking Ahead

The politics of rights provides a new perspective on the
political utility of legal rights. From this perspective, it is
immediately clear that a *strategy* of rights is not really
feasible. Only those who accept the myth of rights could think
seriously about an approach to change which is based
exclusively on rights. Rights are no more than a political
resource which can be deployed, primarily through litigation,
to spark hopes and indignation. Rights can contribute to
political activation and organization, thus planting and
nurturing the seeds of mobilization in ways that were
discussed in Chapter 9. Mobilization thus emerges from this

perspective as the strategy, litigation as a contributory tactic, and rights as a source of leverage.

With mobilization as the centerpiece, it is immediately clear that legal tactics cannot be judged in isolation. Their utility is derived from mobilization and cannot transcend the opportunities inherent in that strategy. Moreover, effective mobilization is surely not the automatic consequence of deploying rights. So far, all that has been established is that legal tactics can make a contribution to mobilization. The extent and circumstances of that contribution remain to be considered. The strategy of mobilization and the contribution of rights will be explored in the next two sections. The remainder of the chapter will focus on the *peculiar* advantages of the legal approach to political mobilization.

MOBILIZATION AND PLURALISM IN THE AMERICAN POLITICAL ARENA

The promise of mobilization can be best appreciated in light of the distinction that Murray Edelman makes between symbolic and concrete uses of politics. Most Americans, according to Edelman, participate in politics only in a symbolic sense. They are not so much users of politics as they are used by politics.

> For most men most of the time politics is a series of pictures in the mind, placed there by television news, newspapers, magazines, and discussions. The pictures create a moving panorama taking place in a world the mass public never quite touches, yet one its members come to fear or cheer, often with passion and sometimes with action.[1]

Symbolic politics are, in effect, manipulative, and they form

1. Murray Edelman, *The Symbolic Uses of Politics* (Urbana: University of Illinois Press, 1967), p. 5.

the principal link between most citizens and "their" government. Only for a relative few in the society is politics concrete and direct; examples of these instrumental uses are "the work of the professional politician who uses politics to get jobs and votes; the maneuvers of the businessman who uses it to get profitable contracts or greater latitude in his economic activities; the activity of the local reform group out for better schools, playgrounds, and sewers." [2] Increasing participation in concrete politics may therefore be reasonably thought of as a useful way to reshape the political arena.

This conclusions rests on a pluralist view òf the American political arena—one which assumes that well-organized interests can effectively compete for the rewards that politics has to offer. It does not, however, presuppose, and in fact casts doubt on, other assumptions associated with a strict pluralist view. For one thing, Edelman's perspective lends a hollow ring to whatever consensus emerges from pluralist bargaining. Most of those in the general population who have ostensibly acceded to that bargain have no real picture of what they have agreed to. Indeed, their attention has been redirected from the concrete rewards of politics to its symbolic gratifications. Consider the matter of financing social programs like public education:

> Here the symbol of "free" education and other benefits, the complexity of the revenue and administrative structure, and the absence of organization have facilitated the emergence of highly regressive payroll, property, and head taxes as the major sources of revenue. Thus, business organizations, which by and large support the public schools that provide their trained personnel and the social security programs that minimize the costs of industrial pensions, pay relatively little for these services, while the

2. Ibid., pp. 10–11.

direct beneficiaries of the "free" programs pay a relatively high proportion of the costs.[3]

The silent majority is not simply short of information. The problem is that the information made available to them is tendentious and misleading. The bargain finally struck is certain to transcend the comprehension of most Americans and likely to be at their expense unless their concrete needs are effectively represented in the intense competition of interest group pluralism.

Two additional reservations about the conventional pluralist vision of American politics are suggested by Edelman's work. First, pluralism's promise of nonviolent resolution of political conflict is stood on its head by the symbolic perspective. What Edelman tells us is that political conflicts are only "resolved" in the arena of concrete politics where actual bargaining takes place. In the symbolic arena, conflicts are masked. As a result, the potential for violence is sublimated but not neutralized. Violence can and often does break out once the legitimating veil has been lifted. People tend to become violent if they become conscious of shared deprivation, but have not yet developed organizational capabilities for functioning effectively in the arena of concrete politics.

> Resort to violence as a form of militant protest is apparently stimulated by the absence of formal organization among the disaffected, though it is widely supposed that the converse is true: that the unorganized are likely to be docile or ineffective and the organized a threat.[4]

Secondly, since symbolic uses of politics induce quiescence and thwart organization, many interests necessarily go unrepresented in the bargaining process. The political arena in

3. Ibid., p. 42.
4. Murray Edelman, *Politics as Symbolic Action: Mass Arousal and Quiescence* (Chicago: Markham, 1971), p. 137.

which the material rewards of politics are distributed does
not, in other words, reflect anything like the full range of
legitimate interests. It is not, as the pluralists tend to argue, a
microcosm of the American society.

Mobilization is of course no guarantee against manipulation. Politically mobilized groups are not immune from
seductive symbols, which history tells us are often employed
within groups by their own leaders. The concrete goals of
organized labor are, for example, heavily influenced by the
symbols of "welfare capitalism," which are regularly employed by labor leaders to shape the perceptions of the
American workingman.[5] Symbolic and concrete participation
are by no means mutually exclusive. Nonetheless, political
organization does bring the membership one step closer to
concrete politics. Just how much closer depends on both the
strength and the participatory quality of the organization.

The fact remains that access to the material benefits of
politics has invariably been associated with a degree of
mobilization and with effective organization. Ordinarily, the
initial stages of mobilization have been accompanied by some
violence—official and unofficial—in defense of the status quo
as well as protest violence on behalf of new configurations of
power and a new distribution of benefits.[6] Once new organizations have been acknowledged as legitimate participants
in the political process, however, violence is ordinarily replaced by bargaining rituals. These rituals often project an
aura of bitter confrontation, as between labor and manage-
ment. In fact, ritualized conflict is symptomatic of accommo-

5. As Edelman points out, there are no necessary connotations of
deception attaching to the symbolic cues provided by organization leaders.
"There is no implication here that elites consciously mold political myths and
rituals to serve their ends. Attempts at such manipulation usually become
known for what they are and fail. What we find is social role taking, not
deception." Edelman, *Symbolic Uses of Politics*, p. 20.

6. For a survey of American political history from this general point of
view, see Richard E. Rubenstein, *Rebels in Eden: Mass Political Violence in
the United States* (Boston: Little, Brown, 1970).

dation, commitment to the existing order, and therefore to a mutually acceptable distribution of burdens and advantages.[7]

The guiding premise of this summary inquiry is, then, that effective organization can make a difference. For the well-organized, politics at the very least ceases to be only a "parade of abstractions" and takes on the trappings of a real contest over scarce resources. Before going on to consider the distinctive advantages of the rights-mobilization tandem, let us take a careful look at the relationship between them.

LEGAL RIGHTS AND POLITICAL MOBILIZATION

Legal tactics do not by any means assure political mobilization. For those in the society who are not caught up in constitutional values, the call of the law will be rather feeble. Conversely, for those who are responsive, the legitimating tendencies of the myth of rights will be particularly difficult to penetrate. Given additional variations according to issue area, it is clear that legal tactics are no panacea. Much will obviously depend on how effectively rights are employed. Even under the best circumstances and with the most creative leadership, however, it is wisest to think of rights as an ancillary tactic to be used in combination with other approaches to political mobilization.

Acculturated Americans may be moved by legal tactics, but will they be mobilized? Those who are most heavily committed to American values are also most likely to be diverted from mobilization by symbolic victories. The statute or the judicial decision may well be sufficient. The myth of rights has, after all, wondrous capacities for reassurance. Failures of implementation are shaped by the myth to look like aberrations, and manifest breakdowns are read as learning experiences. Finally, acculturated citizens with a

7. On the process of ritualization and cooptation, see Edelman, *Politics as Symbolic Action*, chap. 2.

stake in order are likely to have both conscious and subconscious reasons to resist awakening to problems and injustices.

The utility of legal tactics with alienated subcultures is still less clear, because these groups are in a profound sense living in a different world.

> People who inhabit the West Side are not simply poor Americans, who may be viewed as deficient aspirants to affluent American ways of life. Rather, their ways of looking at the social world, their ways of treating one another, the very nature of their knowledge and intelligence, are not the same as those of the America portrayed in the mass media.[8]

The relevance of rights is dependent on some combination of experience and socialization. If constitutional values have never been internalized, the myth of rights will not provide a very inspiring set of political aspirations. Similarly, if rights have no correspondence to daily experience, then hopes will not be kindled by legal victories nor will indignation be aroused when rights are not realized.

The subtle difficulties of mobilization underscore the importance of effective leadership, but the "natural" leaders —that is activist lawyers—are likely to be a mixed and uncertain asset. Indeed, for a number of reasons, activist lawyers may turn out to be the hidden enemies of effective legal tactics.

Activist lawyers tend to be ill-equipped for and (therefore?) ill-disposed toward mobilization. In the first place, activist lawyers who are caught up in their legal world view will be inclined to think in terms of a strategy of rights—that is, exclusive reliance on litigation and its direct payoffs. They will be uncomfortable with the manipulation of rights and particularly ill at ease with the extralegal tactics that will

8. William W. Ellis, *White Ethics and Black Power: The Emergence of the West Side Organization* (Chicago: Aldine, 1970), p. 100.

inevitably accompany mobilization. And how effective will middle class lawyers be with alienated groups living different life styles and responding to different cultural values?

Only a man who has been raised in that way of life, who has been socialized to its norms, and who at the same time has the intelligence and sensitivity to be able to communicate to both ways of life—the mainstream and the West Side—only this kind of man can adequately mobilize and lead the poor black in contemporary urban America.[9]

Finally, there is now and will continue to be a shortage of activist lawyers. There are lawyers for most causes, perhaps, but surely not enough for any of them. In many areas their numbers are woefully weak; they are just not uniformly or dependably available across the full spectrum of public policy needs.

Despite all these obstacles, there is evidence to indicate that legal tactics can be useful. The civil rights experience provides the clearest demonstration that legal tactics—even with reluctant legal leaders—can release energies capable of initiating and nurturing a political movement. But clearly legal tactics are only part of the story of the civil rights coalition and the rebirth of black politics. Nor would it be wise to generalize on the basis of these deeply felt racial matters. When issues emerge which are equally charged with emotion, perhaps legal tactics could work just as well. When issues are less ripe, legal tactics might be capable of doing no more than sparking some initial interest or contributing marginally at later stages.

All this leaves us with a sense of both the opportunities and limitations of legal tactics. If the emphasis has been on limitations, perhaps that is just as well, for it underscores the crucial importance of thinking about legal tactics in combination with other modes of political action. On the other hand,

9. Ibid., pp. 99–100.

there are mobilizing opportunities, and my goal is not to obscure them but simply to offer a balanced view.

Legal tactics are likely to work best in connection with relatively severe deprivations and among groups which are reasonably well socialized. In those situations where deprivation and socialization are found together, legal tactics may well be the most promising approach. This argument applies both to those who are the victims of deprivation and perhaps with somewhat less force to latent sympathizers among their fellow citizens. The obstacles are more serious with alienated subcultures. At some point, they are simply beyond the call of the law and likely to respond instead to appeals with more relevance to their experiences—appeals which can capture their imaginations and evoke images of a dramatically different society. It should be noted, however, that an absolute bar to legal tactics arises only at the extreme point of alienation—that is, when cultural experiences take groups altogether out of the pervasive reach of legal values. Signs that this may be happening at the margins of minority groups were pointed out in Chapter 5. These signals should not be ignored, but militant posturing in the political arena should not be confused with a syndrome of social and psychological withdrawal.

Finally, I return one last time to the activist lawyers, who are indispensable but likely to be undependable. Their malaise will probably run very deep in mobilizing situations. They will lose heart as mobilization takes shape and they are relegated to a secondary position. At these later stages, lawyers' advice may still be sought but their consent will become less important. Their primary service may well be restricted to securing the full measure of constitutional protection for projects and purposes that they oppose. Working themselves into a subordinate position may be the lawyers' ultimate reward and the proof positive that legal tactics can work. For obvious reasons, this reward may not suffice. As activist lawyers find it more difficult to identify with the movement they have helped to create, they will feel they have come full circle—once again the legal mercenaries rather than the principled social activists. Given the outlook of most activist lawyers and the pressures under which they work these problems are inevitable. They cannot really be resolved but they underscore the importance of keeping lawyers in an advisory role rather than signing them on as strategists of rights.

THE PRACTICAL AND ETHICAL ADVANTAGES OF LEGAL TACTICS OF MOBILIZATION

The contribution of legal tactics in combination with political mobilization should be neither overestimated nor underestimated. Under the right circumstances rights can be used as a catalytic agent of mobilization. Mobilization can, in turn, be useful for articulating demands and forging those demands into viable political options. If neither the circumstances most conducive to legal tactics nor the ultimate consequences of mobilization can be forecast with much assurance or specificity, the difficulties are rooted not in the approach but in the impenetrable uncertainties of the politics of change. Be all that as it may, there are some distinct advantages to working toward political change through legal tactics of political mobilization, and it is high time that they be considered.

The Efficacy of Rights

The charge most often leveled against legal tactics is that they are at best conducive to modest adjustments but not at all suitable for programs of fundamental change. Whatever may be the truth of these charges with respect to conventional legal tactics, they lose force when rights are employed in the service of political mobilization. Rights used in this fashion promise to work cumulatively, in a multidimensional fashion, toward redistribution of influence and benefits. It is on these three grounds that the efficacy of rights will be considered in the pages just ahead.

Conventional legal tactics based on the myth of rights tend to be naive *in extremis*. Power cannot be purged from politics by a legalization of political processes. Accordingly, legal tactics directed at introducing reasoned arguments in order to realize the version of the public interest embodied in the Constitution are likely to do little more than divert attention away from concrete payoffs to symbolic gratifications. Moreover, fixation on litigation as a tool of policy implementation tends to promote one-on-one conflicts within the framework of the adversary process. The result is to fractionalize political action—dividing rather than uniting those who seek change.

Mobilization, in contrast, tends to aggregate both demands and capabilities. Rights are employed as mobilizing catalysts. They provide credible goals, cue expectations, and enhance self-images. In thus instilling a sense of purpose, feelings of legal competence, and perceptions of political efficacy, an emphasis on rights lays the foundation for effective political organization. While there is no way to guarantee that these organizations will take hold and grow, legal tactics used in this way do aggregate political energies and bring them to bear on the vital aspect of successful action, that is, building an organization.

It could be argued that mobilization is a slow and problematic process, which even in the long run will not alter the shape of American politics in any fundamental way. Legal tactics provide no alternative vision of social ordering. Since the pluralist premises of American politics are taken as givens, the existing power structure figures to remain pretty much intact. And finally, rights as resources draw their basic sustenance from conventional American values, thus implicating legal tactics still further in the status quo. There is some truth in all of these observations. Before dismissing the message of the politics of rights as just so much warmed-over incrementalism, let us consider just how partial these truths are.

Mobilization is, most significantly, an open-ended process. Legal values and symbols provide the initial or sustaining impetus for legal tactics, but mobilization is by definition unpredictable as to both means and ends. There are surely no built-in limitations on rising expectations. Once mobilization commences, it is clear on the basis of logic and experience that a measure of militancy, transcending the typically comfortable incremental scenario, is likely to follow. One cannot speak with so much assurance on substantive matters. Demands for fundamental change in the social order may emerge and take root, or the people behind these organized efforts may be willing to settle for less. If the settlements reflect significant satisfactions, then whether or not they are "fundamental" is (to some extent) academic. If, on the other hand, the settlements are the products of symbolic manipulation, continued mobilization still provides the most obvious and the most participatory line of defense.

Similarly, it is important to realize that legal tactics based on the politics of rights tend to penetrate deeply into the society rather than focusing exclusively on altering political institutions or changing the power holders. There are those who are inclined to think that the most fundamental obstacles to change are embodied in a conspiracy of society's vested interests. From that perspective, legal tactics doubtless appear unpromising and ineffectual, since the power structure is approached in an indirect fashion and the goal is to make that structure responsive. From another perspective, the behavior of those in power is as much a symptom as a disease. Take the problem of disadvantaged groups. As advocates of the women's movement correctly put it: "In essence, the laws are a formal codification of attitudes toward women that permeate our culture." [10] Must we not say the

10. Ann M. Garfinkle, Carol Lefcourt, and Diane B. Schulder, "Women's Servitude Under Law," in Robert Lefcourt, ed., *Law Against the People:*

same thing about racism, poverty, imperialism, and many other unwelcome tendencies in the American political system? If the problems run deep then the solutions must penetrate just as deep. Legal mobilization is rooted in a new sense of self-respect and collective consciousness, promising new and enduring patterns of behavior based solidly on cultural awareness and assertion.

The Ethic of Rights

The most obvious ethical justification for the legal approach as I have presented it is to be found in its participatory methods and pluralist premises. So long as mobilization is taken as the key technique, the extent and direction of change will be determined in open political exchange. Rights also recommend themselves as one of the least costly routes to redistribution of power and benefits.

More radical positions tend to develop around the ethical imperative of thoroughgoing and precipitous change. From this perspective, legal tactics entail too many compromises with the manifest evil of the established order. Reform, or lesser evilism, is to be avoided both as a matter of principle and because it gives too little weight to the pain of those forced to live with injustice during indeterminate periods of incremental adjustment.

There are two kinds of objections to this radical line of argument. Practically speaking, if it is a slow, tough job to generate an effective strategy of mobilization, there is no reason to believe that a revolutionary movement can be built more quickly and good reason to think that it will take much longer. Moreover, what are the tactics to be in the interim? One thing that radicals find most distressing about reformist strategies is that they are unwilling to heighten contradictions

Essays to Demystify Law, Order and the Courts (New York: Vintage, 1971), p. 120.

in the existing order. Reformists, instead, work to preserve and extend the modicum of social justice that is available within the existing order. What heightening the contradictions means in practice is not altogether clear, but it seems to involve baiting the established order so as to make conditions so intolerable for so many people that revolution will become the only viable response. Heightening tensions is, however, likely to be a dangerous and reckless gamble with fascism. "Unfortunately, there are a few among the Left who are captivated as were their analogues in Germany in the fateful days of the Weimar Republic, by the wishful illusion that open terrorist dictatorship would move people speedily to radicalization and militant struggles." [11] Moreover, even if the gamble succeeds it is premised on an indeterminate period in which suffering is purposefully increased.

If radicals resist rights because they are too closely associated with moderate forms of political action—incremental in tempo and confined by pluralist values—moderates will be equally unhappy with a politics of rights. As a matter of principle, a strategy of mobilization is objectionable because it treats legal and constitutional rights as means rather than as ends in themselves. Beyond this ethical imperative of the traditional myth of rights position, it is clear that the mobilization is destined upon occasion to spill over into extralegal behavior, nor is there any guarantee that the goals of the mobilized will be confined by constitutional values.

In a sense, defense of legal tactics of mobilization to critics at both ends of the political spectrum is the same, and it has already been foreshadowed, in bits and pieces at least. To the moderates all that can be said is that the vision of change without turmoil is part and parcel of the myth of peaceful progress. It is an illusion discredited by American history and

11. Arthur Kinoy, "The Role of the Radical Lawyer and Teacher of Law," in ibid., p. 285.

by experience elsewhere. As Barrington Moore, Jr., puts it: "The first point to get clear is that there has been no such thing as a completely peaceful reformist change, at least not in major modern industrial democracies." [12] Similarly, there is no way in the long run to avoid testing our values in the political arena and, of course, risking repudiation or at least significant alterations. Finally, if Edelman is correct, mobilization will reduce rather than increase violence, since violence is characteristically the response of the impotent and disorganized. [13] Those integrated into the system will be tempered by their stake in the existing order.

Postscript

One last issue remains. It is an issue which in part transcends the scope of this study and therefore will only be touched upon. But because it goes to the most fundamental problems of political change it should not be neglected.

Fundamental change in its most profound form has to do with a transformation of culture. The alternative vision has not yet been clearly identified but it may well have to do with replacing the present syndrome of individual competition and reward with a more communal social order. [14] If this is the standard, it must be conceded that legal tactics, even in connection with political mobilization, hold little or no promise of "fundamental" change. Indeed, legal tactics will, in my judgment, be much more likely at this deep cultural level to reinforce the existing order.

12. Barrington Moore, Jr., *Reflections on the Causes of Human Misery and upon Certain Proposals to Eliminate Them* (Boston: Beacon Press, 1972), p. 154.

13. See also Rollo May, *Power and Innocence: A Search for the Source of Violence* (New York: Norton, 1972).

14. See Kenneth M. Dolbeare, *Political Change in the United States: A Framework for Analysis* (New York: McGraw-Hill, 1974). For an activist lawyer's approach to the matter, see Michael E. Tigar, "Socialist Law and Legal Institutions," in Lefcourt, *Law Against the People,* pp. 327–47.

This is not to say that legal tactics will remain caught up in constitutional goals and procedures as such. The initial energies of mobilization are drawn from the tension between constitutional goals and procedures on the one hand and the shortcomings of real world performance on the other. Nevertheless, as has already been indicated, mobilization will often escalate beyond initial ideals. But how far beyond?

It is in a much more basic sense that legal tactics of political mobilization tend to sustain prevailing values. Mobilization is rooted in the transformation of quiescent Americans into aggressive and competitive participants in the society. This is hardly a way to build the sense of community that is taken by some as the precondition to and the sure sign of really fundamental change. No new consciousness but rather a confirmation and reinforcement of "bourgeois" values is the likely final consequence of the approach to change that has been presented in this study. Whether this is good or bad obviously depends on one's perspective. My own inclination is to look with ambivalent favor on approaches to change that keep us in touch with liberal-democratic values— with what Barrington Moore, Jr., refers to as "liberalism with a difference":

> a liberalism that lives up to its rhetoric instead of using it as a cover for imperialism. To make liberalism a reality is by definition to preserve and extend the historical achievements it does have to its credit . . . civil liberties, protection against arbitrary authority, and a considerable degree of participation in the political process by those whom the process affects.[15]

In this context, the politics of rights can be recommended because it is linked to the ethic of rights but is not caught up in the sterile dogmatism of the myth of rights.

15. Moore, *Reflections on the Causes of Human Misery*, p. 156.

INDEX

Activist lawyers, 5, 139–41, 162, 170–99, 212; professionalism of, 165–66, 169, 171–72; pressures of the bar against, 167–68, 172; shortage of, 178, 211; pragmatism of, 181–82; financing of, 194–99
Adversary method, 123, 171–72
Agnew, Spiro, 191–92
Ambiguity of legal rules. *See* "Open texture" of the law
American Civil Liberties Union, 173–76, 190–91, 195
Aron, Raymond, 47
Attorney-client relationship, 135–36, 163–65, 179

Barnet, Richard, 163
Bellow, Gary, 182
Bickel, Alexander, 28, 33
Bill of Rights, 15, 19, 26, 59; and school desegregation, 101
Black, Charles, 101
Blacks. *See* Minorities
Bok, Derek, 188
Brown decision, 100–01, 109, 137; reaction to, 143, 145, 194
Bureaucracies, 50, 106, 124–26, 130, 139, 182, 184, 195
Burns, Haywood, 126
Busing, school, 103–04

California Rural Legal Assistance Program, 182, 184, 193–94
Case method, 33, 154, 156
Children: legal values of, 63–69; attitudes toward police, 72
Civil disobedience, 51
Civil rights, 4, 95, 120, 123–24, 128–29, 141–46, 168, 211

Cloward, Richard, 140
Code of Professional Responsibility, 162–68
College students: standards applied to, 55, 57; legal values of, 64
Compliance with judicial decisions, 119–20, 123–30, 146, 148
Constitution, U.S., 35, 60, 98–100, 113; as foundation of political order, 15–20, 23, 24–28, 37; flexibility of, 31; updating of, 94; and poverty policy, 105
Culture, legal, 62

Desegregation. *See* School desegregation
Dolbeare, Kenneth, 119, 128
Donovan, John C., 105
Douglas, Paul, 120
Due process, 99, 106, 115, 126–27

Edelman, Murray, 133, 135, 205–07, 218
Education: legal, 29, 151–69, 187–88; public, 206
Environmental problems, 99, 112–15, 121–22, 127, 144
Equality before the law, 19, 54–59, 66, 99, 108
Evens, Lester, 192

First Amendment, 30
Fortas, Abe, 46
Foundations, 196–97
Fuller, Lon, 46, 53, 111

Geertz, Clifford, 14, 17
Goldberg, Arthur, 60
Graham, Fred, 191